PRAISE FOR *THE VOICE COAC*

"This is an exciting and enriching book for both the
importance of the vocal coach (VC) for the speaking v‹
tor who must see the need to engage with the VC at the commencement of the
production process. This book has painstakingly documented lived experiences
of vocal coaches thereby creating job avenues for upcoming coaches."

> **Abímbọ̀ílá Stephen-Adésínà,** *Arts Fellow, Department of*
> *Theatre Arts, University of Ibadan, Nigeria*

"In *The Voice Coach's Toolkit*, Pamela Prather has written a book that is personal, accessible and very practical. As well as telling us the journey of her own
experiences as a vocal coach, Pamela has interviewed a wide range of teachers
that allows us to hear a variety of stories and receive the perspectives and insights
acquired from a professional life in the field of voice. A great read!"

> **Andrea Haring,** *Executive Director, The Linklater*
> *Center for Voice and Language*

"I have often been asked, 'How and what do I do?' Although I am now a 'retired'
voice professional, this book gave me a very comprehensive definition of my/
our professional life journey. It was so rewarding to hear colleagues and former
students reflect on the specifics and dynamics of 'how' we relate to our assign-
ments and clientele. I kept saying to myself, 'YES!'"

> **Barry Kur,** *Professor Emeritus, Penn State University School of Theatre*

"This book is like attending a complete voice conference over a number of days,
and then having a tea date with them afterwards to continue the conversation.
Each session is packed full of useful advice from experienced professionals. It is
a must-read resource for all voice coaches and those just getting into the field.
Well done, Pamela!"

> **Betty Moulton,** *former president of VASTA and*
> *Professor Emerita, University of Alberta (Canada)*

"Providing a comprehensive introduction to the field of voice coaching and full
of wonderful advice from experienced voice coaches, *The Voice Coach's Toolkit*
is an excellent resource both for the beginner and the established professional."

> **David Carey,** *formerly Resident Voice and Text Director,*
> *Oregon Shakespeare Festival, USA*

"What an honor to be included in Pamela Prather's remarkably inspiring and
practical *The Voice Coach's Toolkit*. Her interviews of world renown leaders
of this field make the reader feel they are in the room listening to personal

conversations and stories — gleaning the pathways so they can join in and enter this profession themselves."

Jan Gist, *Professor of Voice, Speech, Dialects, Old Globel University of San Diego Shiley Graduate Theatre Program*

"The world of voice coaching is changing as fast as the rest of our lives, and Pamela Prather's handbook addresses important new themes as well as perennial principles. Her presentation of various subtypes of coaching will especially help those new to the field."

Joanna Cazden MFA, *MS-CCC, Holistic Voice Rehabilitation*

"Pamela Prather ther takes her readers on a remarkable deep dive into the expansive world of voice coaching. This engaging toolkit succeeds at conveying the nuance and complexity involved in professional voice care, all while maintaining a uniquely flowing and conversational writing style."

Michael Lerner, *MD, Laryngologist, Division of Otolaryngology, Yale School of Medicine*

"Aún con la visibilidad que ha alcanzado la profesión en años recientes, el camino para llegar a ser docente de voz sigue siendo confuso. Prather ha tenido el buen tino y la bondad de poner en un solo sitio múltiples recursos de gran utilidad, especialmente para quienes comenzamos en este andar de la voz escénica. (Even with the visibility that the profession has achieved in recent years, the path to becoming a voice teacher remains confusing. Prather has had the good sense and kindness to put multiple very useful resources in one place, especially for those of us who are just starting out on this stage voice journey)."

Oscar Quiroz, *MFA Acting Candidate, Michigan State University and former Voice Teacher, National School of Dramatic Art of Honduras*

"Prather's engaging resource for voice professionals, *The Voice Coach's Toolkit,* is a well-organized interwoven series of interviews that guides one to a rich understanding of approaches. The interviews with luminaries in the field — some of whom are no longer with us — are treasures."

Patricia Raun, *Professor of Theatre, Virginia Tech*

"*The Voice Coach's Toolkit* by Pamela Prather is an invaluable resource for new and established voice, speech and dialect coaches who want to build a career. In an ever expanding field, this book brings together the numerous strands — both methodologies and practitioners — to provide ways and means for navigating training, best practices in teaching and coaching, and building a profitable business."

Rena Cook, *former Head of Voice at the School of Drama, University of Oklahoma and founder of Vocal Authority*

The Voice Coach's Toolkit

The Voice Coach's Toolkit identifies the primary professional vocal coaching opportunities and the avenues by which a student or early career coach can navigate the vocation.

For purposes of this book, the Voice Coach is defined as someone who coaches the spoken voice in three precise areas: the teaching artist, the professional film/TV/theatre coach, and the professional voice-user coach. These three coaching worlds are broadly defined and each area includes in-depth interviews and practical advice from top coaches along with the author's personal expertise.

The book can be read in sections or as a whole, making it as useful for early career coaches as it is for those looking to expand their vocal coaching career or vocal pedagogy students who need a broad survey of all three areas.

Pamela Prather is the Founder of Pamela Prather Coaching LLC and Associate Professor Emeritus at SUNY Purchase College. She has been on faculty at Yale School of Drama and NYU, among others. She is a voice, accent/dialect, and executive presentational coach and a Past President of The Voice and Speech Trainers Association (VASTA).

The Focal Press Toolkit Series

Regardless of your profession, whether you're a Stage Manager or Stagehand, The Focal Press Toolkit Series has you covered. With all the insider secrets, paperwork, and day-to-day details that you could ever need for your chosen profession or specialty, these books provide you with a one-stop-shop to ensure a smooth production process.

The Stage Manager's Toolkit, 3rd edition
Templates and Communication Techniques to Guide Your Theatre Production from First Meeting to Final Performance
Laurie Kincman

The Lighting Supervisor's Toolkit
Collaboration, Interrogation, and Innovation toward Engineering Brilliant Lighting Designs
Jason E. Weber

The Assistant Lighting Designer's Toolkit, 2nd edition
Anne E. McMills

The Projection Designer's Toolkit
Jeromy Hopgood

The Scenic Charge Artist's Toolkit
Tips, Templates, and Techniques for Planning and Running a Successful Paint Shop in the Theatre and Performing Arts
Jennifer Rose Ivey

The Costume Designer's Toolkit
The Process of Creating Effective Design
Holly Poe Durbin

The Literary Manager's Toolkit
A Practical Guide for the Theatre
Sue Healy

The Production Manager's Toolkit, 2nd edition
Successful Production Management in Theatre and Performing Arts
Cary Gillett and Jay Sheehan

The Voice Coach's Toolkit
Pamela Prather

For more information about this series, please visit:
https://www.routledge.com/The-Focal-Press-Toolkit-Series/book-series/TFPTS

The Voice Coach's Toolkit

Pamela Prather

Routledge
Taylor & Francis Group

LONDON AND NEW YORK

Designed cover image: © Xanthe Elbrick Photography

First published 2023
by Routledge
4 Park Square, Milton Park, Abingdon, Oxon OX14 4RN

and by Routledge
605 Third Avenue, New York, NY 10158

Routledge is an imprint of the Taylor & Francis Group, an informa business

British Library Cataloguing-in-Publication Data
A catalogue record for this book is available from the British Library

Library of Congress Cataloging-in-Publication Data
Names: Prather, Pamela, author.
Title: The voice coach's toolkit / Pamela Prather.
Description: Abingdon, Oxon; New York: Routledge, 2023. | Includes
bibliographical references and index.
Identifiers: LCCN 2022041924 (print) | LCCN 2022041925 (ebook) | ISBN
9780367438814 (hardback) | ISBN 9780367438838 (paperback) | ISBN
9781003006206 (ebook)
Subjects: LCSH: Voice culture--Study and teaching.
Classification: LCC PN2071.S65 P66 2023 (print) | LCC PN2071.S65 (ebook)
| DDC 792.02/8--dc23/eng/20221130
LC record available at https://lccn.loc.gov/2022041924
LC ebook record available at https://lccn.loc.gov/2022041925

ISBN: 9780367438814 (hbk)
ISBN: 9780367438838 (pbk)
ISBN: 9781003006206 (ebk)

DOI: 10.4324/9781003006206

Typeset in Times New Roman and Helvetica
by codeMantra

Access the Support Material: www.routledge.com/9780367438838

I dedicate this book to:

My son, Harrison Ozymandias Millman: may your voice always be grounded and true. Thank you for putting up with a lot of macaroni and cheese over the last three years. I love you more than I can ever express.

Aspiring voice coaches: may this book provide wisdom and guidance as you carve your path in the field and honor the shoulders upon which we stand.

Contents

Foreword

I was immensely flattered to be included among the coaches Pamela Prather interviewed for this book, but even more so when she asked me to write the foreword. I have admired her work for a long time, and eagerly agreed.

Reading the manuscript, I realized that I have needed this book for a long time! I hear several times a week from aspiring coaches. "How do I become a voice coach?" they ask. Now I won't need the long but still inadequate reply I've always given. My answer will be much shorter now that I can include a recommendation of *The Voice Coach's Toolkit*, the most comprehensive introduction to the field one could wish for.

Pamela's categorization of voice coaches into the Voice Coach as Teaching Artist (VCTA), the Professional Voice Coach for Actors (PVCA), and the Professional Voice User Coach (PVUC) is simple but immensely clarifying. Seeing that my own practice straddles all those categories will help me rethink and describe my work. Many coaches, like me, reading this, might think that they spread themselves too thin, but *The Voice Coach's Toolkit* shows us we are stronger when we work with a diverse clientele, and that there isn't one best way to be a voice coach. We are better teaching artists having coached professional actors. We are better dialect and accent coaches having helped new English speakers master the vagaries of English pronunciation and prosody. And we help corporate executives tell their company's story more vividly having coached audiobook narrators.

As you see from the table of contents, Pamela has brought in around fifty other leaders in the field to help her tell the story. Many are among the editors of my International Dialects of English Archive (IDEA), several have been guests on my *In a Manner of Speaking* podcast, and I have enjoyed the lectures and books of many others. So, I know most of them very well and am proud to call them my colleagues. Their words of wisdom will help us all: both veteran coaches and those just entering the profession.

This book has made me even prouder of our work, and I believe the veteran coaches among us will be newly invigorated by it, as I was.

Voice and speech is generated by a mysterious cooperation between mind, brain, and body; this miracle defines our species. Helping our fellow travelers respect and nurture this miracle to its full potential is a privilege and a joy for voice and speech coaches. Pamela's words and the words of my colleagues are vivid indicators of this.

They remind us that voice and speech have an awesome power to impart truth, beauty, and goodness, but an equally awesome power to foster lies, ugliness, and evil. With *The Voice Coach's Toolkit* to guide all who aspire to this noble profession, I believe the powers of good are getting a vigorous boost.

Paul Meier, 2022
President, Paul Meier Dialect Services
Author, *Accents & Dialects for Stage and Screen* and *Voicing Shakespeare*
Founder and Director, International Dialects of English Archive (IDEA)
Creator, *In a Manner of Speaking* podcast

Preface

If you want to be an actor, there are plenty of "how-to" manuals that contain recommendations along with advice from working actors. While there are many articles written on various topics of voice coaching and, in fact, there are numerous books about particular methodologies of voice, there has never been a book written about the profession of voice coaching that includes numerous interviews with professionals in the field. This led me to imagine how useful it would have been to have had such a manual when I started my career. It is my goal that *The Voice Coach's Toolkit* provides clarity regarding the three main areas of voice coaching: coaching and teaching students, coaching actors, and coaching professional voice users.

In the first section, you'll find an overview of the field of voice coaching and subsequently three chapters that look into each of the established "buckets": The Voice Coach as Teaching Artist (VCTA), The Professional Voice Coach for Actors (PVCA), and The Professional Voice User Coach (PVUC). I'm in the position of having worked, and also been taught, in all three areas of voice coaching. This background provides me with a rather unique lens which I hope comes through as you dive into the book. I include my own stories and experiences along with those of luminaries in the field. The "My Story" section may or may not be of interest, but is meant to share a possible path and to clarify my experience in each of the areas of voice coaching. This book is written in a conversational style, so I hope you feel like you have had the opportunity to sit down with me and other voice coaching experts and learn something about our field. The final chapter of the first section includes a segment on Vocal Health Topics for the Voice Coach with important guidance from medical professionals.

The second section of the book, entitled "Words of Wisdom," could have been an entire book in itself. Over the course of writing the book, I interviewed close to fifty professionals who work with voice. The purpose of these interviews is to give you, the reader, a moment of mentorship. You will find a list of all our interviewees with an asterisk for those who appear in the printed version. Sadly, we could not include all of the interviews in the printed publication, but you will find that most of the interviewees are quoted throughout. Additionally, the complete Words of Wisdom with all of the interviews live in this book's online eResource materials.

Section three of the book provides additional resource material for you: You'll find a bibliography of publications by the experts interviewed for this book, along with educational resources suggested by them. You will also find a list of vocal health tips, curated by me, and short biographies of every interviewee included in both the printed version of this book and online eResource materials.

This book is for students of voice coaching and teaching, along with anyone who might be curious about what a voice coach does. While it is intended to be utilized by readers internationally, my positionality must be acknowledged: I am a white-presenting cisgender female who grew up in the state of New Mexico in the United States of America. I set out to interview a variety of humans from diverse backgrounds. However, all of this was conducted through a lens that started in North America and it must be true that there are many points of view and perspectives of the field that are not included.

Having said that, I am incredibly grateful to each person who granted me an interview. Time is a currency that we do not get back, and the time spent listening to the stories of my colleagues was a priceless investment. I am simply the conduit, shining a light on all of the talented and innovative coaches I was privileged to speak with. I hope *The Voice Coach's Toolkit* provides a vocational road map along with fuel for the next generations of voice coaches.

Acknowledgments

This book is a snapshot of my professional life and the many amazing humans who have been part of shaping my career as a voice coach. I am humbled and honored to have been the gatherer of this information and to share the depth of wisdom that the many incredibly talented humans around the world generously gifted me with.

My daily prayer is "thank you" and I wish to thank the following:

First, to my parents, Hugh and Kay Prather, who have supported me and believed in me always.

Mrs. Norris, my first-grade teacher, who nurtured and encouraged my gift as a writer and to Meg Wilbur, who mentored me into teaching voice.

My "Friblings," Christy Prather-Skinner and Stephen Skinner, for creating a writer's retreat for an entire year and encouraging me to keep reaching for my dreams.

Elsa and George Sykes for their beautiful friendship, exquisite writer's retreat, and endless words of encouragement.

On the "get it done" front: huge gratitude to Sarah Nichols who has stood by me for years, tirelessly serving as my Editorial Assistant and Project Manager. Rockford Sansom, for his wisdom and eyes an the page. And special thanks to Joe Hetterly and Sammi Grant for early research assistant work.

Thank you to my PPC Team: Michelle Lavine, Evonne Barrier, and Stacey Clarke. Each of whom has touched this project and helped me organize myself.

Appreciation to my tribe of soul sisters Carolina Barcos, Nancy Bos, Kate Clarke, Anne Collins, Micha Espinosa, Debbie "Piggy" Gardner, Elizabet Lahti, Anna-Helena McLean, Teresa Meyer, Christy Prather-Skinner, Maggie Surovell, and Elsa Sykes. Sweet light and encouragement from each of you in different moments. My heart is full. I am blessed.

Thank you to the many students from SUNY Purchase, Yale School of Drama, NYU, Marymount Manhattan College as well as countless workshops around the world. You have been my sandbox and place to learn and play. I thank you from the depths of my being.

Gratitude to Purchase College, SUNY, for granting me sabbatical leave and support.

A very special thank you to the one and only Paul Meier for his eyes on the page and wisdom.

And Flying Star Cafe & Higher Ground Coffee in Albuquerque as well as the Alamo Café in Playa del Carmen for the caffeine!

Section I

What Is a Voice Coach?

To understand what voice coaching is, it can be helpful to get clarity on what voice coaching is *not*. Voice coaching is not singing coaching: While the work of the voice coach can improve the singing voice, the voice coach, as referred to in this book, works primarily with the spoken voice. There is a crossover of singing coaches, however, who also coach the spoken voice. Voice coaching is not voice therapy: Though there are voice coaches who are also trained as speech-language pathologists (SLPs) and voice therapists, the work of the voice coach is to encourage healthy, supported vocal production, and to refer them to medical professionals if we suspect that a therapeutic or clinical intervention might be necessary. Voice coaching is not language coaching: There are multilingual voice coaches who concurrently coach the voice and coach the language. Language coaching requires teaching individuals, often actors, to speak in a language different from their own.

Moving into the positive: voice coaches may coach accents or dialects. This means that you could coach an actor in your native language to speak that language with an accent or dialect. Voice coaches might also coach a non-native speaker to speak with more clarity: For example, if I am an Australian English-speaking voice coach and am working with a client or a student who is a non-native speaker of Australian English, I might provide them with articulator exercises and vocal exercises that will help them communicate more clearly to their Australian audience in what I often term as "international business English." It can often be one of the jobs of the PVUC to help their clients slow down and use more muscularity when addressing people from many countries who are conducting business in English. Ultimately, voice coaching entails helping your student or client to connect to their body, breath, resonance, thoughts,

DOI: 10.4324/9781003006206-2

and, through the spoken voice, to articulate those thoughts with the clarity, precision, and focus that their role and audience demands.

In *The Voice Coach's Toolkit*, I will interchangeably use the terms "voice coach" and "voice teacher." The terms hold both cultural and personal nuances, but I believe a coach teaches and a teacher coaches, so I will leave you to further clarify this for yourself. I also use the words "student" and "client" throughout the book. Students generally refer to anyone who is not already a professional actor or a professional voice user who is making a living through the use of their voice. Clients can be professional actors or any other professional voice user.

Based on my experience and those of the many people I interviewed, it is not uncommon for voice coaches to work in multiple areas of voice coaching. Voice coaches might also be actors, singing coaches, language coaches, English as a second language (ESL) teachers, speech and language pathologists (SLPs), artists, executive coaches, acting teachers, directors, or belong to some other profession entirely. For the purposes of this book, I break voice coaching into three buckets: The Voice Coach as Teaching Artist (VCTA), The Professional Voice Coach for Actors (PVCA), and The Professional Voice User Coach (PVUC). The following chapters will define each of these and you will gain further insight through my personal stories and those of experts in each area. The book is meant to serve as a road map and can be read in sections or as a whole. If you are an early career coach, an individual looking to expand your vocal coaching career, or someone who is interested in hiring a voice coach, you might be interested in more deeply examining one area, while a vocal pedagogy student might want to survey all three areas.

Although voice coaching is a relatively new field, it is a profession and that means getting paid for the work you do. This may be stating the obvious, but communication is key in securing contractual agreements and payment for service. When it comes to negotiating your rates in the area of productions, if you are starting out, the best advice is to speak with your peers. In the case of film and television, there is often a precedent set by previous coaches. This is also true in the area of coaching PVUs. I believe it is really important to be transparent with other coaches in all areas of remuneration because there is currently no union that sets the bar. The Voice and Speech Trainers Association (VASTA) is an excellent resource to connect with coaches in your area of specialty and in your region to compare salaries and fees charged for voice coaching services. It is my opinion that undercutting other voice coaches' fees devalues our field. It is important to acknowledge the years of training, expertise, and life experience that you bring to the table as a professional and to be paid for that. Rates will certainly vary depending on where you live and how much experience you have.

Finally, regardless of the specific skills required for each of the areas outlined, a voice coach will need to have a foundational understanding of the mechanics of vocal production along with the knowledge of how to help students and clients develop healthy practices. It is an exciting time to be in the field of voice coaching because there is more and more science that supports the efficacy and importance of the work we do around breathing, vocal production, warm-ups, and cool-downs for our students and clients. The final chapter of this section explores vocal health topics and provides additional resources for deepening your knowledge of the vocal instrument.

CHAPTER 2

The Voice Coach as Teaching Artist (VCTA)

This chapter explores possible venues for coaching voice in settings other than working with professional actors or professional voice users. For the purpose of this publication, I have chosen the term "Voice Coach as Teaching Artist" (VCTA) to cover teaching and coaching the spoken voice for students in secondary school, college, university, a conservatory training program, Master of Fine Arts (MFA) programs, or privately for individuals who are either training to be actors or training to be voice coaches. For this section, I primarily interviewed coaches based in Africa, Australia, Canada, Central America, Europe, and the United Kingdom as well as the United States, where I am based. This section is meant to provide a basic overview of the field. While I have attempted to include many voices in the field, this book is written from a US perspective. Depending on where you live, there will inevitably be location-based considerations for the aspiring VCTA.

DOI: 10.4324/9781003006206-3

VCTA JOB DESCRIPTION

As stated previously, I will use the terms "coaching" and "teaching" interchangeably. The job of the VCTA can include teaching voice, speech, dialects, accents, and text as well as possibly coaching student productions and teaching voice coaches how to teach. Some voice coaches might specialize in one area of voice, while others will work in many areas. There are a variety of venues where the voice coach can work as a teaching artist. This person could work with children or teens in a school setting as part of a theatre program or even in a performing arts camp or summer program. It is not unusual for coaches to also specialize in another area of actor training such as movement, directing, acting, or some other component of theatre training. The majority of VCTAs work in university or conservatory settings. This includes post-secondary BA, BFA, MA, MFA programs or actor conservatory programs. Within this area is a subset of MFA programs that specifically train future vocal professionals. Several voice coaches who lead, have led, or created vocal pedagogy programs were interviewed for this book. However, the focus of this section is on how *you* can train to become a coach for student actors.

MY STORY

I come from a long line of educators. My grandfather and his sisters were all teachers in Tennessee. My grandfather moved west to Colorado and met my grandmother at a teacher's college. He went on to become a superintendent of schools in New Mexico where my grandmother was also a teacher. My father also started as a teacher and became a superintendent of schools as well as a professor specializing in early childhood education. He later ran a consulting business, which helped train educational leaders and enhance communication between school boards and their constituents. He was even inducted into the National Educators Association – New Mexico Hall of Fame. With a pedigree like that, I firmly vowed that I would *not* become a teacher. My plan was to become an actress in New York.

My parents were not quite sure what to do with their wild child, but did their best to support me in my theatrical dreams. During my senior year of high school, I auditioned for one BFA program and was not accepted, so I decided to take a more practical route and go into broadcast journalism with a full scholarship to the University of New Mexico. There, my love for storytelling and the spoken voice only grew. I spent my junior year abroad at the University of Essex in the UK, where I began my foray into the world of the DJ. My first on-air experience was at University Radio Essex (URE), spinning 1980s vinyl. I went on to become a club DJ and worked as an on-air talent at a commercial big band radio station in Florida. I subsequently worked at several KISS FM radio stations and NHK Radio in Japan. Back in those days, we actually cut our own tape and recorded commercial spots on four tracks. I loved creating soundscapes and inventing various voices. But, despite my growing success in commercial radio, I never lost my passion and dream of becoming an actor.

Finally, after going out into the world and working, I auditioned for, and was accepted into the MFA acting program at UCLA. It was there that Kristin founded I met Meg Wilbur, who learned her craft directly from Kristin Linklater at a teacher training workshop at LAMDA prior to the conception of Shakespeare & Company, the actor training and performance company that Kristin founded. Imagine my surprise when she called me into her office and said, "You seem to have a thing for voice." It was the mentorship and opportunities that Meg provided for me to teach undergraduate voice and speech that unknowingly paved my path into the field. She retired from UCLA, went on to work with Marion Woodman, and specialized in creating Jungian-based journeys to help women unearth their voices. She bequeathed to me her original Edith Skinner paperback training manual from Carnegie Mellon and her original hand-typed pages of interviews she conducted with Kristin Linklater and Catherine Fitzmaurice from the 1970s.

I laugh now when I think of my twenty-year-old self digging my heels in and saying, "I will never become a teacher!" Armed with a few years of teaching voice and speech to undergraduates at UCLA and an MFA in acting, I moved to New York City. I knew I needed supplemental income to support my acting career, and I had no desire to wait tables. I did the 1990s version of cold-calling and sent out about thirty headshots and curriculum vitae to any school or program in the New York metro area that seemed to offer a voice and speech class. A few weeks after moving to New York City, I received a phone call from Beth McGuire, an interviewee of this book who taught voice and speech at the Yale School of Drama for over twenty years. When I first met Beth, she was heading a voice and speech program in the city. I remember my job interview with her at a quaint Belgian waffle and coffee place in Chelsea. It all feels so cinematic looking back on it now. She hired me for my first east coast teaching job at the School for Film and Television. Like any relatively new teacher, my classes were a combination of experimenting and learning on the job. I was fortunate because Beth was extremely organized and her style certainly informed and influenced my own voice as a teacher. What I hope to illuminate by telling my story is the importance of being open to what appears and seizing opportunities. At one point, in my early career, I was teaching at Marymount Manhattan College on the Upper East Side NYU, in the Village, and the American Academy of Dramatic Arts on the Upper West Side. The different types of students and the different mediums, along with the quantity of classes I was designing, helped me create my own style.

During this time, Barbara Adrian, Head of Voice and Speech at Marymount Manhattan College and the author of *Actor Training the Laban Way: An Integrated Approach to Voice, Speech, and Movement*, advised me in the importance of diversifying and specializing in other teaching areas if I wanted a career in voice and speech. Her advice led me to complete a variety of workshops and trainings. I became certified in Prana Yoga, went through the third Fitzmaurice Voicework © teacher certification that Catherine Fitzmaurice offered in 2002, certified in Reiki, certified as a Laughter Yoga Teacher, studied Estill Voice and Butoh, and began creating my integrated approach as a voice and speech teacher. I dug into learning the International Phonetic Alphabet (IPA) and studied with

Dudley Knight and Phil Thompson prior to the Knight-Thompson Speechwork (KTS) certification days. Beth McGuire and I co-created a method of teaching phonetics that we called "Kinesphonetics" (body shaping sound) and co-presented our work at the International Phonetic Association Conference at University College London. We also co-taught workshops with Phil and Dudley, and at one point Catherine Fitzmaurice brought us in to share our work with her teachers in training. My path has certainly been eclectic, but it led me to teach at Yale School of Drama for eight years and then to gain a tenured position at State University of New York (SUNY), Purchase.

That is my story, but as you will learn, there is not one single way to become a VCTA. Several of the seasoned and incredibly talented trailblazers in the field of voice did not complete an MA or MFA or have any particular certifications. Teachers of my generation tend to have started with a degree in acting and then followed a mentoring path along with certifications in specialized areas. It has become more common in recent years to complete a vocal pedagogy MFA program, potentially along with one or more specialized voice methodology certifications. Ultimately, the best way to become a better teacher is to follow your passion and receive meaningful feedback from experts in the field who can help you improve and refine your skills.

WHAT DOES THE LIFE OF A VCTA LOOK LIKE?

Like all the areas of voice coaching outlined in this book, the individual who works as a teaching artist may coach part-time, or it could be their entire professional focus. The VCTA could act as an independent contractor or work as an adjunct instructor for one or more institutions. They might also be a full-time lecturer or professor of some rank at an institution. A full-time position tends to happen early to mid-career and comes with other responsibilities, which can include serving on committees, holding auditions, and even heading a department. As a teaching artist, you might teach voice, speech, dialects, acting, or movement, or you might serve as an entire department. In some cases, you will be part of a voice and speech team and work with colleagues to build and create a meaningful curriculum for your students.

Most voice coaches I interviewed started in the field of VCTA and have continued to make that their primary focus. As with all areas of voice coaching, each path is unique, and it has been important to me to collect stories from many experts in the field. In this section of the book, I will include commentary and anecdotes from Eric Armstrong, Jane Boston, Andrea Caban, Jan Gist, Andrea Haring, Nancy Houfek, Katerina Moraitis, Betty Moulton, Christina Shewell, and Shane Ann Younts. Their perspectives, advice, and suggestions will help clarify the career path of the VCTA. Their individual stories and biographies of other voice coaches along with the full versions of their "Words of Wisdom" are available in the online eResource materials.

SELECTED TOPICS FOR THE VCTA

- Training to become a VCTA: Mentorship, MFA, and Vocal Pedagogy Programs
- Teaching Professionally: higher education, conservatories, secondary school, and performing arts camps
- The business of the teaching artist: finding your identity in the field

TRAINING TO BECOME A VCTA: MENTORSHIP, MFA, AND VOCAL PEDAGOGY PROGRAMS

There are three primary ways that people train to become VCTAs. First, there is the mentorship model. This happens when an expert in the field works with an individual and helps that person grow as a teacher through observation, hands-on experience, and one-to-one guidance. The next model is one where the individual originally begins in the field of acting, completes a rigorous MFA program where they learn voice and speech along with acting, movement, and other elements of the profession. That person may work as an actor for some time while also becoming interested in the discipline of voice and speech. Usually, this transition from actor to VCTA entails additional training through certification programs, perhaps concurrently acting while finding their way into teaching. Finally, and most recently, there are several MFA and MA vocal pedagogy programs in existence. Receiving a degree from such a program has become a highly respected avenue for learning how to teach voice, speech, and dialects. This section will explore each of these areas in more depth. It is possible that any combination of these models can be the foundation for a successful career as a VCTA.

MENTORSHIP MODEL

The mentorship model is the oldest and original path for becoming a VCTA. I share this with you because, while these days it is almost imperative for a VCTA to have an MA or MFA, there are some extremely talented and seasoned experts in the field who came to their positions through a traditional path of studying with and working alongside other professionals. One especially notable and highly respected individual is Shane Ann Younts, who is the co-author with Louis Scheeder of *All the Words on Stage, A Complete Pronunciation Dictionary for the Plays of William Shakespeare*, along with the Audio Shakespeare Pronunciation App: www.audioshakespearepronunciationapp.com. Shane Ann's story provides insight into the traditional method of becoming an expert in any field: learning first-hand from the best. I would like to invite you into our candid conversation so that you can gain a clear picture of the many years it takes to develop and embody the craft of the VCTA.

At the time of our conversation, Shane Ann was working as a Professor at New York University's Tisch School of the Arts teaching voice, text, and Shakespeare classes in the Graduate Acting Program. She opened our conversation with an infectious smile as she graciously shared:

> I think I mentioned this to you, and it makes me laugh even as I say this: I have a BFA—a Bachelor of Fine Arts—but I teach in an MFA program. I do not have an MFA. If someone was starting out now, they would not get my job. I don't know of anybody starting out in the last five years who does not have an MFA. So that would be crucial for new teachers. The reason I mentioned that is because someone going into the field now needs to complete an MFA program. I'm one of like three people who've been there [at NYU] the longest. And of those three, none of us have MFAs.
>
> *—Shane Ann Younts*

Based on my research, I agree wholeheartedly with Shane Ann's observation. I would add that her story and those of other VCTAs who came through the ranks via mentorship offers guidance in helping the aspirational voice coach find their authentic voice and depth as a teaching artist. Shane Ann began her career studying with Robert Neff Williams. Robert, who taught at Juilliard from 1970 to 2011 and headed the Speech Program at Columbia, lived to the age of ninety-four. He touched the lives of such notables as Elizabeth Smith, Tim Monich, Wendy Waterman, and Ralph Zito. Shane Ann recounted her experience with Robert:

> I studied with Robert Neff Williams. Back then it was a two-year program. I teach the same thing, and now it's thirteen months; those are the times we live in. (laughs) His class was the only one that was voice and speech and he combined it with Shakespeare. Nobody else did that. There were people who'd taught voice, people who'd taught speech, and people who called it text work. He did not call it that. But that's really what he did. Nobody else combined everything. So that was my attraction to start off with.
>
> At the time, he was head of the speech program at Columbia University. I'm not sure if he was head at that time—but if not within a couple of years—he was also the head of voice and speech at the Juilliard School. So, I knew his credentials were good, and it turned out that he was so brilliant that the rest of us can only attempt to be as good as he was. I tell my students that when you look up "voice and speech teacher" in the dictionary, there is a picture of Robert Neff Williams. He was in some whole other category. I've worked with some pretty famous teachers—a workshop here, a workshop there—and they were all very good, but nobody is in his category.
>
> When I finished with Robert, I had a brief acting career for about five minutes. But what happened is that instead of being a waiter or working on computers, he just called me and told me that there was a school that had a voice and speech [course] in their evening program. He was so busy, he couldn't

do it. And he said, "Would you be interested?" And I said, "Mr. Williams, no, I don't want to do that." And he asked me why and I said, "I wouldn't know what to do." And he said, "Oh, yes, you would." (laughs) So anyway, I ended up taking the job. But this was absolutely not anywhere on my radar. Having come from this extraordinary teacher, there is no way that I would have thought of myself as being a voice and speech teacher.

—*Shane Ann Younts*

In Shane Ann's case, as with most voice coaches that I have spoken with in all areas and stages of their career, she said "yes" to her interests and took advantage of opportunities that aligned with her cultivated talents. As she went on to say:

I thought it was a lot better than being a waiter or computer processor. (laughs) Then he just started sending me individual private students, and there was the realization: "Oh, I can actually earn a living doing this." So, honestly, again, I did not go searching for this at all. Through Robert, there was an acting teacher here in New York who had ten or twelve students and she taught privately in this two-year program. She wanted him to work with all her actors, but there was no way he could take it on. So, he asked me if I wanted to put together a class, and again I said, "No." I don't even remember the rest of the conversation, but obviously I ended up doing it (Pamela laughs), so I started the same way he did twice a week. He let me use his material, and at that point in terms of my own training, in terms of being a teacher, I just learned how to teach from going and watching him. Robert was a brilliant teacher in the classroom, but he was not specialized in training teachers. He was not one to say, "Well, the first thing I would do would be X, Y, Z. And then if they're not doing this, etc." This is what I do when I train teachers, but he never did any of that.

So, I just watched him and figured it out on my own. I actually have somebody right now who's watching me. And when we get together, I will go through a pattern: "Start with this, and then do this, then do that." Robert never did that with me; nevertheless, I got to watch this master teacher for a year, a year and a half. I still pattern much of the way I teach from him; it is still from him from all that time ago.

—*Shane Ann Younts*

Shane Ann has also mentored several apprentices over the years, including Beth McGuire, mentioned earlier in my story. While Beth did earn an MFA in acting, she worked with many expert teachers over the years to develop her style as a VCTA. Shane Ann recalls:

The way Beth got started is I sent her some private students. And then, when I got some good feedback, I sent her some more. I think maybe she called and said, "What should I do with this person or that person?" Then I don't remember who it was, but a program called me and wanted me to teach there.

And at that time, if I'm remembering this correctly, I was teaching at Juilliard and at the NYU Grad Acting Program, and thought, "I can't do a third school." Whomever I was talking to asked me if I had a suggestion. I said, "Well, I have someone who's just starting out, but you could at least interview her." She took my two-year program. I mean, I basically gave her the voice and speech training and then [she] went off and took other things. But she had her basic voice and speech and Shakespeare training from me.

I don't have a training program like Kristin Linklater or Catherine Fitzmaurice. The people who—and I have quite a few out there: Beth McGuire, Scott Miller, Donna Germain—the people whom I would say came from me had the training from the class itself. And then most everybody I just mentioned came and watched me teach because that's all I really knew. (laughs) I watched Robert teach, so I'm like, "Well, come and watch me teach," you know. And then people like Scott Miller, who also learned from Robert, has developed his own method. But there are still a lot of elements of it that came right from the training. People have asked me about offering a specific voice and speech training … I like the idea of having more good voice and speech teachers. I don't like the idea of me setting up a school: "Shane Ann Younts' School for Voice and Speech." I do not see that happening, no. (laughs)

—*Shane Ann Younts*

Another VCTA that I spoke with, Eric Armstrong, has spent over twenty-five years in the field. He spoke to me of his journey as an apprentice which began at York University with David Smukler, who is also interviewed in this book. Eric recounted:

So, I went to York for two years and studied with David, and part of that process was a requirement to do an apprenticeship of sorts at The National Voice Intensive. That was part of the core of the Voice Teacher Diploma Program at York; you would have to have done The Voice Intensive before you did your MFA training, and then midway through, you would return as an associate. Maybe at the end, you would return again. So, by the time I graduated, I had participated with The Voice Intensive three times, once as a participant, two times as an associate. So, that really helped set me on a path. All along, I'm keeping up correspondence with Andrew Wade (Royal Shakespeare Company: Head of Voice, 1990-2003), writing him letters once a month and sharing frustrations and challenges, and he's giving me very different points of view.

After I graduated, I had an opportunity to return to Banff and assist Judith Koltai, who teaches movement at The Voice Intensive, and Andrew Wade, and I got a grant to do that. As part of that grant, they covered my flight and my room and board. I arrived in Banff and they went, "You're doing too much for us to not pay you. So, we're going to pay you for the whole thing, and your room and board is going to be entirely covered." And so, I then had this grant money. So, I called the grant organization, and I said, "You gave me this grant to come here, and I'm here right now, and they're willing to pay me. So, I'm wondering whether I could use that money to go to England and hang out with Andrew Wade and observe him teaching and coaching in that setting." And they were like, "Sure. That's okay."

So, I had three opportunities to go to the UK and just hang out with Andrew Wade, and I think that was partly just due to our close friendship. He really didn't have this kind of mentorship with other people. I really had the privilege of being his friend as much as he was a mentor to me. It was a very fortunate position, but really, I was kind of like a bug on the wall. I just got to observe. There was very limited opportunity for me to observe, and a lot of the time was just me hanging out with Andrew and interviewing him. I started to record these interviews while we'd be sitting around having a coffee. I would record them, and eventually, I edited that material into my first article in the *Voice and Speech Review*. Andrew was very keen on me being like him: being a coach for professional theater and using my skills in the area of text to head in that pathway. David Smukler, on the other hand, was very much setting me up to be a voice teacher. They're both wonderful in their own strengths, but they were very different kinds of voice professionals. So they offered different points of view. Of course, David did a large amount of professional coaching outside of his teaching, but pedagogy was always at the heart of what he did. Andrew did a lot of teaching, but coaching and the professional actor was always at the heart of what he did. So, that was a really great counterbalance of those two forces.

Eric had the opportunity to learn from two very different mentors. In order to be and stay relevant, it is necessary to cultivate a mindset that allows you to continue learning and growing from experts you admire, no matter how widely they differ from one another. Ultimately, it is the individual plus their influences—few or many—that contribute to each coach's unique style and approach. Eric went on to say:

I feel like people coming up have an opportunity *not* to be like their predecessors.

I think when I was being mentored, I wanted to be like them. I really wanted the people coming up to be saying, "I don't want to be like you." I think that's been at the heart of what my thoughts are about VASTA, and what we needed to do for a long time. I remember saying that what VASTA needed to have as a mantra was that we have to be different. We can't stay like what we are, and I think VASTA's working hard at that and our goals around diversity, inclusion, and equity are really, really important. But it's a personal thing. We all have to take it on as a personal thing.

Today, that's the thing that's really loud in my head. My students are—they are on us. They are on us to be better and different, and it's just not good enough anymore. I wish that we had gotten to the change that we needed to make before it got to the place that we're at, but we didn't, and so, now we have to.

—*Eric Armstrong*

Andrea Haring, who has served as Executive Director of the Linklater Center for Voice and Language and was a founding member of Shakespeare and Company, spent years working with and learning from Kristin Linklater. When she began teaching at Dartmouth, her years of teaching at and building Shakespeare and Company were accepted as a professor of practice. While she has been incredibly successful in all areas of voice coaching without an MFA (and she is certainly a role model in her own right), she shared with me:

> I *always* tell my trainees they have to go and get an MFA. I think the best voice teachers in this day and age have an MFA in acting. The Royal Central School of Speech and Drama's MFA in Voice Studies: Teaching and Coaching is very well thought of. As you write your thesis, you vocal coach with a theater [or institution] and you do out-in-the-field work. So, I would have done that. I think you need the degree behind you. We're all very degree-oriented. It is really, really difficult to get a job with a university if you don't have an MFA. Just to make sure you're getting a well-rounded education. And why I prefer acting training, as opposed to just voice pedagogy, is the people you're going to be coaching are actors. You need the acting vocabulary. You need to know how this is going to awaken the actor. If you come in just pedagogically, it may be a little too heady. And you as a vocal coach should know what it feels like to be in the hotspot. You should be a performer. You should really have the opportunity to track what happens [with] *your* chatter in your brain and tension in your body. And you need to give yourself opportunities to be afraid. (laughs) You know? You need to give yourself an opportunity to feel nervous.
>
> —*Andrea Haring*

It seems clear that, these days, mentorship is generally not the primary path for becoming a VCTA. However, it is extremely valuable to find leaders in the field whom you would like to learn from, and find opportunities to shadow them or to study with them to deepen your knowledge and experience as a voice coach.

MFA AND VOCAL PEDAGOGY PROGRAMS

When I began as a teaching artist, most of my contemporaries came from the acting MFA Acting background. The trend in recent years has been toward vocal pedagogy programs, and the number of programs that specialize in training voice coaches has grown tremendously. One clear advantage of an MFA in acting is that it really helps the individual build a deep understanding of the process of the actor. If coaching actors is something that you are interested in, most coaches suggest the experience of also being an actor. One of the advantages of an MFA or an MA vocal pedagogy program is that you will experience a deep dive into the mechanics of the voice and how to facilitate vocal production. In this section, I share my conversations with several voice coaches who created vocal pedagogy programs in their respective institutions, along with others who teach in such programs. These conversations are meant to provide more insight into how you might engage in specialized training to become a VCTA.

Nancy Houfek led a program educating voice teachers for about fifteen years at the American Repertory Theatre (ART) program at Harvard University. Teachers that she trained have gone on to coach and teach at premiere actor training programs, including NYU and Yale School of Drama. Nancy designed a program that focused on working with one teacher per year. One could almost consider the model that Nancy designed as an MFA based on mentoring. The MFA she created was focused primarily on learning how to coach and teach actors. Nancy shared a bit about the training methodology:

> The voice program was under the umbrella of the whole MFA (which also included dramaturgy and acting) within the ART. Because it was a Master of Fine Arts and a voice pedagogy program, it was based on teaching and coaching in the theater and was rigorous and all-encompassing. The voice students got to participate in all of the actor training, including my classes in voice, speech and dialects. They were also teaching fellows for undergraduate classes and had an ongoing teaching practicum culminating in their Moscow Art Theater School (MXAT) residency.
>
> Both the professional main stage and the MFA acting program had full seasons of productions. Each voice student would be assigned one or two MFA productions to be lead coach on. They would also assist me, helping me out in a myriad of ways, on the main stage productions, sitting in the room with me while I was working with the whole cast or in individual actor coaching. It was six days a week, Tuesday through Sunday.
>
> On Saturdays, at the end of all our classes, we would have a "voice seminar." We would just sit in my office for a couple of hours talking about what's going on, how to handle it and how to manage different people, how to work with different groups, how this particular director worked and what were the pitfalls and how to be better. We would talk about how to work with an individual actor giving you issues and what is the best way to coach for this particular show. We talked a lot about teaching challenges, too, and what to bring to the table every week, so it was a real open dialogue of brainstorming and troubleshooting. And I had some amazing experiences with amazing students.
>
> —*Nancy Houfek*

While the program Nancy created was more of a mentoring model of training, there are several programs that host larger cohorts and focus on vocal pedagogy in a wider sense, rather than being housed in an MFA program.

I spoke with Jane Boston when she was serving as Principal Lecturer at the Royal Central School of Speech and Drama. She discussed the Voice Studies: Teaching and Coaching program with me.

> We call it "voice studies." So, the pedagogy is a large part of it, but essentially, it's a synthesis of all the facets, all the ingredients that contribute to making voice studies a subject, if you like. Ultimately the goal is to generate coaches in the field. But more than that, because we're an MA/MFA program, there's an intellectual component; that is part of the MA-ness. (laughs)

I asked Jane about her thoughts on the apprenticeship model. She spoke about the complexities of teaching in the world we live in now and balancing the expert's experience and wisdom with that of the student or client's innate knowledge. Jane talked about when she first started working in training programs:

> There was a kind of an assumption (by the students) that excellence was in the room; there was just an assumption that this would be done this way, for the best kind of reasons, but I think I'm more unpacked now. And that led to allowing the expert to be them, and seeing myself as a conduit, a guide, in a sense, to their own best intelligence. That their own sensation is the self-verification process that each individual has. If I work with that, we can all be greater somehow, rather than me coming in with, "*I* will do that." Again, it's not that people intentionally want the pedagogue to do it for them, but there is a sense of previous patterns in education where you hand over authority to the person at the head of the room.
>
> I have to say that this does cycle back to my interest in alternative, child-centered education. I was a child of the 1960s; we were reacting against certain pedagogical hierarchical structures of power that had existed, you know, since the 19th century and beyond. So part of that movement that I yearned for was the ASN (A.S. Neil Summerhill project), which is: you as a child need to be listened to because otherwise you're infantilized and excluded. So, there is an origin there in theories of education that I have translated into and relate that to Augusto Boal, if you like, or Paulo Freire that say there is a tendency in certain kinds of pedagogies to disenfranchise the possibilities of the learner.
>
> —*Jane Boston*

One of the values of a voice studies program is that theories and best practices in teaching are consistently being updated and shared with vocal pedagogy students. In recent years, more attention is being paid to equity, diversity, inclusion, and accessibility when training actors. That means it is essential for new VCTAs to steep themselves in what works best with their students. Jane shared with me that this topic is a key element in training up and coming coaches:

> The boundaries of the role have changed with the knowledge we have about learning difference, and about diversity and equity in theater practice and performance; we need to be aware of this in the classroom. I don't think it was like that when I first started. I had a lot of passionate engagement offered

by coaches, for example, but I was less informed about how to transmit the knowledge. So, at my peril, I stood by the side of great teachers, or great "heads of"—almost iconic presences. Where I struggled was getting the learning from them because of their own lack of awareness about pedagogical positioning.

Maybe the important thing to say is the impact Cicely Berry had on me was huge. I positioned myself in a deferential way, as a younger woman, to her seniority, and she didn't actually want me to do that in any case. I found some kind of tussle in relationship to these significant others, you know. I think this is ultimately deeply productive because I formed a great sense of using their experience to guide me and give me inspiration. I think there is an inheritance in the voice field that is recently, in the last decade, informing much more widely about how it operates. And that's where I hope I can contribute a bit.

—Jane Boston

I asked Jane what she thinks this shift from "teacher as expert" to "teacher as guide" means. How, for example, does a person with a lifetime of experience manage positionality as a VCTA? Jane went on to explain that this is part of what she discusses with her vocal pedagogy students:

I found it's got easier as I've matured to take that position in the classroom that says, "All right, I don't have to jump in and fix this. But I can take my position of authority in the capacity to listen and orient." So, I would say one of the skills in developing voice practitioner coaching is to know where you are at any given point in sensation and in identity assurance—in a sense that you're not asserting that, but you're not de-asserting it. You're existing in relation to what and who is in the room. And that makes a lot of difference: if you can live in that truthfulness or awareness of that, of who's there and what you want to do together and, "What are the learning outcomes? What is it you can achieve?" [It's] transparency and the capacity to hear and notice, both for yourself and for them on behalf of them, and model that as best as possible.

—Jane Boston

Vocal pedagogy programs are not limited to training teachers to coach actors. The focus of most programs is training coaches to work with the human voice in a broad sense. Betty Moulton, a former president of VASTA who started the voice pedagogy program at the University of Alberta, shared with me:

One thing I was really dedicated to in the MFA I started was the amount and variety of coaching that MFA students had an opportunity to do. You can learn all you want through books and videos, but you *have* to be in the room coaching for many, many hours to really start to understand what it is that's required of a coach. Our MFA students were coaching for hours a day: they were coaching BA individuals and BA classes, warming people up, or coaching shows by BA people or shows by the Professional Actor Training program BFAs. They were in the room with new directors, coaching dialects and text. They did Shakespeare, they did Restoration, they did poetry, they worked with lawyers, they worked with teachers, and they worked with voiceover broadcast stuff in the recording studio we had.

—Betty Moulton

Aside from learning how to teach, another important component to voice peda-gogy programs that differs from MFA acting programs is that there is a deep dive into anatomy. This can be very helpful in identifying exercises that might benefit your students. Betty went on to discuss this:

It was really important for me to give the new voice students an understanding and a comfort level in the scientific world, so they could go to any science conference or any session and have an idea of the language and the focus of research and how people present it. They found—and they said this time and time again—that they would take the anatomy and physiology and speech science courses in their first year, and they would struggle through because it was science-based. They'd be in tears in my office, and I'd say, "Don't worry, it'll be fine."

In the second year, when they were teaching more and more and coaching more and more, they would say, "I use this information every day." The level of legitimacy it brings when you can, with authority, talk about a semi-occluded vocal tract or the vocal folds and what happens with the arytenoids and cricoid cartilage is important, and it adds legitimacy to legal clients, educators, and politicians because you know what you're talking about on an anatomic level. And science always trumps the imaginative work in a lot of people's minds. So, to have both ends of the stick is important. If you want decent clients to stick around for a while, and they feel that you know what you're doing, then that's another tool in your toolkit.

—Betty Moulton

This can be very helpful if you are working with vocal challenges. (I discuss this more in the section entitled Vocal Health for the Voice Coach.) If a student or client comes to you after working with a speech-language pathologist or a physician, the idea is that you will be able to work with them more intelligently because of your experience from a vocal pedagogy program.

It is a clear trend in the field of VCTA to complete a postgraduate degree of some type. If you imagine yourself continuing to act, direct, and work in the world of the actor outside of voice coaching, it might be more advantageous to complete an MFA in acting and supplement that training with mentoring and additional certifications in the field. However, if you see yourself desirous of primarily working with the spoken voice in all areas, it could be a better fit to train in a vocal pedagogy program. The VASTA website continues to be an excel-lent resource for the most up-to-date programs and certifications available. It is outside the scope of this book to attempt to name or rank institutions or training programs. However, referring to the Words of Wisdom section in this book, or the full version included in the Support Materials online, will likely help you in your personal research. Networking and connecting with other people who are doing what you imagine yourself doing is always a great place to start as well.

TEACHING PROFESSIONALLY: HIGHER EDUCATION, CONSERVATORIES, SECONDARY SCHOOLS, AND PERFORMING ARTS CAMPS

Once you have the necessary training, the goal of the VCTA is ultimately to teach professionally. Most opportunities for serving as a VCTA exist in higher education, conservatories, secondary schools, and performing arts camps. This section will describe these areas along with a brief overview of what the job picture might look like in each sector.

The VCTA who works in secondary schools or performing arts camps will likely combine the teaching of voice with other disciplines. When I was in graduate school, I was invited to teach in a summer program called EXPLO. This was a three-week summer residential program where I taught voice, speech, and acting to high school students on a university campus. I also worked with the California Shakespeare Festival in a program for elementary school children. In that case, I assisted the director in areas of voice, speech, text, and embodiment of the roles. There are also secondary school programs that specialize in the arts. In the United States, these school-based opportunities generally require a person to also specialize in movement, acting, or directing. The advantage of working in secondary school programs is that the schedule is usually quite predictable. Depending on your personality, you might like to teach several disciplines to the actor, and it is almost certain that you will, if you are working with this demographic.

Conservatories and university programs are generally a place where you can specialize in voice, speech, and dialects. Conservatory programs can be stand-alone programs that grant certificates to their graduates, or they can be housed within a BA, BFA, or MFA program. The entry-level for the VCTA is likely as a visiting instructor or an adjunct. It is not uncommon to have placements at multiple institutions when you are starting out. The goal is to learn how to teach the work in relatively low-stakes environments so that you can experiment and find your voice as a coach.

My first job in New York City was at the School for Film and Television. I also worked at the American Academy of Dramatic Arts. These types of positions can be excellent arenas for developing your teaching style and accumulating hours in the practice. Next in line would generally be an undergraduate program of some type. BA programs will tend to offer more introductory classes.

There are times when a BA program also includes singing, which is not the focus of this book, but singing can be a complementary field to voice coaching. Depending on the size of the program and whether it is rooted in a conservatory model, you might solely coach elements of voice, or you might branch out into other areas of actor training as outlined above. BFA and MFA programs require more specialization than BA and MA programs. At some institutions, there is a head or chair of voice and speech and a community of other teachers who work within that program. At others, there is one person who is responsible for teaching all voice, speech, and dialect work. Most post-secondary programs will have some type of on-camera or stage production requirement for the students, and this often means that coaching productions is part of the VCTA job description. It is quite common that your students in a professional training program will be the next professional actors on stage and screen, so it is not surprising that many individuals will start out as teaching artists and move into voice coaching professional actors.

It will be important for you to build your network. I highly recommend starting with the Voice and Speech Trainers Association, or VASTA: www.vasta. org. This is an international organization with yearly conferences and numerous interest groups that periodically hold in-person and online events. There are student membership rates, opportunities for you to present at conferences and volunteer for the organization along with chances to learn directly from experts in the field, many of whom have been interviewed for this book.

THE BUSINESS OF THE VCTA: FINDING YOUR IDENTITY IN THE FIELD

As a VCTA, you will need to consider how you show up in the classroom or studio and what areas of the field you are interested in specializing in. Whether you come from an MA, MFA, mentoring background, or some combination, it will be important to deepen your knowledge in your areas of interest. This could be accent and dialect work, breath work, certifications or lineages of voice and speech work, movement, yoga, or any other area of actor training that will help you find your identity in the field. It will also be important to keep building and cultivating your network of colleagues. This will help you further identify your areas of interest, and you can consider whether you might want to present your work at conferences, in written form or at workshops and training. If you are choosing a tenure track path, it will be important to find out what the current best practices are at your institution. The trend in higher education has been moving away from tenured teaching positions and toward professors of practice. The most current resources for you will be your colleagues.

As I've stated previously, there is not one single path to becoming a voice coach. You will find that the VCTA could spend an entire career working in academia and researching topics in the field, or they could work in some combination of other areas of voice coaching. Christina Shewell, who teaches voice teachers how to teach, shared her thoughts on finding your identity as a voice coach. She said:

> I often start by saying to students, "Okay, so in pairs, imagine you're at a party and you meet someone and they say, 'So what is this thing called a voice coach or a voice teacher?' What do you say?" It's really difficult, and it's really, really interesting. And the reason I do that is because then I go into my way of *analyzing* voice, *hearing* voice. It's interesting because very often none of them mention, "Well, you listen to someone's voice, and you ..."

Christina encapsulated the identity of voice coaches in the complexity of a rainbow, something to consciously create and evolve in your career. Christina spoke of her own role in the field:

> I suppose my role nowadays is mending and extending voices. I definitely see my role as being a healer, as having healing in it, mending broken voices. But no ordinary people know what voice teachers do, really, because everybody takes it for granted. I always say, "This sound that flows out from our head and our hearts." I never say I'm a speech and language therapist or patholo-gist. It's interesting. I say, "I work in voice therapy, mending voices. And I work with people who want to develop their voice or extend it in some way."
> —*Christina Shewell*

In any endeavor, it can feel daunting to start. Betty Moulton advised the new voice teachers she was training when they were starting out:

> "How do you know where to start in a session?" I think when you're a more mature teacher, you have confidence that if you start somewhere, you'll get somewhere. (laughs) If you start somewhere and you start things moving, you overcome the inertia of not having worked yet; then, other things will occur to you as the work is happening in front of your eyes. And that's what guides the process. So, as a young voice teacher, I would encourage them: "Start somewhere, just anywhere. It probably doesn't matter where." Now, where that spot is, of course, you have to assess. Try to assess where your students are. You're fed by everything that they're doing in that moment in front of you.
> —*Betty Moulton*

The path of listening, looking, and leaning in becomes more familiar with expe-rience. I advise the voice coaches that I've mentored to approach each human with a desire to engage in and teach compassionate, clear communication. This means listening to what your student says along with the mechanics of how they say it. Betty echoed this when she shared with me the qualities to cultivate as a voice coach:

> ... Human, compassionate, empathetic, people who are able to allow their own vulnerability, and yet have a core of strength. And often I use the word "bravery." You have to be brave enough to be with a person in their moment—

in your moment—to be able to withstand whatever it is they're doing and feeling and thinking and to help guide it, or to be a kind of rock they can throw themselves against and know it won't shatter. You're a solid presence in the moment so that they feel safe in that they can explore and climb higher. So, I think bravery is a huge part of it, which means you're brave enough to stand for what you believe is truth in the moment.

That's true especially with text, really good text. That's why Shakespeare is so great to work on. Good text is so much about the truth of a human being, expressing what's in their heart in the moment and asking for a response. I believe a voice coach is privileged to be able to be in that same moment with an actor—a communicator, and the coach also has the incredible responsibility to gently provide whatever guidance you can to help the person feel like they can express themselves safely, strongly, and clearly, because that's a huge shout out in the world—a human truth. When people open their mouth, they are seen. So, when you help facilitate that, you must be able to handle what they respond to, *how* they respond to being seen. And sometimes, especially in young student actors, it can be really overwhelming at times. You need to be strong enough to stand firm and say, "There's a lot of emotion going on there. I see that there's lots of stuff flowing through you. Can you take it again? We'll try it again."

—*Betty Moulton*

One particular challenge as you are creating your identity as a coach is holding space and redirecting your students when necessary, while also recognizing when they might need professional help. The work the VCTA engages in can often be therapeutic, but it is not therapy. As Betty went on to say:

We're shaping for artistic expression rather than therapy. That's one thing I think someone who's a voice teacher needs to have a very clear border or knowledge of: what is useful emotional energy and intellectual energy for artistic expression, as opposed to the emotion and intellect for therapy. I never was interested in being a therapist. I would always try to feel like there was a professional approach I gave off that was, again, safe for the people I was working with. I would not broach that; I would not cross that boundary. And if I found that they were trying to veer toward that and needing it or wanting it, then I would turn it right back into the work for the show or for the character.

I think it's a safety to be that strong. To say, "This is where we are and this is what we're working on." And I think that's, again, a bravery in the voice teacher and a strength to know the boundaries and to help shape toward what the purpose is. With, hopefully, authentic communication as a public speaker to move an audience, to create more humanity, or to accomplish this task together … Being in the now, being in the moment with the person, which goes right back to having the bravery, and the empathy, and the passion, and a sense of fun, curiosity, mischievousness.

—*Betty Moulton*

Eric Armstrong emphasized the importance of cultivating a community while you are building a career:

> When I finished my diploma and my MFA, I joined VASTA right away and I was on VASTA VOX [an email list for voice trainers]. It was the early days of the internet, and I was on there all the time, and I must've been pretty annoying, I think. I just wouldn't shut up. When VASTA asked me to do the website, I said "Yes," in a millisecond, not really knowing what that meant. But I found an opportunity, and those opportunities just kept presenting themselves over and over and over. I firmly believe that VASTA was hugely responsible for my success, and it is at the core of my ideas around collaboration and mentorship, openness and generosity.
>
> —*Eric Armstrong*

A powerful component of VASTA that can help to buoy your growth is the breadth and width of methodologies and humans that are represented within the organization. VASTA has grown from a small US-centric organization to an international group of voice professionals. Eric added his perspective:

> With some approaches to voice, there can be a kind of "circle the wagons" mentality. It's us against the other methodologies, and VASTA is the opposite of that. It forced me to encounter methodologies that I was unfamiliar with and to abandon protectionism philosophies that some of my mentors had. I think my personality is different. I wouldn't say I'm a gregarious person in any way, but I am a joiner, and I very much believe that a community of ideas is enriched by people sharing their ideas together, and that protecting what you do and how you do it makes us all poorer, not richer. That is very much at the heart of the way I have worked. I think that closed some doors for me, but it opened others. There is a cost to service, but the benefit of it far outweighs that. I have to say that some of my dearest, closest friends are people that I know through VASTA. The summers where I don't get to go to the VASTA Conference, my life is poorer. Then the other thing is word of mouth and referrals. I'm constantly having the opportunity to say "no" to work and offer that work to other people. I am in that place of privilege now, but it's a two-way street: you offer work to other people, they're going to recommend you for work as well. Creating relationships like that is vitally important to finding work.
>
> —*Eric Armstrong*

All coaches that I interviewed emphasized the importance of building relationships and authentic connections with colleagues. One of the values of these connections is the opportunity to compare notes and discuss field-specific questions that come up for the VCTA. It is inevitable that, in most institutions, the job of VCTA will involve assessing your students. The area of voice can feel very subjective at times, so one of the most challenging areas of teaching for many is that of framing assessments in a format that addresses the individual's growth as well as their growth opportunities. While you can administer a test on your student's knowledge of anatomy or the International Phonetic Alphabet (IPA), there is an element of learning how to *feel* someone's improvement in a particular milieu and helping that person become consciously aware of their personal strengths and growth opportunities. It will be important for you to develop assessment plans that clearly lay out the particular aims of the course(s) you are teaching along with desired outcomes. These will vary depending on the size, length, content, and capabilities of your students. It is vital that precise feedback is delivered to the student along with a clear path forward. Feedback could contain exercises and other tools to help students address specific challenges so they can continue to improve and expand their voices. I asked Christina Shewell to share her thoughts on how to measure student success, and she started by sharing a story about an Ear Nose and Throat (ENT) surgeon who presented to a group of voice professionals in the UK some years ago:

> He came over, and it was in the very early days of what's now the British Voice Association; it was called the Voice Research Society then. He stood up, and he said, "Ladies and gentlemen" in his lovely American voice. "I'm really glad to be here because I am the world expert ..." And you could just feel people going, "Oh God, arrogant American." He said, "I am the world expert on the sound of my own voice." And it really stayed with me, that. He then went on to say, "If a singer says there's something wrong, there's something wrong." The ultimate judge needs to be the person whose voice it is, or the student who's auditioning, or the public speaker who's speaking.
>
> —*Christina Shewell*

I appreciated what Christina said about the client's or the student's experience of their own voice being integral to teaching. What this means is that it's important for me, as the voice coach, to help students learn how to hear and feel and sense themselves with mindful attention. The reality is that very few of our students will have the luxury of private coaching. If they do, they will likely have spent years being their own voice coach prior to working privately with a professional voice coach. You will need to help them learn to identify their own challenges and give them tools and techniques that will live with them long after your course with them is over. As Christina went on to say:

> I think mindfulness, the mindful attention to the inside of the body, is incredibly important for our clients. You can have too much mindfulness, and it gets in the way of you dancing in a musical. But actually, when you're trying to solve something, to really know what you're feeling in terms of your physical body – whether it's emotionally in the felt sense or whether it's, "Wait a minute, what does happen when you as a voice coach say I'm constricting, what does that actually feel like?" – mindfulness is important. It's essential the person feels that, because then they'll be talking to someone in a bar and they'll

suddenly go, "Oh, wait a minute. That's what I'm doing." So, that recognition of physical and emotional feeling is incredibly important.

—*Christina Shewell*

With the increased number of online and virtual activities during the post-pandemic era, it has only become more important to help students be aware of their breath, voice, and bodies. I spoke with Katerina Moraitis, while she served as head of voice at the National Institute of Dramatic Art (NIDA), a leading Australian center for education and training in the performing arts, based in Sydney, New South Wales. I shared with her the challenge that many new teachers and coaches have in developing meaningful assessments for their students. She concurred with this challenge and added her advice:

> How do I measure that somebody is able to connect with their breath? How do I measure that they're able to connect that thought to the breath? How am I able to measure that the thought and the breath can connect into action and body? Right? It's so process-based. What we do, my team at NIDA and I, is we always mark together so that we discuss the students. That's the first thing; we always have two or three markers. […] And we discuss their journey before we give them a grade. My boss doesn't like us to give grades at all. But unfortunately, we're an institution and we have to. So, I always say to the students that it's about the process, not the product, and it's about where *you* are in the process, not the product.

> Sometimes people come to the work already with voices in a good place. I've got first year actors at the moment. I feel like I have nothing to teach them in terms of voice; their voices are in such a good place. But what I *can* teach them is to connect the technical work to the expression. Because what they are unable to do is let what they're doing vocally and physically change them in an inner way. They're not allowing their inner life, their inner creativity, their inner imagination, their inner emotions to respond to what they're saying. They just sound good. And I don't want students to just sound good. Because for me, it's not about sounding good. What sounds good today didn't sound good at Central School of Speech and Drama in the 1920s. You know, if Laurence Olivier, who is known as "The Voice," was in my class today, we would be saying, "Well, it's a little bit too … big." Right?

—*Katerina Moraitis*

Jan Gist, retired professor of Voice, Speech, Dialects at the Old Globe/University of San Diego, inspired a laugh-out-loud response when she responded to my question about creating grading—or marking—rubrics. Jan said:

> When I hear the word "rubric" I want to murder someone. I hate that word. I don't know what it means. It just turns the process of teaching, coaching, and theatre into something that is—I don't know what it is. When you talk about cause and effect, goals and strategies, and honesty of what you can

deliver or not deliver, and feedback, I'm all for it. But the word "rubric" sounds like someone is trying to nail metal on my forehead. (laughs).

—*Jan Gist*

Teaching is an organic process, and students are humans with their own challenges and experiences that will continue to shift as the world we live in shifts. We, as voice coaches, need to stay present to what the needs are in front of us. We need to be able to help our actors, our clients, and our students contextualize the work they are doing. They need to understand how to calibrate and execute their breath, voice, and body to serve the needs of the situation. Katerina and I discussed how student learning outcomes will most certainly change:

> Understand what voice is needed in terms of when you're in film, when you're on television, when you're in the theater, when you're in, I don't know, a basketball court, if you're doing drama in education. What is the need at any given moment? I often say—well I don't say it, somebody else said it and I can't remember who it was now—good acting is knowing what style of play you are in. I often equate that to voice as well as my students. Good voice work is knowing what style of text, language, or space you're in. You need to be able to adapt at any given moment. So that's what we do. I also often say to my students, "I don't teach voice, I teach awareness. I teach you to be aware of what you're doing, so that you can choose to use your instrument in any way you choose to use it."
>
> If I want to go around speaking in an Irish accent, I should be able to do it. That's my choice. If I don't, that's my choice. If I want to speak with a glottal on open vowels, like a lot of Australians do—I don't recommend it—but if I choose to do it in my everyday life, that's my choice. As long as I know I'm doing it, and I can let go of it when I have to play Lady Macbeth. Right? Those are the key things: knowing who you are, what you want, why you want it, and how you use your voice to communicate what it is that you want to communicate. Those are the four key things: who you are, what you want, why you want it, and how you get it. And that is whether you are a human being or whether you are an actor.

—*Katerina Moraitis*

Additionally, it is imperative for the VCTA to continue to train in specialized areas of interest. There are many forms of specialized voice training that you can certify in, as well as movement or acting techniques. Some MFA programs have a precise course plan, while other programs have a more elastic approach like the one that Andrea Caban created at California State University, Long Beach. Andrea explained how the voice coaches in her program come in with different interests: some want to be teachers and some want to coach actors. She shared:

> In LA County we get a lot of mid-career actors coming back to learn the art of teaching and get a terminal degree, and that had been the focus of the program for many years. But I started to recruit people who were more early

career and knew they wanted to be voice and speech pedagogues, and that's worked really well for me. I have two students who graduated this month, and they both secured tenure track positions while they were still students with me. That's pretty hardcore in terms of being competitive, and I think it was layering on the Cal State Long Beach curricula and the KTS (Knight-Thompson Speechwork) curricula at the same time.

Now I've got four women coming in and their focus isn't necessarily on going into academia, as opposed to my cohort that just graduated. They want to be actors, and they also want to coach professionally on set, so I'm going to prep them to be speech and accent experts. I'm not going to train them so much in research, grant writing, development, and all that kind of stuff, which I did with my cohort that just graduated. So really, it's kind of plug-and-play depending on whatever the specialist wants to focus on, because I can help them carve out a path.

—*Andrea Caban*

Learning is a lifelong process and there is always more to absorb and to try, and you will likely find that your interests change over the years. A key piece of advice that I come back to again and again is the importance of seeking balance and time to replenish. Voice coaches are always giving so much to their students. There is one of you and possibly hundreds of students who all need and want your attention and guidance. Remember that you always know more than someone who has never studied this work, so you have value to offer. I really appreciated Christina Shewell's advice when I posed the question to her asking what advice she would give her younger self:

Well, (laughs) that's a huge question. On an emotional level, I would say don't be so afraid, so anxious, so self-critical, and so self-conscious. But saying "don't" to anybody isn't the right thing. I think the loving kindness meditation—the mindfulness approach—had I learned that earlier, it would have benefited me but also my clients. Also, the honoring of working from who we are, knowing that we are complex. When I'm teaching, students laugh at me sometimes because I talk about PBs: we're complex Precious Beings, and we're working with complex Precious Beings. I have learned so much through working with people, and I'm very comfortable working with people. So, I don't think I'd have done anything differently. It's been a long journey. But I think the mindfulness approach, if I'd known that earlier, would have been very useful.

—*Christina Shewell*

The longer you work in this field, or any field for that matter, the more you are likely to feel you know very little. It is useful to remember that your unique experience and your path into coaching is an offering to your students. I have found it imperative to my growth and health as a teacher to take care of my voice and to offer transparency around my process. I have grown to think of my voice teaching and coaching as also helping my student actors understand and share their voices in the world, in whatever way feels authentic and connected for them. Christina agreed with me and added:

> There's one other thing I'd say, which is don't neglect your own voice. I think I would say to my younger self, "Listen, you can sing. Just sing as well, that can go along with it. Sing, act, dance. You can be a performer as well as working with performers." I think it's really important for voice coaches. Yes, you're in service to someone else. But actually, you have your own fire as well. It's really important to take care of yourself, whether you're president of VASTA or not. You know, to actually make that time, to take time, not to be afraid of being on one's own, to understand the nature of truly taking care of yourself. And body work is an absolute vehicle for traveling, for oneself. And for others. What's that saying? Something like, "Take care of your body. It's the only place you live."
>
> —*Christina Shewell*

I believe that your own body, breath, and voice is the only place you can teach from, so consciously caring for and feeding your instrument is vital as you embark on this career. This includes developing your listening skills. As you cultivate your ability and awareness around listening, you can also train your students to do the same. This level of acuity will certainly help them beyond the walls of your classroom. I think of teaching listening as teaching the silent voice.

There is a vibration to active listening that is the counterbalance to spoken voice. As Jan Gist said:

> You have to be an extremely dedicated lover of listening. You have to love listening and you need to hear on many levels: you need to hear as a member of the audience who has never heard of this play before; you need to hear as a heart listening to the heart of the actor; you need to hear the play as you're reading it. So, you're listening constantly. One of my favorites, of the thousand favorite things I do, is listening to the acoustics of the space you're in. I've worked at a lot of theaters for a number of different shows. The same stage in the same house has very different acoustics depending on the set design and the staging of the play. The acoustic changes depending on how many people are in the house and that kind of thing. So, really, it's important to have elephant ears to listen.
>
> When I'm teaching students and coaching individual actors, I ask them to listen to the others: "What are you hearing in each other and how do you put it into words? And how do you hear deeper?" I ask three questions about this, and I tell everybody I work with. I listen to you and I think to myself: *Can I hear you? Can I understand you? And do I care?* So, if I can hear you and understand you but I don't care, something's wrong. If I care but I can't understand you, something's wrong. (laughs)
>
> —*Jan Gist*

These questions are important to consider as you craft your own classes and think about what and how you want to teach. While I do take play seriously,

I remind myself and my students that the actor's work is often on a play. As Katerina shared when I asked her what she would advise her younger self when she first started teaching:

> Don't take it all so seriously. Have fun, play. Don't be so anxious about the future. If you go with your heart, and if you know what you're doing and feel what you're doing is right, then it *is* right. And follow that. Stop worrying about what other people think. It doesn't matter what other people think. Because leaders don't follow. That's what I would say.
>
> —*Katerina Moraitis*

Jane Boston offered her advice as well:

> I always think I'm deeply privileged to be in this capacity, and I feel that the students I work with are in a place of privilege equally, because we are at a place to exchange lifeforce moments with other people. Why did I choose this career path? Because there's something about being alive, something about engaging with the life force possibilities and engendering that, even marking out how remarkable that is to codify and authorize expressive experiences in a public way. What a wonderful thing to do to think, "How can we live this together?" I see voice and voice coaching very much in that area. To embrace those possibilities, it's more than a sandpit, it's more than a swimming pool, it's more than a gym, more than a studio. It's a place of confluence, of energies that we can talk, experience, sing, and move towards better capacity for all of us.
>
> —*Jane Boston*

The VCTA is often the starting place for voice coaches. Based on the interviews I've conducted and my years in the field, I've found that most voice coaches start out as teaching artists. That is not to say it is the only way to move into the areas of coaching professional voice users or professional actors. Coaches I interviewed like Mary McDonald and Amy Stoller are exceptions to the trend. However, the skills learned as a VCTA can be translated into the other fields. Coaching student productions and finding your voice in a conservatory or university environment can set the stage for your career as a Professional Voice Coach for Actors (PVCA). This is exemplified by coaches like Doug Honorof, Beth McGuire, Leith McPherson, Paul Meier, and Erik Singer, to name a few, who all spent time as a VCTA. Managing a classroom and finding your voice there certainly translates into helping a professional voice user find their voice in their field. Professional Voice User Coaches (PVUC) like Rena Cook, Nancy Houfek, and Patty Raun, who all started their voice coaching careers working as teaching artists. The classroom can indeed be your laboratory for developing your unique voice in the field.

CHAPTER 3

The Professional Voice Coach for Actors (PVCA)

In this chapter, we'll explore who the Professional Voice Coach for Actors (PVCA) is, possible avenues for preparing to coach a professional actor, and some types of coaching that you might encounter when coaching working actors. For the purposes of this publication, I have chosen the term "Professional Voice Coach for Actors" to cover voice coaching for working actors in the fields of film, television, theatre, voice over, video games, and other professional performance avenues. The needs of these productions vary and can include elements of vocal prosody, breath, resonance, dialect/accent, clarity, and connection to fellow actors and the text. The PVCA can be credited in a production as voice coach, voice/dialect coach, and dialect coach, and recently there has been a move to use the term "dialect designer" rather than "dialect coach" in credits. I

DOI: 10.4324/9781003006206-4

will use the terms "dialect" and "accent" interchangeably and will be addressing the coaching of productions in the English language. My intention is not to get granular in each specific venue, but rather to provide a broad overview with thoughts and guidance based on my own experience and that of other professionals working in the field. I will primarily use examples from coaching film and theatre. Although each of the specialty areas within PVCA has its own jargon and particular nuances, the following information and anecdotes provided will offer a possible road map for the aspiring PVCA.

PVCA BRIEF HISTORICAL OVERVIEW

The field of Professional Voice Coaching for Actors is relatively new. Edith Skinner published the original *Speak with Distinction* in 1942, and for a period of time, professional actors were coached to speak in a "Mid-Atlantic Standard." This style of speech is one that you might recognize from 1940s and 1950s American film actors who sounded neither British nor American. This led to the concept of "General American Speech." There is much written on this topic; the late Dudley Knight (2000) provided an incisive article in the *Voice and Speech Review* VASTA's academic journal, entitled "Standard Speech: The Ongoing Debate" that gives an overview of the history of an American Standard. Over time, audiences began to expect actors to reflect reality more authentically. Trey Taylor's (2013) article, "The Rise and Fall of Katharine Hepburn's Fake Accent" in *The Atlantic* gives a more in-depth history of this shift, including a story about Rita Moreno, who was cast in many roles requiring dialects or accents that were not her own. She recounts having to make up accents to fit various roles.

While it might be difficult to imagine a time when voice, speech, and dialects were not identified as a specific design element in productions, it was not until 1986 that the Voice and Speech Trainers Association (VASTA) was born.[1] The British Voice Association (BVA), which grew out of The Voice Research Society, was founded in 1991.[2] The Australian Voice Association (AVA) was founded in 1991.[3] These three organizations include members from both the medical and teaching fields, as well as individuals who coach professional actors. As I write these words, the field is changing, and it is important for voice professionals to stay connected with organizations such as VASTA, BVA, and AVA to keep current with best practices. Many voice coaches are also members of other specialty organizations such as the International Phonetic Association and The Pan American Vocology Association (PAVA), along with organizations particular to their modules of training and certifications. A partial list of these organizations is provided in the bibliography of this book.

The role of the PVCA as designer and coach has evolved to include the accent/dialect and voice of the character(s) to serve the vision of the production, director, and actors. Like all of the areas of voice coaching outlined in this book, the individual who serves as a PVCA may coach part-time or it could be their entire professional focus. The PVCA might come from an acting, teaching, or professional training program background. The PVCA coach could work as a resident coach for a theatre or film studio, but more likely they are hired on a production-by-production basis. Some coaches are brought in to work with one actor or an entire cast.

There are agents or liaisons who work with voice coaches such as Diane Kamp[4] and Amy Landon (Big Timber Artists), Pamela Vanderway (Dialect Coaches Worldwide),[5] Emmerson Denney, Jill McCullough, and Sarah Upson, to name a few. Generally, big-budget film productions will work with agents to find a coach with the appropriate experience for the project. Doug Honorof, a well-established PVCA, further elaborated:

> Sometimes, a production assistant is asked to search the web for several coaches to be interviewed, but usually the production will not hire a coach who has not come through a recommendation. Sometimes a producer knows an agent and reaches out directly for submissions. More often, productions are routed to a specific coach by a creative: a cast member, or, for film, the director or for tv, perhaps the showrunner. If not, someone from the production side—often the line producer, unit production manager, production coordinator, etc.—will reach out to a coach they already know or have had recommended to them. The coach then connects the production with an agent to work out a deal. Or, if the coach is unavailable, the coach may send the Production to an agent who might be able to submit another coach. So having representation can help you find work once you are established, but being known from past projects helps the most. And, however you find the work, agents can help with the deal itself and can troubleshoot issues down the road. In my case, I also have my agent and an attorney review consulting agreements for my loan-out corporation when studios require them. That is a step beyond the agent's deal memo.

As indicated above, having an agent is not the only way in. Whether you have an agent or not, you would likely benefit from connecting with someone who has deep knowledge in the field. It is not uncommon for the elite number of dialect coaches who are represented by agents to open the doors for newer coaches to gain agent representation. This can happen by virtue of being a protégé of someone who is currently represented. As film and television dialect coach, Erik Singer, shared with me:

> There are not that many dialect coaches working in major film and TV. So, everybody knows everybody, or at least knows who everybody is. And if you're on a job, you can't do another job simultaneously. So, you're going to recommend somebody else. That may be one way that you can build up a career: get really good at what you're doing and cultivate. Go to VASTA, cultivate relationships with colleagues, collaborate with them, and make friends. And you may then be in a position to be recommended for jobs when other people can't do them.
> —*Erik Singer*

It cannot be overstated that building relationships is very important. Many of the coaches I interviewed were re-hired by directors or production companies who were happy with the voice and dialect work they executed on the initial hire. Credentials from reputable production companies and "A List" and "B List" actors can also ultimately lead to representation.

MY STORY

I was fortunate to serve on the Acting Faculty at Yale School of Drama from 2002 to 2010, where I had the opportunity at times to work as a Voice/Dialect Coach at the Yale Repertory Theatre. It was there that I developed my style as a PVCA, working on productions directed by James Bundy, Liz Diamond, and Evan Yiounoulis, among others. It is not uncommon for a training program to be associated with a professional theatre, and that was my road into the field of PVCA. It was 2007, and I had been teaching at Yale School of Drama for five years. I had coached eight or nine professional shows and had worked on off-Broadway productions in New York City by that point.

The Hartford Stage, a regional theatre that has sent productions to Broadway, called me to coach Hal Holbrook and the cast of *Our Town* in a co-production with the Tony Award®-winning Alley Theatre, directed by Gregory Boyd. I seized the opportunity, did my homework, conducted interviews, and prepared materials for the actors. Apparently, it went well, as I ended up coaching twenty-eight productions for the Alley Theatre over the next ten years, along with numerous New York City productions and a fair amount of film and television too. But everyone has their own story, as you'll find when you read the Words of Wisdom section in this book and in the Support Materials online.

THE ROAD TO PVCA

There is not one way to become a PVCA. While I have shared my story, I think it is important to provide some insight into many possible avenues that can lead to coaching actors professionally. I interviewed a number of voice coaches who focus primarily on the world of PVCA coaching so I could provide their perspectives along with my own. Throughout this section of the book, I include commentary and anecdotes from Ben Furey, Doug Honorof, Mary McDonald, Leith McPherson, and Erik Singer. While there are many other notable PVCAs in the field, it is my hope that the stories of those featured here will offer you a glimpse into the world of the PVCA. You can also read more about them in their Words of Wisdom in the online e-Resources of this book.

WHAT IS THE JOB OF A PVCA?

As a PVCA, you are responsible for coaching each actor you work with to embody the voice, accent/dialect, and text of their role in a production. This production could be in film, television, theatre, voice over, video games, or any venue in which a professional actor is working. Your day will be as varied as the work is. If you are working in theatre, you will likely start sometime after noon and could work late into the night. In film and television, your call time and obligations could be at any hour. Your job is to have your vocal or accent/dialect material fully prepared prior to meeting the actor, and ideally you will have the opportunity to work with the actor prior to production. This means getting clear about what the director's vision is.

There are times when a director is unwavering in what they want, and there are other times when you have more leeway to bring in your suggestions and thoughts based on how you read and understand the script. You need to find out how much access you will have to the actors. There can be contractual limits because of actors' unions that need to be considered. Find out who your point person is for scheduling time with your actors. This contact could be the stage manager or the assistant director. In rare cases, I've been able to work with an entire cast to teach vocal warm-ups, and the director even participated. However, it is more likely that you will only have a limited time with each actor, and you will need to make sure you know how to creatively secure as much time as you can with each actor you are working with.

Theatre typically offers more opportunity for building in rehearsal time than other avenues. Nevertheless, if you are called in last-minute to work with an actor or on a production, you need to decide what you can realistically accomplish within the parameters provided. For the scope of this publication, I will focus on some of the skills you might want to cultivate and then look precisely at film and theatre coaching, because most of what you encounter in those mediums is transferable to other areas.

SELECTED TOPICS FOR THE PVCA

- IPA/Phonetics for Coaching
- Ingredients of a Successful PVCA or "Pronunciation, Posture, Prosody, and Pixie Dust"
- Coaching the Professional Actor: Notes from the Field
- Finding your Way

IPA/PHONETICS FOR COACHING

Most actors who come out of a conservatory or actor training program have encountered a voice and/or speech coach and some training in phonetics for accent and dialect work. However, not all professional actors come from a training program. In my experience, one of the reasons directors have shied away from voice and dialect coaches is that they don't want the actor to lose the authenticity and special "*je ne sais quoi*" that got them cast in the role. Somehow, there is a lingering belief that the coach will deliver a heavy-handed approach and turn the actor into a disembodied caricature. While the PVCA coaches that

I spoke with undoubtedly have their own styles, there is a through line that all coaches share: a desire to serve the actor, director, and production by helping actors find an authentic, embodied, healthy, and sustainable voice/dialect/accent.

One of the coaches I spoke at length with was Doug Honorof, who primarily coaches for film and television in English and other languages, and he manages a team that provides transcreation services: translation for shows with multilingual dialogue. Doug trained as an actor and writer as well as a linguist, and he has worked professionally in all three of those areas. While pursuing postgraduate studies in articulatory phonology at Yale (PhD, 1999), he became curious about the ways in which accent acquisition was different for adult actors working in their own primary languages as compared to adults acquiring another language. At the Yale School of Drama, he collaborated with Jill McCullough and Barbara Somerville on "Comma Gets a Cure," a diagnostic passage for accent study that includes all the sounds and major sound combinations of English. "Comma" has been adopted widely not only in phonetics research but also for archives used by actors and coaches who rely on primary source recordings in their work including the International Dialects of English Archive, founded by Paul Meier. Doug spoke to me about the origins of "Comma Gets a Cure":

> We were working on accent training materials for actors using HyperCard, which was this cool little multimedia application on early Macs. You would press a button and the software would play a sound, which was a big deal back then. (laughs) Anyway, HyperCard is no longer. We got pretty far, but then Apple completely re-engineered the operating system, and HyperCard stopped working altogether. So we dropped the project. But "Comma" came out of that partnership. This was when I was sitting in on classes as part of my mentorship in the MFA acting program at Yale. Barb ordered copies of John C. Wells for her speech students to read: *Accents of English,* three volumes. I don't know how many of my classmates worked through all of that. Some of it was very technical. But I did. And it got me thinking.

> I had been working on my doctorate at Yale and doing speech research at Haskins Labs with Louis Goldstein and Cathe Browman who developed Articulatory Phonology. At the time, Articulatory Phonology was considered a fairly radical linguistic theory. Louis and Cathe were saying that phonetics and phonology are really just different ways of looking at the same thing—the physiological gesture and physiological coordination in speech. I'll spare you the gory details for the moment, but the key point is that my research in the gestural basis of speech got me looking at the phoneme with a raised eyebrow, if you will. Basically, I don't trust phonemic transcriptions, and I barely trust my own phonetic transcriptions. I guess I really don't 100% buy the idea that speech is always divisible into segments in nature. Good chance the segment is often just an illusion that so many linguists impose on the speech stream because we know these languages like English that are written with an alphabet. Reading and writing have warped our view of linguistic reality in a way. In real life, gestures can be longer than or shorter than an individual letter of

the alphabet or IPA symbol, and they don't come one right after another. Speech gestures are overlapped in time. Like maybe gestures are the more psychologically real units of speech.

Now, at the time, most people who were doing accent training for actors were teaching sound substitution. "Signature sounds," some people called them, or "key sounds." A lot of people still do it that way, but certainly, back in the 1990s, we really weren't talking about lexical sets for vowels in the drama world the way Wells did in the linguistics world. I mean, there were sets of words in [*Speak with Distinction* by Edith] Skinner like the "ask list," but only for one accent. The lexical sets work for all English accents because they are based on the history of English sound systems. And also, they don't require letter-based transcription. And I was really thinking of transcription as a shorthand for gestures at best, but usually just a distortion.

So I started thinking we should really be shifting our consciousness about speech; that we should really start to focus more on the gesture, and that is where I was getting stuck on our sound-substitution tradition. I say our tradition, but to be fair, sound substitution was also used by lexicographers and language teachers. But in the acting world, I would see these handouts with sets of symbols from an implied standard accent on the left, then a little arrow pointing at a symbol for that sound in the target accent on the right. It was talked about as a process, you know, "In this accent, this sound goes to …" So, letter goes to letter. And part of the problem was that not everybody was starting from the same standard accent on the left, so those starting-point symbols didn't mean the same thing to every actor, plus static letters are not great stand-ins for actual articulatory gestures and their patterns of coordination. Space and time were getting lost in that manipulation of symbols. And a lot of actors don't naturally learn that way, anyway; the phonemic segment is too abstract.

Sometimes I just found it all very confusing. And I think that abstraction is part of the reason that so many actors hated their speech training, and why they shy away from phonetics, which really is not about transcription at all for us phoneticians. Even for phoneticians who still divide the speech stream into segments, not gestures, practical phonetics—that's what we call it when we teach transcription to "nubes"—that IPA stuff is really just about ear training; budding phoneticians learn it, then move on. And I thought actors should do the same thing, you know, do some ear training, but then actually use lexical sets to make sense of the vowels of the sound system of a dialect. So that's why I proposed "Comma" to begin with; it's organized around lexical sets, at least in part.

—Doug Honorof

One of the challenges for the PVCA is creating a road map of sorts for performers using accents. Coaches at least want to have some method that gives actors the tools to speak the text in an embodied and authentic way while using an accent. "Comma Gets a Cure" is used for a majority of the primary sample interview recordings housed in the invaluable online resource, the International Dialects of English Archives (IDEA).[6] The IDEA is the brainchild of Paul Meier, also featured in this book, who is Professor Emeritus at the University of Kansas, redundant. just University of Kansas. The IDEA holds more than 1,600 samples from 135 countries and territories and more than 170 hours of recordings and is currently the largest archive of its kind.

Voice/Dialect Coaches are called upon to help actors understand that the spelling of a word or a sound in English doesn't necessarily map perfectly to a corresponding sound for a character from another country. As Doug concurred, coaching an accent/dialect is more nuanced than simply substituting a particular English spelling with a sound in a dialect or accent:

> It's not just the idea of discrete sounds that I have a problem with. The sub-stitution part of sound substitution is a problem, too. "Just substitute the closest sound that you have in your own accent!" Of course, you're gonna sound ridiculous if you blindly substitute letter for letter; you're really just speaking a distorted version of *your own* accent at that point—that approach doesn't teach anyone to transform. It's no wonder a lot of actors who learn accents that way can sound awkward and stilted. But I think if acting students start by learning actual phonetics—and I don't mean phonetic symbols for English—but if they actually learn to make all the sounds of all the world's languages, even if they never really retain the symbols, using the whole instru-ment to imitate wildly different sounding languages in a more fine-grained way can be hugely helpful as a first step. And I mean that—a first step, because I almost never use phonetic transcription in coaching.

> I am glad I learned it; my transcription training reshaped the way I listen for sure; it built a kind of sensitivity to sound and gesture that I needed as an adult learner. But "Comma Gets a Cure" was meant to be used after that phonetic training, where the actor learns to explore the whole vocal instru-ment. And Barb was really dedicated to teaching the anatomy and physiology of it all to her actors, so my classmates had that foundation. But the idea was, after that, you could teach the lexical sets without referencing a standard accent, and that's what was new and hadn't really been done. When you look at the history of English, those words in the lexical sets hang together across accents for the most part. So, if you learn one of each of the sets or subsets within them—one word as an exemplar—and how it's said in the new accent, you'll then know how to make the vowels in roughly all the other words within each of those sets. And that's something that you can do if you are a native speaker of English no matter what accent you have. Even if you've never studied those sets, you know which words hang together because you know which words rhyme for you. So that's kind of what we did with "Comma."

> But it's not just about vowels. We wanted to have a passage that was con-versational and phonemically balanced. "The Rainbow Passage" isn't. People

keep making the mistake of assuming that, because "The Rainbow Passage" has been used by speech pathologists, that it's phonemically balanced. It wasn't meant for dialect study; [Grant] Fairbanks didn't include every sound of English in roughly every order. The passage is really more like written prose— and the content is very "scientistic." It doesn't mirror spoken language. But "Comma" isn't just about being conversational and balanced; there were lots of other considerations that went into shaping it—some additional lexical sets that aren't in Wells. His lexical sets are organized around RP and so-called "General American" English, so Wells gives subsets and so on. And we considered consonants that tend to vary across accents. We also added turns of a phrase that we hoped would bring out a variety of intonational phrases across accents. And when we had a draft of "Comma" done, we had the passage checked by English speakers from around the world, so it would not seem too strange no matter where it was used.

I wrote a *Voice and Speech Review* paper breaking down the passage in terms of what to listen for in each part, but now I think that paper may have been too technical for some coaches-in-training. And "Comma" is just a starting place. You also must study spontaneous speech recordings—oral histories and so on. But all of that is really just for the initial listening phase where you build sound memory and gestural memory. The real work doesn't start until you are done with *Comma*, until you get into embodied dialect and all the ways we need to push past that initial learning phase, so the learning itself doesn't get in the way. But at least if you are not fixated on phonetic symbols, you aren't bouncing from letter to letter trying to hit some string of symbolic targets in your head.

I know I can be snarky about phonemics, but I can't really be so ideological in my actual practice. I've actually worked with quite a few actors who are able to start from transcriptions or sound-substitutions, and then they fill in the blanks and come out the other end sounding great. So I can't honestly claim that there is never a use for the IPA after drama school, for actors who went. And I even occasionally make a note on my own copy of a script in the IPA, but I don't share those symbols with actors unless they ask. A few clients have used them, but it's rare. I usually just let the actors write their own notes, anyway—those who take written notes at all. However, I have some actors who ask me to learn their own "fauxnetic" system, and then I mark up the text for them, which I do because I figure they know what works best for them. Unless we realize that they don't know, and then we talk about trying something else. But the "something else" is never the IPA. Because I tend not to look at my own IPA transcription notes after I make them, when I do.

I guess I think the value of narrow phonetic transcription after your initial training is just in being forced to listen more closely, so you can make choices among symbols. Then once you make the choice, you move on. I might even listen to a native speaker recording of "Comma," and from that, I transcribe each of the lexical sets in a list. But a lot of times I don't; I just plot the lexical set keywords on vowel charts. Or, maybe I just internalize it all without writing much these days. I coach a lot of TV; there isn't much time for prep. You cut every corner you can. Our days are long enough.

—Doug Honorof

When coming from an academic background, it is important to remember that the IPA primarily gives the coach clarity and tools for coaching. And while most training programs teach actors some version of the IPA, it is not the job of the PVCA to teach a professional actor how to read and write symbols. As Erik Singer stated:

There is a long and storied tradition of voice and speech and accent teachers using very imagistic language to move actors toward a desired result. Sometimes those things work, and they're great. And sometimes they don't. And it's going to vary according to the individual person. Everybody has a different learning style; everybody's going to receive things in different ways and be able to hear things in different ways. There's no one thing that's going to work for everybody. But the deep and fundamental insight for me was, if *we* know the physical shape, the physical speech action, that is desired—that is our target thing and here's the thing that *you're* doing—then I can try any number of ways to get you from one to the other. I directly physically describe it and try to give you the kinesthetic feel and experience of being able to do it. I do that a great deal, and I think it ends up being very powerful and accessible for almost everybody. [But] if I can get you there by telling you to, "Make a slightly rosier sound," and it does it, fantastic.

—Erik Singer

The IPA can be very useful for the coach, but ultimately when coaching professional actors, it is important to meet the individual where they are and lead them to an embodied and authentic performance using all of the tools in your disposal.

INGREDIENTS OF A SUCCESSFUL PVCA OR "PRONUNCIATION, POSTURE, PROSODY, AND PIXIE DUST"

While many PVCAs feel that an in-depth knowledge of the IPA is essential to their coaching work, there are also very successful PVCAs who have a cursory knowledge of the IPA and spend more time working with other methods to help their actors embody the voice and dialect of a character. Each coach brings their own magic to the process. One of the qualities I noted in every person that I interviewed was a love of learning and an almost insatiable curiosity. As PVCA, Mary McDonald said:

I think the coach needs to know as much as they can know, and they certainly need to be lifelong learners. I will say this: my expertise in [the] IPA is very shallow. I can make my way through [it] about as well as I could make my way through Paris with my French. I can answer any question I need to answer, but possibly not on the same day—quite likely later that afternoon, but quite possibly not in the moment. So that's number one. Number two: for me within KTS (Knight-Thompson Speechwork), I embraced the lexical sets. And though I have a fair understanding of the biomechanical system here, I've discovered different things. One is, no matter what an actor says, they don't know IPA. No matter what. And if they do, the rare actor who does is also an actor who is fear-filled and stuck in their head. If they're relying solely on the IPA, they're clinging to something as a form of superstition as opposed to releasing and surrendering and opening to being in their body. I use the "four pillars." My four pillars are pronunciation, posture, prosody and pixie dust, which is what the actor brings.

—*Mary McDonald*

As mentioned earlier, the IDEA is an incredible resource for spoken word samples. It is also very helpful to see what the mouth and the body are doing in a primary sample: the facial and physical gestures contribute to the authentic embodiment of character. The "Accent Tag" feature on YouTube can provide glimpses into accents and dialects. I've included select resources in this book and will direct you to join the Voice & Speech Resources page on Facebook for up-to-date suggestions for finding primary accent and dialect samples. Often coaches will have their own collection of primary samples, which can help with the specificity of prosody. At one point I was coaching a theatrical production of *The Lieutenant of Inishmore* by Martin McDonagh, and I Google searched "local businesses in Galway, Ireland." I found the name of a pub and cold-called the owner in the town of Inishmore who was willing to speak with me. The director and the actors, in the production that I coached, loved the recording, and that resource certainly contributed to a deeper and authentic experience of the dialect's unique prosody. Doug Honorof elaborated on the importance of coaching the melodic components of a dialect:

One of the aspects of speech that's specific, to specific accents, is the melody. The intonation contours: both what those contours look like and also which ones are used for which intentions by native speakers. It's a super complicated problem, but it's also something that actors *have* to be able to manage in order to sound like native speakers, because they are expressing a wide range of meaning in character. If you get all the sounds right but keep your native accent's intonation contours, it still sounds super weird. The rhythm, the intonation, those global properties, the length of sounds, how long they are relative to other sounds, where people slow down in a sentence and where they don't, where they get loud and where they get quiet—these things can also be specific to a voice.

In other words, the global properties can also be character-specific: Some people just have idiosyncratic things that they do with their voices, but also, there are global patterns bigger than any gesture—or phoneme if you must; those patterns can be part of an accent. They can be "phonologized"; they can be part of the system. And so, you have to learn all of the prosodics—the suprasegmentals, and it can be tricky to teach. Barb had us use *Better English Pronunciation, New Edition* by J.D. O'Connor to learn a sort of old-fashioned RP. And in chapter seven O'Connor, particularly at the end of the chapter, lists different intonation contours and how they're used in sentences according to what type of intention you have. And I thought that was very useful for actors. O'Connor has four tune types, but the way they're applied multiplies them. And, obviously, there are many more intonation contour types in any given accent, so that's just a start.

Kenneth Pike and Dwight Bolinger did a lot of descriptive work on intonation back in the day with similar types of notation. It's worth a trip to the stacks of your local library. I don't teach any of those systems in production work, though. I use impressionistic terms when we are doing our imitation exercises together; I learn with the actors because most jobs are customized for the part. Then, once it settles in a bit, I mostly just talk with the actors in dialect whenever I see them, and I hope the melody, loudness contours, rhythm, and all of that is absorbed by exposure. And when it slips, I remind them to go back to the primary source recordings and play with just the melody or what-have-you. For the actor, it's all art, not science, but the suprasegmentals part is doubly so.

—*Doug Honorof*

There is undoubtedly an element of design to coaching dialects. I think the "pixie dust" that Mary McDonald referred to earlier could also apply to the individual coach's approach to working with each actor and production. We are not meant to be linguists who are creating an exact replica of a dialect. The director's vision, audience's expectations, and elements of intelligibility need to be considered. Many of the coaches I spoke with emphasized the importance of coming from an acting background. This can build a deeper compassion for the delicate and complex process that the actor faces in embodying the character. Erik Singer concurred:

Do as much acting as you can and learn as much as you can about acting. You need the anatomy, the linguistics, the phonetics, the science, the mechanics, and the understanding of the physical actions at as deep a level as you possibly can. But you also need to know how actors work and how acting works. You're supporting the process of an individual actor, and you're supporting the storytelling of that actor and the director and all the rest of the people collaborating and telling that story. Everything you say and every choice you make—it's always a choice—adds to that. An accent is always a design, even if you're like, "We are doing Martin Luther King, Jr.," you're still designing that accent. You're still choosing what and how, and you're still morphing it through the filter of that individual actor's vocal tract, but also there's the actor's soul, being, imagination, and creativity.

—*Erik Singer*

It is ultimately your job to use your tools as the dialect coach or designer to help the actor breathe life into the character.

COACHING THE PROFESSIONAL ACTOR

Coaching the professional actor comes with its own unique challenges. Ideally, you will be able to schedule sessions to work with the actor prior to the start of a production. This could be as few as one or two in-person or online coaching sessions. As stated previously, you need to be prepared to meet the actor and production and do this as effectively and efficiently as possible. The stakes are particularly high in film, and if you have a good relationship with the actors, they are often open to working with you between scenes or takes. You will develop your ability to read each situation and in doing so, create the best outcome possible. As Erik Singer shared:

> Every set is different. Wildly different. A lot flows from the director. There are directors that hate dialect coaches. Perhaps, to give them the benefit of the doubt, they've had bad experiences with not very professional dialect coaches. The absolute imperative is not to cost the production money. I never keep this exactly in my head, but every minute on set in a big budget movie is worth [about] $10,000. And so, if you are taking an extra minute giving a note to an actor when everybody else is ready and the director is ready for a take, that costs the production $10,000 or maybe more. You don't want to do that. That is an absolute no-no. So, there is a whole other layer of things you have to get good at very fast as a coach on productions like that, which is understanding the flow and rhythm of the set, having eyes in the back of your head, making sure you don't block the way when equipment is coming through, knowing that when they yell, "Points, points!" you have to get out of the way, making sure that you're aware of when the first AD [Assistant Director] wants to go, etc.
>
> —*Erik Singer*

If you are working in film, you will have a precise call time, which you will likely not know until the night before. You need to make sure to be at the appointed location with plenty of extra time, so you can arrive on set in time. Theatre is a bit more predictable. If you are located in the same area at the theatre you are coaching, you will likely meet with the actors in person. If you are in a different location, you may work primarily or entirely remotely with your actors. Prior to the COVID-19 pandemic, I was often flown in to work with actors during the first read-through and first week of rehearsal. I then would be available remotely during the bulk of rehearsals and subsequently fly out again to work with actors on the production during the technical and dress rehearsals.

Since the pandemic, the employment of the PVCA has changed along with numerous elements of production. Some of the coaches I spoke with have been conducting all their work via Zoom or some online method for many or all of their PVCA gigs. Undoubtedly, the world has undergone a tectonic shift, and the post-pandemic coaching environment will continue to evolve.

When you are coaching actors online, it is important to make sure that you and they have a solid internet connection so that time is not wasted. Additionally, it can be challenging to help your actors take the coaching from an online medium and translate it effectively to stage or set. An astute coach can build in methods for helping the actor explore the varied vocal and physical dynamics appropriate to different mediums, even when coaching online. Remote coaching has the potential to be particularly effective for coaching dialects and accents as well as audiobooks or voice overs. It can be very helpful to give your actor permission to record the coaching session, or obtain their consent for you to record it and send the recording to them afterward. My preference is to have the actor record the session, so there is never any question that I hold any materials that the actor might feel ownership over.

There is not one clear path to becoming a PVCA. Most PVCAs have varying degrees of acting and teaching experience prior to focusing solely on coaching actors. You can work with regional theatres or specialize in certain genres. If your goal is to become one of the elite go-to coaches in the field, it can be difficult to juggle other areas of voice coaching. Especially if your chosen specialty is coaching film, you could be called on to be in various locations for months at a time. Leith McPherson started her career as a teacher, which led to coaching at the Melbourne Theatre Company. Her work coaching actors in theatre opened the doors to coaching actors for screen, which ultimately took her to New Zealand to work on *The Hobbit* trilogy. She still takes on an occasional teaching gig, but she balances her time between stage and screen. When I asked Leith for her advice for the PVCA, she emphasized the importance of developing the following:

The ability to be flexible and collaborative. The ability to know when *not* to give a note is as important as when to give a note. If you can develop emotional intelligence, you can improve your flexibility and your ability to read a room. It's important not only to know what an actor needs, but it's also important to know where your place is in the bigger collaborative process in a particular moment—not to feel that you need to assert yourself. If you feel the need to assert yourself just for the sake of contribution, then you're in approval mode. You're not attending to the task, which is to serve the text and serve the production in whatever context that applies, whether it's in theatre or on screen. In a classroom, your ability to adapt to the moment is something that you can develop, and so is your ability to empathize with the other.

Empathy is also something you can work on, not to assume that the behavior you are interacting with is actually the root issue. Ninety-nine-point-whatever percent of the time you're working with anxiety, and if you can't see that, you will attend to the wrong thing. If you *can* see that, and if you can help someone move through that into a mode that is going to enable collaboration and flow, well, woah! Those are the most joyous moments for me in my work. It started for me with David Carey at the [Royal] Central School of Speech and Drama. One of the first things I noticed in him and his work was humility and the ability to say, "I don't know." That means that in the moment you are correctly assessing the landscape and finding a way forward as a team, rather than feeling that you need to be someone who espouses an answer. I don't know how it's possible to feel that you know all of the answers when all of the questions haven't been imagined yet.

—Leith McPherson

Leith was one of the over 200 voice teachers who studied under David Carey at Central School. David was the Course Leader of the Voice Studies course for seventeen years before becoming Resident Voice and Text Director at Oregon Shakespeare Festival in Ashland, Oregon. When I spoke to David, his advice to the PVCA was this:

Going back to my own experience, it's about being clear about what your strengths are and what kind of work you want to do. If you're coming straight out of any kind of training, you might be thinking, "I've got all this wonderful training, I can do anything." Well, yeah, but what are your strengths and where's your passion? One of the pieces of advice I gave my voice teaching students was to be prepared to build a portfolio of work over the first two to five years of graduating. You're not going to walk straight into a full-time job. You may be extremely lucky to do that, but my basic advice was not to expect that.

Also, be prepared to have a part-time job that has nothing to do with your profession. But maybe use it to forward your other skills in building up your business acumen, so that you know what you need to do for taxes or what you need to do for keeping records. There's so much you need to do, so many skills you need to acquire in the professional world. You can build those skills when you're not being a voice teacher. It's hard, particularly because today, there are far more people who are interested in being vocal coaches and who know that coaching is a professional option. So, you need to be prepared to take time to build up that portfolio and seek the work. And perhaps outside of the area that you might most want to work in.

—David Carey

Some coaches prefer to be more invisible, while others have a more obvious presence. As you gain more experience, you will find your style. Whatever your personal "pixie dust," it is vital for your success as a PVCA and for the production that you learn to focus on the task at hand. If you are one of the many PVCAs coming from an acting background, you will have to shift from an actor to a coach mindset. Actors are always auditioning for a role, and you are not the actor. In fact, if anything, you are playing the role of vocal coach because you were hired to fulfil the demands of that role. It can be a bumpy transition to go from being the one who was given notes to the one *giving* the notes. Using your actor tools to play the role of voice coach in a fulsome and authentic manner can certainly help you serve your clients.

Finding a way to clearly articulate the changes you would like to see and hear the actor engage in can present challenges. Leith McPherson elaborated when she shared her experience of learning how to function in a healthy and effective way in the role of the PVCA while navigating the complexities of coaching on a big-budget set:

Actors generally don't like being corrected, but [one of the actors in the cast of *The Hobbit*] particularly did not like being corrected. So, on a daily basis, it would be my job to step into set and say, "Actually, the line is such and such." He hated it, and he yelled at me a lot. A lot. I started to crumble. When somebody that you revere is yelling at you, of course you assume that you've done something wrong. I thought, "Okay, I'm not coping. I am not coping." It was a lot of stress and self-doubt, and I thought, "Wait a minute, there must be tools for this. I need to develop resilience. I need to find a way to work with and through this self-doubt that I feel, and this level of stress."

And so, I did a lot of reading and that led me to an epiphany, which changed *everything*. It changed everything in me and around me, which was the realization that two of the modes that we can be in when we are interacting with other people are whether we are *task* focused or *approval* focused. And I realized like a bolt from the blue that every time I stepped toward [him], I was in approval mode. I was hoping for a special moment of connection or validation from an actor who was under incredible pressure, who had received the lines at maybe 5:00 that morning, and it was now 12:30 before the lunch break. His frustration was with himself, not with me, and it was egotistical to think that it had anything to do with me. I was looking for something I was never going to get. I was looking for love in all the wrong places.

And in that moment, I thought, "My God. Stop." (laughs) "Just stop! You have to stay in task mode. It is your job, especially when we're quoting from Tolkien, but we're trying to get a script in the can. Stick to your task and don't look for validation when you're not going to get it from somebody who is in a state of anxiety and stress." It has *nothing* to do with you. I had to remind myself because the fight/flight/*what-have-I-done* instinct reflex is so strong that I would have to write it on my call sheet every day. I would write a little mantra going, "Breathe, ask what's really going on, stay *task* focused." When I did that and when I reminded myself, I became invulnerable, because it just wasn't about me; it was about the job. And in that moment, I also got this landscape vision [that] almost every actor I was working with was in approval mode. And yet, the director was in task mode.

It was a matrix moment; it was a lightbulb moment; it was amazing. What I realized was that, especially with actors who come on to set just for the day, they weren't doing their best work; they were re-auditioning. They were trying to show why they should get the job when they were there to *do* the job. That realization—and practice, because it takes practice on a daily basis, on an hourly basis—that realization changed everything and meant that I was a much better coach. I was a much better crew member. I could step to the director, who had to answer four hundred questions before breakfast, in a moment and ask him something to do with my work, because it wasn't about having a special moment with [him]. It wasn't about saying, "Am I doing a good job? Please give me any kind of sign that I'm doing a good job." It was doing the job. And that is its own reward, but it also takes you out of fight/flight/freeze, and it lets you be there for the other person. That's the definition of a coach, isn't it? You are there for the other to empower and to support.

—*Leith McPherson*

Getting clear about what you are there to do as a coach makes all the difference. I remember when I was an actor and I worked with a voice coach who was probably a bitter actor. This person really wanted to be an actor and seemed to want my job rather than their job. As the voice coach, you need to "stay in your lane" and love the lane you're in! Ben Furey offered another key to success in the field when he told me this:

Don't approach anything to do with acting in your coaching. Phrase everything in terms of what the actor and the director are talking about. [In] the first coaching job I did, the director had been really put off by a voice coach who basically started to redirect the actors. That's not what we're there for. So, get out of the way and say, "What do you (the director or actor) need? What are you looking for? How can I help you?" And be gentle in giving notes. I had a 65-year-old veteran Broadway actor say to me on the last show I did in New York, "It's been great working with you. *You're* not scary." And it shocked me that this guy [who] had done so many shows was used to dialect coaches being scary. It was a horrifying thing for me.

—*Ben Furey*

There is an alchemical quality to the work of a coach. We are coaching human beings, who each have their own stories and psychology that they carry with them. We have an obligation to approach our work with sensitivity and care.

FIND YOUR WAY

As with any of the areas of vocal coaching, it takes time and experience to develop your style. Inevitably there will be new venues that present themselves, and creating your inner circle of trusted mentors and coaches will help you continue to grow and flourish in the field. Mary McDonald put it beautifully when I asked her to share her advice for those new to the field of the PVCA:

Do the work. That's the best way to ban imposter syndrome. Do the work. Ask for help when you need it. When you're scared, check in and seek whether or not you really need to be, because so often that fear is not coming from a reliable narrator. Embrace your beautiful authority. Give it wings. Never stop learning.

—*Mary McDonald*

NOTES

1   https://www.vasta.org/
2   https://www.britishvoiceassociation.org.uk/history.htm
3   https://australianvoiceassociation.com.au/about-us/
4   https://www.wmagazine.com/story/diane-kamp
5   https://www.dialectcoaches.com/
6   https://www.dialectsarchive.com/

The Professional Voice User Coach (PVUC)

In this chapter, we'll explore who the Professional Voice User (PVU) is, possible avenues for preparing to coach a PVU, and some types of coaching that one might encounter as a PVUC. For the purposes of this publication, I have chosen the term "Professional Voice User" to cover voice coaching for executives, politicians, motivational speakers, public figures, clergy, broadcast journalists, and anyone who is not coming from the background of a trained actor. The needs of these individuals vary and can include elements of vocal prosody, storytelling, clarity in message, authenticity, and even body language and code-switching in order to connect with different audiences.

DOI: 10.4324/9781003006206-5

PVUC JOB DESCRIPTION

There are many avenues to this field, and it is not unusual for a client to need more than voice coaching. Their needs may fall under the larger umbrella of Communication "comms" Coaching or Executive Presence (EP) coaching. Importantly, many communication or executive presence coaches do not necessarily have a specialty or background in voice coaching or actor training. This gap creates an opportunity for someone with an actor training or a teaching artist background to differentiate themselves in the field of PVUCs. There are thousands of companies and individuals who can use our services, so there are a multitude of possibilities to create a niche for yourself and to explore how your unique background, training, and voice can be of service to PVUs.

MY STORY

I didn't set out to become a PVUC, although about half of my professional work at the time of writing this book has been with executives. PVU coaching came to me without my seeking it out, although (unsurprisingly) my work in all fields of voice coaching helped to prepare me for this path. After completing my MFA in acting and fulfilling my initial goal of being a theatre artist in New York, I found myself called to the field as a Voice Coach as Teaching Artist (VCTA). I was hired for my first voice teaching job, outside of graduate school, in 1998 by Beth McGuire for The School for Film and Television in New York City. Four years later, Evan Younoulis hired me to teach speech at the Yale School of Drama, where I spent eight years as part of the acting faculty. It was during that time that I started to receive requests for PVU coaching. I began to parlay what I had developed working with actors and apply it to executive coaching. After all, as William Shakespeare famously stated, "All the world's a stage and all the men and women merely players."

Through happenstance, I connected with Barry Nalebuff, co-founder of HonestTea and Professor at Yale School of Management, to help him with his on-camera executive presence. At that time Barry was being asked to do a number of classes and speeches that were being recorded. I began to translate the exercises I used to help actors look natural and authentic to the world of the executive. The plethora of TedTalk opportunities, and with them the expectation to look and sound polished on camera, had not yet become the norm. Working with Barry opened the door that led me to found Pamela Prather Coaching, LLC, a concierge coaching firm that has worked with "C-suites" from PepsiCo, Netflix, Facebook, Noom, and Care.com, along with executives from financial firms such as HIG Capital, Bain Capital, The Carlyle Group, APAX Partners, Silverlake, Global Endowment Group, Harren Equity Partners, and TA Associates—to name a few. When the global pandemic hit in 2020, the expectation for executives to appear camera ready and present like actors grew. While in-person coaching will always be a "stage" that professionals will need to appear on, I believe the online and hybrid meeting business model will only continue to grow as new technology develops, allowing for more efficient and inclusive virtual meetings and presentations. This means more opportunities for the PVUC.

WHAT DOES THE LIFE OF A PVUC LOOK LIKE?

Like all the areas of voice coaching outlined in this book, the individual who coaches PVUs may coach part-time, or it could be their entire professional focus. Generally, the PVUC either works as an independent contractor for a larger organization or gains work as a solopreneur. You might work with large groups in a workshop or training program or with smaller groups in targeted management team workshops or skill-building sessions. Or you may work one-to-one with any type of PVU, preparing them for team meetings, keynotes, or helping to enhance the efficacy of their communication delivery style. If you are working within an organization, you would likely be freelancing as an independent contractor. If you have decided to explore the world of PVU coaching on your own, you might decide to specialize in certain areas and create a niche for yourself.

I interviewed a number of voice coaches who focus primarily on the world of PVU coaching so that I could offer their perspectives along with my own. Throughout this section of the book, I will include commentary and anecdotes from Hilary Blair, Tom Burke, Andrea Caban, Rena Cook, Andrea Haring, Nancy Houfek, Amy Hume, Jenny Kent, Leith McPherson, Scott Miller, Bonnie Raphael, and Patty Raun. Each of these phenomenal coaches has taken their own unique path into the field of PVU coaching, and their stories offer a glimpse into the world of the PVUC. Full versions of their Words of Wisdom are available through this book's Support Materials.

WHAT DO YOU DO AS A PVUC?

While working with a PVU client often starts as purely "voice coaching," this work frequently expands beyond vocal skills into messaging, non-verbal communication, and even clothing choices. This evolution means helping the PVU understand that they are playing a role as a CEO, yoga teacher, lawyer, or politician. I often talk about helping the individual consciously create their "character" at work. Inevitably, someone will say, "I'm not an actor." I reply, "Imagine picking up your cell phone and your best friend from high school is calling. How would you speak to them? What would you say?" You can see that I'm already asking them to "act as if." They might not realize it, but they are already playing a role with me. I give that thought a moment, and then I say, "And now imagine your boss just walked in and asked you how your latest project is going." Without question, every person I've tried this exercise with experiences a shift in vocal and physical expression. "See?" I say, "You are playing roles all the time; you just have never thought of it that way."

At this point, I usually get an affirmative nod, and the PVU gets curious about how a voice coach can help them. I might help my clients identify the roles they play, how they work on a variety of "stages," and I teach them voice, speech, and performance techniques that will help them play their role(s) more effectively. I might help them identify the different venues they work in and how they will need to show up both internally and externally, with or without electronic audio enhancement, in either a live or virtual setting.

In my experience, and in the opinion of every PVUC that I interviewed, the keys are to connect with the needs of the client, find your authentic voice as a coach, and deliver exercises and techniques that serve the needs of your clients. There is no "right" way; every coach just needs to find *their* way. Below you will find common topics and questions with thoughts from working coaches that might help.

SELECTED TOPICS FOR THE PVUC

- Breath Coaching
- Translating Exercises for the PVU
- What about "Accent Modification" for the PVU?
- Practice
- Simple is Not Simple
- Helping Your Client Transform and Getting out of the Way

BREATH COACHING

Spending time working on the breath is fundamental in helping your client connect with their audience and fully embody a role. The challenge with the PVU is that they don't usually have the time or "bandwidth" for long-term coaching engagements. They will come to you looking for a quick fix, and you must remind them that a theatrical play rehearses for a certain period of time (weeks or months) or that an actor training program can be two to four years. Nevertheless, one thing that you can help your clients with is breathing. There are myriad of breath exercises that you can adapt from your own training and background. You will often find that your clients are able to intellectually process the idea of breathing and sounding, but it can be challenging for them to feel it in their bodies.

When I began dipping my toe into the arena of PVU coaching, I became certified in a coaching program recognized by the International Coaching Federation. I found that experience helped me begin to adapt actor exercises for the PVU. As a coach, you must know your audience well. Early in my career, I remember working with a group of executives and wanting to show them their diaphragm and the holistic connection of breath to performance. So, I pulled up a Tom Myers *Anatomy Trains* deep-front line dissection video. The room turned green, and I just about lost my audience. I learned my lesson, and fortunately the story became a bit of a joke.

Rena Cook shared the importance of introducing breathing when coaching her clients:

> Breath is also, as you know, absolutely key, and the first thing is just encouraging clients to breathe and be aware that if you just exhale gently, the inhale comes in by itself. [*She demonstrates.*] Exhale gently, wait, release your belly, and the next breath comes in. So you get them to access the deep central breathing in a natural and organic way. Then, we find the moment when the inhale becomes the exhale and mark it with the word "Now." Then expand that to include the phrase, "And now I am ready to speak."
>
> —*Rena Cook*

Hilary Blair recounted a moment when one of her clients was simply not breathing. She was trying all her tricks, and then she found out that the woman had lost her husband recently. And while it is not our job as coaches to dig into the "why" of such matters, we can be curious, observe, and then help our clients become aware that they are holding their breath or bracing their bodies. Then we can provide them with exercises to help them feel and find their presence. While this might seem elementary to coaches, it is actually a huge revelation to many clients, and there are ways to support people in connecting to themselves without crossing the line into therapy. Hilary shared:

> So that one was a classic one for me—understanding when people are holding their breath, how much of an impact it has on them, when they are nervous with a new position at work or, when they're having home trouble. It's impacting their productivity. So, if I ask someone to think about something in their past, I simply say, "Think about that. That's not for me to know." I'm really very, very clear about that line. That's super important: coaching goes forward, therapy goes back, in that if you're not trained there, *do not* go there.
>
> —*Hilary Blair*

The PVUC is inevitably coaching more than the voice, and often, when someone hires you, they don't know what they need. It is incumbent upon you to ask questions and understand the needs and expectations your client has. You need to be clear in how you message and impart the lessons that will best serve your client. I send a questionnaire to my clients prior to our first session to get the ball rolling and help frame our conversation and expectations. Scott Miller believes that by educating his PVU audiences about the profound importance of breath, he can help them more consciously obtain desired outcomes:

> Voice [coaching] is the vehicle by which I can get into the room, but ultimately, it's breath, right? And breath is inhaling, and breath is exhaling;

and breath is holding or doing neither. And neurologically what we find is that there are very specific things that happen when you're inhaling, when you're exhaling, and when you're doing neither. And we find that these actions are deeply connected to decision-making, interpretation, bias, and anxiety. The way we literally take in oral information is through our skin … I don't have a stake in the game as a scientist. My job, as I see it, is to share information. And I believe once that information is shared, different outcomes will occur.

—Scott Miller

PVU clients tend to be more product-oriented than any of the other clients or students mentioned in this book. If you engage your client in the most amazing breath exercises you have ever encountered, but don't contextualize that for them or give them clear signposts that help them understand the destination, you might not get a second session with them. It is up to you to connect the dots for your clients and set up clear deliverables and desired outcomes.

TRANSLATING EXERCISES FOR THE PVU

If you are coming from the world of actor coaching or academia, you might be wondering: how do I take all of the process-based exercises that work in the classroom or the rehearsal space and translate it into the PVU world? How do I dial up those skills from working with actors, and the myriad of "weird acting exercises," and make them palatable for the executive? From my own experience, as well as the experience of the many coaches I interviewed, there is a collective view that seemingly simple exercises can be significant and impactful. Additionally, it is useful to translate the language of acting into that of the world you are coaching in. Your PVU clients are performing on their stages, so you can help them to unpack their particular "given circumstances," which will enable meaningful growth for your clients. Patty Raun shared her experience with me:

First of all, I start out with really simple and easy things like doing a basic warmup. People can experience a change in their relationship to the physical world and to one another in a ten or fifteen-minute warmup—or a "performance practice" if you want to call it that rather than calling it a "warmup." The process [of performance practice] is actually one of the most important things. We're not warming up for anything; this *is* a thing. So, allowing them to experience that change in their own perception and ability to just make sound, and to hear other people's ability to make sound, is vital. It's really tangible. Here's proof. "And now, if you choose to follow me a little farther (we don't have to go too much farther, but if you choose to follow me just a little farther), I'll put you in relationship with somebody else. And we'll experience how that connection and those vibrations—both literal and figurative vibrations—can change the relationship between the two of you."

—Patty Raun

And while in many ways helping clients tune into breath, vibration, and text can seem rather elementary, it's important to remember that most of your PVU clients have had little to no training in vocal health, breath, vocal prosody, storytelling, and connection to text. Most clients in this category are more comfortable behind a desk than they are breathing and speaking in an embodied way. Patty continued:

> And so, it's really one tiny step at a time. I also make it very clear in any promotional materials that I have, or blurbs that people write about the event, that they understand that it's *very* participatory. That they're not going to come in and take notes; they're not going to be recording on their cell phones; they're not going to be watching a PowerPoint. They're going to be in a big open room. They're going to be rolling around on the floor, and they'd better wear comfortable clothes. And they're going to be out of their comfort zones. And one of the things that I'm finding right now with people, especially early career scientists and engineers, is that there's a real hunger for things that *do* take them out of their comfort zones—that help them imagine their own work in different ways. So, there's not enough time in the day for me to do the work that I'm doing because there's so much demand for it.
>
> —*Patty Raun*

It has become clear to me from my discussions with voice professionals around the world that we share a collective view regarding the concept of voice as being more than simply vocal production. Being a voice coach includes the vibrations your client exudes in the room, the words they choose, the way they listen, and their overall presence. As Patty shared in our conversation:

> I feel like, in some ways, voice teachers have this trained and intentional ability to listen and to hear the subtleties of what other people are expressing, and what they're not expressing, and to sometimes help them bring those things forward. And I think what the world needs right now is better listeners. I would say probably 80% of what I teach and what I do is listening. Especially with scientists, and again, the folks in highly technical fields, what they often don't do is listen to the people that are going to be most affected by their work. (laughs) My initial contact with people quite often is, "Could you come in and teach us how to do a presentation?" And I have a standard reply, "That's really not what I do. What I do is teach people how to be in relationship, not unidirectional.

Patty went on to explain an exercise that she uses with her clients from Kristin Linklater's work:

> There's one exercise that I just did in class this week. It's part of the River Story Sequence that Kristin Linklater [taught]. It's a profound experience for those of us that have had that, and I've been teaching it for nearly thirty years. It also is connected to a phrase that I always start the River Story Sequence with, which is, "I am here in this room with all of you." That phrase that starts

with the word "I" and ends with the word "you." And then to think about how those two words are exactly the same thing if we just switch places: you're my "I" and I'm your "you."

That sense of taking the other person's perspective and really trying to understand how you might be experiencing the world, how you might be receiving my communication or connection. That's what voice is to me—it's empathy, and it's understanding that my visual vibrations, my physical vibrations, my vocal vibrations are all part of this connection, as are yours to me. And that, to me, is the definition of empathy. It's not sympathy; it's not compassion. It's literally trying to say, "You and I are switching places, or both of us are in the same place at the same time, back and forth."

—Patty Raun

I spoke with Nancy Houfek, another academic who has bridged into working full-time as a PVUC. She took the rigor from the MFA program that she headed at Harvard University and translated actor training concepts into a language for the PVU. Nancy offered some clear advice on finding a way into PVU coaching:

When I left Harvard after seventeen years at the ART, I thought that a lot of my non-theatre work would dry up because I didn't have that Harvard connection. In fact, I've booked more clients and workshops since then because, without theatre classes and coaching, I'm available more. I offer workshops in corporate communication, storytelling, negotiation, or leadership, depending on the needs of the client. All of my workshops are linked to the theatre and have aspects of the theatre in them. For example, when I lead a negotiation workshop, I talk about having a clear purpose and using a variety of tactics. I always include a section on vocal production and clarity of speech in whatever content I'm offering. Word of mouth, repeat workshops with previous clients (some of whom I've been working with for decades), and my website and LinkedIn presence are how work comes to me.

—Nancy Houfek

WHAT ABOUT "ACCENT MODIFICATION" FOR THE PVU?

I toyed with whether I should even use the term "accent modification" in the book and decided it was necessary because both "accent reduction" and "accent modification" are still widely used in the non-actor world. In a recent conversation with Paul Meier, he reminded me that many PVUCs have clients from countries around the world who find coaching via internet searches.

People still go looking for "accent reduction" or "accent modification" whether we like those terms or not. My Google search today returned 13 million results for the first term and 16 million for the second. The two search terms are alive and well because, presumably, coaches design their websites to attract as many as possible clients who search that way. "American Accent Training" is a more popular search term (46 million results), and my search for "British English Accent Training" returned 15 million results. "Accent Softening" is another popular term. So, although coaches often personally prefer terms that suggest that they *add to* someone's speech rather than *subtract from* it, they are wise to include as many different descriptors of the process as possible. Whatever we call it, it's a privilege to help clients through the minefield of English pronunciation and prosody and achieve the most comprehensible and effective English speech style possible.

—*Paul Meier*

I chose to include the concepts to suggest the possibility of working together as PVUCs to educate our clients. "English language enhancement" might be another way to describe what the coach does.

In any case, the voice coach often receives an inquiry from a company's HR department seeking help for an executive to "modify," "reduce," or "get rid of" their accent. The PVUC who specializes in helping clients to speak modern business English often comes from a theatre or ESL background and might cringe at the idea of "reducing" anyone's accent or dialect and could perhaps even feel a bit triggered by the term. I have found, at a high level, that requests for "accent reduction" can be an opportunity to educate and serve. In fact, it is not just humans who grow up speaking multiple languages who might seek a voice coach, but also those whose first language is English. The PVUC is adding to the toolbox of their client and is not interested in reducing or modifying any human's identity. The first thing I always say is, "I can coach dialect 'enhancement'." What I mean by that is that I can help my client become more aware of the physical experience of phonemes—the sounds they grew up with and the sounds of the language (in my case, usually American English) that they wish to have more command of. I will do this by working with them on their articulators and leading them into more oral muscularity in speech, along with elements of vocal prosody.

One of the awesome humans and researchers that I spoke with for this book was Andrea Caban, Co-Director and a Master Teacher of Knight-Thompson Speechwork™ and Head of Voice and Speech at California State University Long Beach. She also holds a research appointment at the UCI Department of Neurology. Andrea is not only seeped in this accent work from the perspective of training voice teachers and coaches, but she also works with PVUs herself. Andrea explained:

I have to manage their expectations. A lot of people come to me and want "accent reduction." And I don't do that work. I don't actually reduce anybody's anything, and I don't believe it's a thing that's possible. So, what I do is I help people empower their speech choices. And then it's really about communication. So, it's less about speech and more about what you are thinking about when you're communicating. Are you thinking about how you sound and your accent being judged? Because if you are, you're thinking about the wrong thing. And so, how do you practice thinking about the right thing? It's what we know as actors to be true: you think about what you want from the other person, or you think about how you can be of service to the person that you're talking to. And that person can be one person, or it can be 1000 people. So, that's helped me the most, getting really clear with people about what I do, how I do it, and cutting through the shame and anger that typically comes into a first session of working with a professional.

I generally say, "Look, you've had this experience of being shamed for this. And it's okay; it's not bad. You know, how you're communicating is intelligible; I hear you, but you're just focused on the wrong thing. So can we let go of other people's idea of what you should sound like, and even your own idea of what you *should* sound like, and can we zero in on something that's attainable in a short amount of time?" Then I tell them, if they put a lot of work in, the improvement can be testable because we can record them today, and we can record them in three weeks. Do you hear a difference? Do other people hear a difference? And that's learning outcomes. I emphasize personal work. If a client does not do the homework that I give them, and they don't do it daily, then they shouldn't expect results. And they won't be my client anymore. I have such a small amount of time for private clients because I do so many other things that I only want to work with people who want to put some work in. I'm working with this non-native speaker of English right now: he's the Dean of this Pan-Asian business school. He puts time in every day, and I meet him for six sessions–twice a week for three weeks–and he sounds like a different person.

—*Andrea Caban*

PRACTICE

In the world of PVUs, it is important to keep expectations realistic and to get buy-in on the necessity of practice. I liken it to sports. For example, I might say that my client from China has the speaking muscles of a ballet dancer, and American English uses the muscles of a weightlifter. The ballet dancer is never going to be an Olympic weightlifter; however, they can certainly change their musculature and move in that direction, while also continuing the practice of ballet. Additionally, if someone can afford to work with me every day, that's great! But usually it is once per week, or even every other week for super busy executives. In those cases, I remind them that the coaching I offer is only as good as the practice in between.

Again, the sports anecdote seems to resonate with most of my clients: If you work with a personal trainer once a week and spend an hour doing a variety of abdominal exercises, some incremental progress will happen over the course of three months. If you add twenty minutes of practice per day in between the weekly coaching sessions, then you will have a six-pack of abs in three months. I ask my clients: "Which do *you* want? Some slightly better abs or a six-pack?" A favorite book that I like to share with my PVU clients is *Atomic Habits: An Easy and Proven Way to Build Good Habits and Break Bad Ones* by James Clear (2018). Clear provides research that demonstrates how tiny and relatively easy changes can deliver big results. The book is full of excellent strategies that are very practical and digestible.

One of my favorites is hooking a new desired habit to something that you are already doing daily. I ask my client something laughable such as, "Do you brush your teeth every morning?" To which they usually crack a smile and say, "Yes." Then I ask them what the most important exercise they want to work on is, and they then are directed to incorporate the jaw release exercise or the mouth warm-up PRIOR to the teeth brushing on a daily basis. My executive clients appreciate that the homework I give them is hooked into the latest evidence that indicates change will happen with focused, precise practice.

Andrea Haring shared some insight on her experience of working with executives. Like many in the field of voice coaching, she started primarily working with actors prior to expanding into the field of executive coaching:

> I've been doing a lot of corporate coaching over the last ten, fifteen years: I've worked with the World Economic Forum for over ten years with Kristin; I've been coaching the Obama Foundation Scholars since they started the Scholar Program; I worked with the Columbia Senior Executive Program. So, I do quite a lot of corporate coaching, Ted-type talks, things of that nature. But really, how do you bring the benefits of acting training into the corporate world, so that you're not looking and listening to yourself? You're really finding, "What am I talking about? Why am I saying this? How can I reach my audience?" One of the essential acting tasks is to take your focus off of you and put it onto the person who you're speaking to, and ask the question, "What is the event that's taking place between us in this moment?
>
> *—Andrea Haring*

I asked Andrea if she found the core process of coaching students, actors, and PVUs to be similar:

> You know, I would say the core process is similar, but I must have a slightly different focus when I go into the corporate world. For the most part, they're really in their heads. They're really into, "Bottom line. What's the strategy? Give me a takeaway." (laughs) And I respect that. I absolutely do. There's money riding on what they do. They have people above them who are expecting results immediately, and many of them are not used to being in a process and/or a self-opening, awareness process. So, initially, I would say my corporate people are a little stiff, a little shy, not quite so apt to do all the physical work that I do. I have to tailor it; every group is going to be different. And I also need to explain things and really give a framework around the purpose

of the work and what they're going to get out of the work. They have to know what the payoff will be up front.

Whereas I think actors in their training, whether they've gone through an MFA program or whether they've just acted in shows, they understand that in the process of developing the character and exploring the events of the play, there's going to be a lot of moments where they don't know what's going on—where they're really investigating, using trial and error, and working stuff out. That's what the rehearsal process is about, so actors understand that there is a rehearsal process of trial and error. And it takes a while for the corporate people over the course of a three-hour workshop, a one-day work-shop, or a five-day workshop to really understand. Everything is building on top of each other. There is always a reason for what we're doing. And without feeling like I'm going into dangerous territory, "Can I be okay with not knowing, and just making mistakes and feeling foolish, and kind of giving it a go?" That whole idea of saying "yes." The actor's initial acting lesson is, "I'm going to say 'yes' to what's happening and know that, inside me, I have everything I need to respond, react, and keep the ball in play.

—*Andrea Haring*

In my experience, one of the biggest shifts in moving from the world of actor coaching in academia to working with PVUs is finding your way of condens-ing exercises into the most valuable elixir for your particular client. The more clients you work with, the more you will start to see common challenges, and this will provide opportunities to experiment with your way of coaching for your client's needs. It can help to have a few programs in mind when you speak with a potential client. Sometimes I break down this programming into "Quick Fix," "Moderate," and "Intensive." Additionally, I have found that offering a six-month retainer model can be very helpful for my top C-suite clients. It is not uncommon for someone to come to you and want to have one session to be ready to perform a particular speech or fix a problem. Again, it is up to you to educate and to know your own capabilities as a coach, so you don't overpromise.

Many of my clients are in the world of banking and private equity, and I say to them, "Actors spend anywhere from two to four years working on their craft to make performance look natural and effortless. How many years did you study to become an accountant?" They often look at me, knowing where this is going, and they nod their heads. I continue, "So you wouldn't expect me to be able to work out the complex formulas you calculate after working with you for an hour, right?" I usually get a laugh. The point for the coach is that people seem to think that just because they have a voice and just because they speak, it must mean they should be able to perform like an actor does after a short ses-sion. Ideally, I like to create four-to-six-month customized training programs for individual PVUs. I price my offerings so that there are incremental discounts based on the amount of time they commit to. I also know that with additional time I can more precisely target the training and they will have better results.

Andrea Haring concurred and shared her thoughts around emphasizing listening so that she is not pushing her agenda. She works to help PVUs hook into the "why" of what they are doing, so she can lead them to achieve a collectively designed, desired outcome:

> Some people just think, "Oh, one session and I'm going to be fixed," you know? But the big thing is—and I think this is true with everybody—to really try to be present with them. What does it mean to be present? To ask questions that can help them define what it is they want out of the session. And then, I will tailor my work to serve their needs. So, although the Linklater work has a progression of exercises, I may condense it. I'll always work on releasing physical tension, loosening the breath, and finding a clear connection to resonant sound. But I may not go into the details of laryngeal (back of the tongue) tension. I may simplify and do a simpler exercise to give them an experience of speaking with an "open throat" as opposed to a "closed throat." Or I might create a little game where we play with range, as opposed to going through the "resonating ladder."
>
> So, [to frame the training] I will ask: How much time do we have? What do they feel they need to work on? What am I hearing in their voice? How can I [use] all of those things *and* my own intuition as a teacher? And I will come up with something that really works with them—not overwhelming them with exercises. Yet, for the exercises that I choose, I can talk about why [we are] doing these exercises. It's a natural progression so that by the end (even if it's only through humming and moving it through the body, and a little bit of articulation), they can feel something more awake and alive in themselves. I want to give them a payoff. I want to give them a takeaway.
>
> —*Andrea Haring*

SIMPLE IS NOT SIMPLE

Many early career PVUCs are coming out of the realm of an MFA training program either in acting or in vocal pedagogy, and they have spent many years working on voice and breath. If you are mid-career and making a shift to work with PVU clients, you are even more steeped in the voice coaching for actors world. Because of this it can be easy for the voice coach to forget that basic exercises can make a huge difference to the layperson. What might seem simple and obvious to you could be a big "ah-ha" for your client. It is important to remind yourself that linking the exercises you know well to something that matters to your client can result in meaningful and measurable results. It can also be fun to invent and create training programs for the PVU. There is a skill in distilling information into bite-sized manageable chunks, coaching your client into a sustainable practice and measuring the change.

Amy Hume spoke about her experience in working with PVUs:

> Work with non-actors is incredibly rewarding because there [have] been experiences where people have said things to me and I've realized that, "Their life

is going to be different now." I'll never forget when one woman, who was a professor, came to me because of feedback she got in student surveys. She was renovating her home at the same time; she came in one day, and the renovations were going on everywhere. It was just chaos. And [because of the work we did] she got the building manager back on track because she had the skills to say what she wanted to say. She got her home renovations back on track because of some work we were doing on her presence in the lecture theatre. That's pretty rewarding. (laughs)

—Amy Hume

Whether working with PVU clients is a side gig or a career, there is a certain skill and "code-shifting" for this audience that is necessary to maximize successful outcomes, and such skills are required to help your client build and create feedback loops for their work. Amy Hume concurred:

It is a practice and not anyone can do it. And I think that some voice coaches— and actors, even—kind of want to supplement their income with that type of coaching. But I think it would be naive to expect that you can just do it: "Oh, well I can speak in public, so I can teach public speaking." Well, how? The psychology that you're working with in that type of person [PVU] is totally different. The language that you use has to change; the "way in" has to be different; it's a body of work.

One of the things I teach my non-actor clients is self-assessment. I have a form for them, and they go through it. It's simple. It's things like eye contact, pitch range, and modulation. Throughout that one-minute speech or whatever they had to do: Do they do it always? Do they do it sometimes? Or is it still developing? Those are just three options that make it quick. And always when they practice something and they say, "How did I go?" I say, "Well, how *did* you go?" I ask it back to them. It's that thing: you're always training people for you to not be there.

—Amy Hume

The world of PVUs who can benefit from coaching seems to be growing, and there are so many markets that can be tapped into. You can choose to offer a wide range of programming, or you might want to specialize in a particular area. Bonnie Raphael has worked with a wide range of PVUs:

I've worked with politicians. I've worked with lawyers. I've worked with members of the New York Stock Exchange. I've worked with a sitting President of the United States. (laughs) I've had my share.

And, in Bonnie's words:

It's the same stuff. You're looking for a different door into the same room— making better choices, not making your voice a sacrificial victim in the process of doing your job. It's the same stuff, but it has to be presented very differently depending on the receiver. Listening is important, not coming in with an agenda that is not possible to change at the last minute in huge ways. You can pre-plan. But I think Eisenhower said, "Plans are useless, but planning is indispensable."

—Bonnie Raphael

Flexibility and a creative mindset are really important because not one plan is going to work for every client. However, the preparation and experience with each subsequent client will lead you to be present with what is in front of you. Whenever possible, I also try to approach the work with my clients as a co-created experience. I don't assume that I know what is best for my client or what they "need." As Bonnie said:

> Even if you're individual and you're very good at what you do, it's not going to fit everybody. It's a shock when you realize your perception of the universe is not universal. (laughs) I don't think I ever got over it.

Bonnie went on to share some of the qualities that she thinks are important for the coach to cultivate:

> I think they have got to be a wonderful listener. I usually use the loose phrase "talk half as much as you teach." Don't spend the whole time advertising yourself, even though you deserve it, of course. But impart knowledge that is useful rather than trying to impress the client. And usually when I work, I try to start with one or two [of] what I call "quick fixes": something they can hear and something they can use and do almost immediately, rather than get buried in lots of instructions or handouts. I try to start with something they can do, where they will notice it makes a difference. And then once they figure out that I'm on their side, I can take bigger chances so *they* can.
>
> And sometimes the "way in" is not what I thought it was. Often, I'll think I know the way in because this person is an actor with a specific problem, or that political candidate has been criticized about thus and such. So, I think I know the way in, but I try to say [to them], "Okay, if I were a magic fairy and I had a wand, and I could do something immediately to change you, what would that be?" And this whole thing about their perception of what they need does not usually include their ability to accept themselves making a different sound. "I want to be more authoritative. But you want me to talk deep in my voice? I'm a woman; I don't want to come across like a demon." So many women have been educated to not make waves, to charm their way into teaching; a lot of the voices are very insipid. When I work on a musical, some of the women who are beautiful sopranos talk that way also. For the singing voice it's fabulous, for the speaking voice it's a little insipid. (Pamela laughs) I don't use those words with them, but you know what I mean.

—Bonnie Raphael

As you build your voice (pun intended) as a PVUC, it is important to think about how to distill exercises and hook them into what matters for your client. Voice can often be a pathway for the coach to focus on a myriad of other performance and personal growth-related topics. Sometimes, voice coaching can be about helping to lead your client to a more fulfilling life, both personally and professionally.

As I began to branch out from teaching in academia to coaching professional actors, I started to examine voice in a larger sense. I've mentioned this general topic before, but it is an important idea to consider as a coach. When you work with PVUs, there will be times when you are called upon to work with CEOs and thought leaders in their fields. In the world of coaching PVUs, you may find that your clients want to present in a particular way or create a certain impression with their audience, yet there can be a resistance to what's called upon to get there. You will need to help your client connect to their vocal and performance vision, as well as a path for getting there.

HELPING YOUR CLIENT TRANSFORM AND GETTING OUT OF THE WAY

Part of your job can be helping the individual explore how they are perceived now and how they wish to be perceived. I often carry out what I call a communication "mini-360" or "collegial feedback" with two or three of the client's colleagues. You can usually get guidance on this from a Human Resources person, if that's who brought you in to coach. Sometimes, your client will have a few people in mind, and in some cases, the assessment of where they are now and where they want to go will simply be between you and your client. The key is to create that vision and then educate your client about how you will get there.

You will need to introduce them to tools involving breath, volume, vocal prosody, intention, and storytelling to help them move the needle in their desired direction. The paradox is that stepping into who they want to be can sometimes feel paralyzing to them. Humans get comfortable in patterns and can become uncomfortable when they are called upon to make bolder choices and change their patterns. In fact, you may discover that your client is quite happy with the sound of their voice, but they may be dealing with hoarseness or vocal loss with added speaking demands. As Bonnie noted about one of her clients:

> "Nobody will recognize me. I'm known for my voice." Yeah, not good if you're running out of voice after ten minutes.

People can be afraid of change—afraid of what it takes to change. And when you finally get them to make meaningful changes, they can feel like, with all the work they have put into it, these differences register significantly when, in fact, for the rest of the world it is subtle. Bonnie continued:

> With a lot of people, I remind them over, and over, and over, and over that what feels like a giant change to you may not even register with somebody. You feel like you're changing your voice 100% and the person doesn't say anything. And you wonder why. (laughs) It's like sometimes when a guy shaves

his mustache, and he comes into class, and nobody notices. He feels naked: "Oh my gosh, my whole face, and nobody says anything. What's that about?"

—Bonnie Raphael

Leith McPherson, dialect coach for *The Hobbit* movie trilogy, occasionally still works in executive coaching. One of the tenants in Leith's work is distinguishing between approval mode vs. task mode work. In her experience: when one is focused on "approval," there is a need for one to seek personal and/or professional validation. This takes one away from the task at hand. When one is trying to lead a client toward goals, there can be a desire for a special moment or validation. It is important to facilitate the growth process of your client, and this comes from being in task mode. You have the job, and it is your job to do the job. Then, the client's mood or state of mind is irrelevant. You are just doing your work by asking yourself, "How can I best help this client to achieve their goals?" Leith spoke of her time working with PVUs:

> So, at the moment, my focus is totally screen work. But back when I started, even before I went to the Royal Central School of Speech and Drama, I started doing a bit of professional coaching, or coaching for professional speakers, which is such a broad term, of course. And there have been times when that has drawn me back. For example, I will give an introduction to a play at the Melbourne Theatre Company for a corporate event, for their subscriber event or a corporate sponsorship gig. And from that, they go, "Oh, can you come and help us with that kind of corporate work?" And I really love it when I do. It really is fun.
>
> And to work with civilians is always really refreshing as well. To take the people who "have no intention of lying on the floor, thank you very much." (laughs) "Let's work with your patterning; let's work with your sense of self and relationship to sound and communication." I love that challenge. I love it whether it's in the creative sphere or the corporate sphere, if there's a difference between those two. It is often the same work; it's just about the way that you're framing it in order to find that connection that allows the person to essentially give themselves permission—rather than giving you permission—but give themselves permission to expand, and to explore, and to work with the parts of themselves that are less secure, rather than doing what most people want to do, which is show you the most secure parts of themselves.
>
> *—Leith McPherson*

I often say that one of the jobs of the PVUC is to make themselves irrelevant. What I mean by that is that you are ideally coaching your clients to get familiar with their personal challenges, learn exercises and techniques to address those challenges, and develop self-assessment techniques to measure personal growth and areas to attend to. You are working on helping your client to find awareness and autonomy. As Jenny Kent called it, "making yourself redundant." Jenny also said:

> I think corporate work's really rewarding because you can talk about the simple things like claiming your space and using the energy in your voice to

project, and even if you're nervous, that will project an image of confidence. It's a light bulb, and you sort of think, "Oh my goodness, that just made a big difference in that world!" (laughs) It's so exciting.

—*Jenny Kent*

Scott Miller, the founder of the Miller Voice Method, emphasized that coaching PVUs is a valuable component of his career as a voice coach. Scott approaches his work with deep intentionality and a desire to help impact change makers by leading them to pause, breathe, and bring more consciousness into their voices. Scott teaches and communicates how breath and clarity can impact not only yourself, but also the world around you:

> What I'm doing, and most interested in doing, is really affecting and impacting leaders of the world. People who are making decisions, systemic decisions that affect large masses of people. I'm trying to get the work that I do to them with the hope that when they're in the work [Miller Voice Method], they will be exposed to information that will influence their decision making in a way that's, frankly, more archetypal feminine: More flowing and less destroying, or a larger and sustainable picture versus a temporary removal of the pain picture.

—*Scott Miller*

The American paleontologist and scientist, Stephen J. Gould, introduced the theory of punctuated equilibrium in 1972. Simplistically, this theory postulates that change is not always gradual, but that things can move along at a relatively stable pace and then there can be a moment of great change in a short period of time, such as the extinction of the dinosaurs (Gould 2007). This term has found its way into the business world: Professor Bernard Burnes applied the punctuated equilibrium theory (PET) to the world of business, identifying where relatively long periods of stability in organizations can be followed by short and intense bursts of revolutionary change (Burnes 2009).

I think that the COVID-19 pandemic provided that moment of punctuated equilibrium around the use of video technologies such as Zoom, GoTo Meeting, Google Meet, and Microsoft Teams among others, for coaching and training. Prior to the pandemic, many PVUs requested that coaches meet primarily in person. Since 2020, the field of PVU coaching has undergone many changes. Human Resources teams are now commonly looking for virtual "lunch and learn" programming, or prepackaged modules of online training. As a response to the increased demand, many coaches have created online courses around voice and presence that have synchronous and asynchronous components. Tom Burke and I spoke about his move from being a speech and language pathologist to coaching business executives. He encourages voice coaches to be clear about their business plans and to clearly identify their "zones of genius." Tom said:

> I think I've had controversial views thus far that are now a little bit less controversial. It's this idea that, eventually, one comes to the realization that time

is finite. And energy. With each passing year, you want less and less of your energy spent on any B.S. that detracts from your genius zone. So, there's a joy that comes through only doing things that you just excel at. And so, I think that breaking free of the one-to-one model is huge. And I don't mean eliminating one-to-one, but just opening oneself up to scale. You can only work X-amount of hours per week. And at a certain level, there's only so much you can charge for an hour, right? But if you figure out a way to provide faster results in a shorter amount of time and work with more people in a way that doesn't drain you, that's the ultimate and underlying question I'm always asking. And you *can* do that online more effectively than in person. But I feel like there's either explicit or implicit bias against a lot of these things.

I don't know if folks are questioning where the forty-hour workweek came from. Or, "Why is a voice lesson 60 minutes or 45 minutes? Why isn't it 54 minutes?" (laughs) It's so arbitrary, where these things come from. A lot of the stuff is Industrial Revolution: 40-hour workweek, factory line. We're not Henry Ford building cars here. So if you really go back to this idea of *what's the minimal effective dose to elicit the target transformation*, that might be done in three minutes, or it might take three hours. I kind of experimented with, "How do you release the time constraint and focus more on [what the goal is]? And what's the shortest pathway to do that?" I encourage my colleagues to experiment with creating products, membership programs, video trainings, masterclasses, one-on-one coaching. It's like a combo platter, so they're (a) introducing themselves to more people and (b) minimizing the reliance on one cash flow stream. That's what's been helpful for me—having multiple streams of income. So I'm not relying on just one.

—*Tom Burke*

Reflecting on conversations with Tom and others, along with viewing my own career pivot to PVU coaching, it is clear to me that creating a successful career in the PVU coaching realm often includes stepping out of an artistic or academic world, and this means adapting new models. It means asking yourself questions about your clients' needs and getting curious about how different types of people learn. As I've said before, most professionals in our field come from either actor training, a vocal pedagogy program, or a mentoring background. This means shifting from a common "old school" model: "Okay, I teach at a university; I'm going to get benefits there. Then I'm going to coach professional actors. And I'm also going to do a bit of PVU coaching on the side and make a little extra money, because I don't really make a livable wage doing the other jobs." The challenge here is that it could mean you're now working sixty hours a week. The hour model continues to go up as you look for different revenue streams, so it becomes imperative, in order to sustain your energy and create work-life balance, to get clear with yourself about what your "zone of genius" is.

In her book *The Genius Zone*, Gay Hendricks (2021) poses this question: "How can I spend the majority of my time doing what I most love to do while making my greatest contribution to the world?" You need to know that there is not another single coach in the world who will approach voice, breath, text, and presence in the way that you will. When you are on fire and coaching from a place of passion, connection, and genius, you will find a flow in your work. Experiment with finding what the "minimal effective dose" is for your clients so that you don't get stuck in a model of scarcity and "over-delivering."

One of the challenges for creatives who move into the corporate world is undervaluing themselves. This challenge exists for a many reasons, including the proclivity for under-funding universities, conservatories, and arts-based programs, It can be useful to create a personal business plan with clear financial and outcome driven goals. This could include connecting with local small businesses and/or entrepreneurial organizations, or getting involved with VASTA's BizCore interest group and seeking out current best practices for delivering training to PVUs. Tom Burke created a training program called "Six Figure Voice Studio" particularly tailored to voice teachers that helps them think about what they deliver and how they might create offerings, not only in the performing arts realm but also in the corporate world. With the initial onset of the 2020 pandemic, he noticed that many voice professionals were challenged by figuring out how to transfer their formerly in-person model into the virtual world. Tom used this opportunity to follow his own advice and explored how he might leverage his superpowers to help other voice coaches find their own. He said:

> Part of my "pivot party"—courtesy of COVID—was that I just offered one-to-two free classes on how to get on Zoom back in March of 2020 for folks that were freaking out or were new to "online." And that evolved into working with about sixty or seventy voice teachers, or voice coaches, or performing arts coaches, who all wanted to ride the wave of "online" and work toward building their business. It's called Six Figure Voice Studio. It's how to grow your business to multiple six figures as a voice coach. Which seems unfathomable for most folks, but it is possible in a way that you're still not charging clients astronomical amounts; you're just rethinking the delivery model. So that's been really fun over the past year or so to really be digging into that.

I asked Tom what he noticed when working with voice coaches who are in the process of growing their businesses. He noted:

> I would just say that imposter syndrome comes with the territory, and just have a sense of humor about that from day one. Try to learn that lesson as early as possible, meaning that you're always going to feel like an imposter. You're always going to look back and be like, "Oh, what was I teaching those people? What was I telling them?" You're always going to feel that. So just be light about it and just give what you can. At the end of day you want to be like, "Did I give them the full Tom show?" I always say that to myself: "Did I give the full Tom show?" And the full Tom show is: Did you make it? Were you empathic? Were you entertaining? Did you try as hard as you could in the moment? That's all you can say. And don't worry about what other people are saying about you.
>
> —Tom Burke

In my own work, I have found it helpful before starting my day or before leading a workshop to write down my personal check-in. I keep it in my "work journal," but you could easily record it in your smart device as either a voice note or by writing it down. I ask myself: How do I want my client/audience to feel after working with me? What change will happen for them? Are there any key personal challenges that I am working to overcome? How will I feel at the end of the day/ workshop? Because what we are often doing involves being a "solo performer", I allow this to act as a preview of the experience I intend to have. For example, I will write: "I see the team feeling a sense of exuberance and joy. They each have more and more insight into their vocal/presence strengths and growth opportunities. They saw/felt how some of the exercises really made a difference for them, and they now have a variety of techniques that they can practice. I was a great listener and had dynamic and impactful insights, tips, tricks for them. Everyone feels rejuvenated and full. I can see that my work made a difference. I feel satisfied and I'm excited to reflect on how I can make it even better next time." I asked Tom if he followed any plan prior to the "Tom Burke" show. He said:

> I did learn from Dr. Asher (MD, FACS, board-certified Otolaryngologist) in New York this idea of, at the end of each session, doing a "white light cleanse." Pretend whatever just happened in that last session is now over; that moment is gone. And then I tell myself, "I have to turn into Tom Burke now." I think the secular version of myself has more issues and is lazier, but when someone is sharing your time, you have to go *up* a little bit more, or something, and be generous. That's why it protects your energy. Because if you're going to go there and try to be in your highest self in that time together, you have to make sure that you're energetically able to show up and be present. And then as long as you can say, "Hey, I did my best." That's all you can ever say, right? So, have a sense of humor about that as early as possible.
>
> —*Tom Burke*

I asked Tom if he had any advice or a story that he might share about his current journey as a bit of inspiration for anyone who was coming in the field of PVU coaching:

> I think I was disappointed when I wanted to work more online and I saw how possible it was—this was years ago, maybe seven or eight years ago. If we skip to the meat of the story, I wanted to travel the world. I got down to two suitcases full of clothes, sold all my possessions, left my partner of ten years, and saw what was possible online, with YouTube, and with meeting people from around the world. But lots of my [in-person] legacy New Yorker clients didn't come with me. I was disappointed, and that's what changed me. I was thinking, "What is it about in-person?" I think I had to deal with that and be okay with leaving a certain percentage of my population behind.
>
> The funny part of the story is, now, all those folks are online saying how amazing it is and how it's changed their perspective on what 'online' could

be. I've also, then, had to not go down the dark road of, "I told you so." I don't like that energy either. What that taught me was: stop looking at anyone else's yoga mat; just stay on your own yoga mat. I would have told my younger self, "Hey, this is what you want to do; just do it and don't look back, and figure it out. And it'll be okay." Because it did wind up being okay, even more okay than it was. And then, when you do that, when you let the pendulum swing the other way, you develop a greater sense of nuance. What I mean by that is I did come back to a hybrid version of in-person and online coaching.

As my dad would say, "If you're gonna do it, do it." Which is, go fully into a world, immerse yourself in it, complete the criteria for success or mastery within that discipline, and then move on. And fold in other stuff. I think certifications are good, because it's like a community agreed-upon criteria for success and mastery. It's like, "Okay, we community believe *this* is the definition of mastery within this domain. Let's all agree to that." And once you're there, great! There's always something else; there's always something new that you can fold into it. When you look back on that certification, you realize what was or was not useful for you personally. And also, in context of your clientele: What's most useful? What unique mixed bag is most right for your clientele?

—*Tom Burke*

The message from all the coaches that I spoke with is to know yourself, know your audience, and allow your vision as a PVUC to develop from there. Just as there is not one single path to becoming a voice coach, there is not one methodology or way of coaching PVUs. You will keep evolving your style to meet the needs of the people you serve and that will most definitely lead to a rewarding and fulfilling experience of coaching from your personal genius zone.

CHAPTER 5

Vocal Health for the Voice Coach

TOPICS ON VOCAL HEALTH FOR THE VOICE COACH

There are many books, articles, and specialized training packages that focus on vocal hygiene and the mechanics of the voice. I did not try to replicate that here. My goal instead was to sit down with a team of medical professionals trained specifically to work with professional voice users and performers and gain insight into how we can create a triad of support for our clients and students. Michael Lerner, MD, and Andrew Keltz, M.S., CCC-SLP, from the Yale Voice Center, share their perspectives on creating a team to work with. Joanna Cazden MFA, M.S.,CCC-SLP, and author of *Everyday Voice Care: The Lifestyle Guide for Singers and Talkers*, shares her thoughts on vocal health and partnering with professionals. It is my hope that you will gain insight into how to leverage your own skills as a voice coach in conjunction with those of medical professionals to maximize the vocal health and longevity of your students and clients.

A CONVERSATION WITH JOANNA CAZDEN

In this book, I've generally broken the areas of voice coaching down into that of coaching students, professional actors, and professional voice users for the purpose of exploring career areas of specialization. However, for this particular section on

DOI: 10.4324/9781003006206-6

vocal health, I would like to use Joanna's Cazden's definition of professional voice user along with occupational users. Joanna is a longtime member of VASTA, a performer, a coach, and a speech language pathologist. She is in the unique position of deeply understanding the intersection of arts and medicine in voice.

A CONVERSATION WITH JOANNA CAZDEN

How would you define a "professional voice user"?

In my world, "professional voice user" is a relatively broad category that includes performing artists, clergy, politicians, courtroom attorneys … in a way, anybody that makes their living with the sound of their voice is a professional. Now, within that, there may be an elite group of vocal professionals who are artists. They may be international rock stars. They may be jazz singers who are mostly instrumentalists, but they do some singing. And pretty much anything in between. There's a kind of related category of people whose jobs and livelihood depend on their voice, but it's more about the *adequacy* of their voice, not the actual tone.

A classroom teacher needs to have enough vocal stamina to talk for seven hours a day, nine months out of the year. But the exact *sound* of their voice is not as much of an issue as it is for an opera singer … That's not really in our category of "professional voice user." They're an *occupational* user. And so, there are occupations that are at high risk for problems: Fitness instructors and teachers, and music teachers, especially. Voice coaches, perhaps. Music teachers, we know for sure. Theatre and acting coaches, we don't know as much. But generally, the "professional voice user" is where the sound of your voice and the quality and range and full ability of the voice is important in your public livelihood.

How much anatomy and physiology do you think a voice coach needs to be aware of?

I'm going to refer to one of the grandfathers of my field, a gentleman named Thomas Hixon, who, along with his wife, Jeanette Hoyt, did really important basic research on breathing. I mean, he put people in vats of water and measured the displacement as they breathed. He had ways of measuring rib cage movement versus abdominal movement, and which body type seemed to prefer one or the other, and so on. This was in the 1960s, 1970s, and 1980s. His really deep scientific text is called *Respiratory Function in Speech and Song*. And that gets into pretty deep physics and stuff. But he has another very accessible book called *Respiratory Function in Singing*, that just goes through the basics of how the rib cage moves, how the diaphragm moves, and why ribcage expansion versus abdominal expansion can work equally well … [it] goes through a lot of the basics on that.

A very important point that he makes at the beginning is that many, many artistic vocal coaches—and he's talking, again, more about singing coaches than speech, but it probably applies—these folks tend to know too much anatomy and not enough physiology. Anatomy means you've memorized all the names for things in Latin and Greek. That's useful. It's usually done in two dimensions on a page, right? It doesn't tell you anything, or not very much, about how this incredibly complicated three-dimensional organ works in the throat. And getting that 3-D physiology is much more important, or at least is underweighted, in a lot of "vocal pedagogy" classes. That's changing, because there is a new generation of experts who are really able to integrate basic science and physiology with artistic demands. Again, that is more developed in the singing community than in the theatre arts community.

If you were to share your top three areas of Anatomy and Physiology for the vocal coach to understand, what would they be?

The most important thing—most coaches kind of get this, not all—is that your vocal cords are part of your airway. They have a physiological job to do, protecting the lungs. That's their day job. Vibrating is extra. "Evolutionary gravy," if you will. Icing on the cake. The main thing the vocal cords do is they are guard gates for your lungs. They are in the airway, they're part of the airway system. Nothing that you eat or drink is going to touch them. Unless, "It goes down the wrong way." Your breathing tube and your swallowing tube are separate.

It feels like we all have one mouth and one throat, right behind your tongue, right out of sight. Right where things start to get unconscious, it divides into a double pipe. So, your vocal cords don't care whether you're having lemon in your tea or honey in your tea. What they care about is that the tea doesn't touch them at all. Because if it does, it's going to make you cough and get it out. Because your lungs don't want any of that, okay? So, most of the recipes for, "Drink this, it will soothe your voice." Yeah, they feel good a couple inches away in your throat, they might soothe the rest of your body. The liquid in them is going to help your vocal cords stay plump and hydrated *after* it's processed through the rest of your body. That's the bottom line that answers all other questions. (laughs)

There are a whole lot of tips out there, but "hydration, hydration, hydration," right?

Yeah. But again, at the moment you're drinking, it's not touching your vocal cords and it's not helping your body. It gets processed; it keeps the fluid level in your body at a certain good level so that the jelly vibrating layer of your vocal cords stays plump and healthy and they don't get tired as fast. But that's from the water that you drank four or eight or twelve hours ago.

That's such a great "It just can't harm anyone" kind of tip for somebody who's thinking of coaching anybody. Tell them to hydrate and that it really doesn't matter what they're drinking, as long as it's not *de*hydrating them.

Right, or something that they're personally allergic to … Let me make another comment about anatomy. About the Latin and Greek names for things: I think it is important for teachers and coaches to know that stuff. It's a shared vocabulary across all of the voice disciplines, it's a way to communicate with fellow professionals, and it's a way to understand a lot of the medical and scientific literature. I *don't* think that terminology is very useful to students. And I think it's very important to separate teaching someone *skill* from teaching someone *information*. Those are two very different learning processes.

For instance, I was once in a class with an accent, dialect, [and] articulation maven/wizard/specialist who was giving us this guided tour of subtle changes in sensation of tongue position and so on. And at the same time, they were throwing out anatomical terms of, "And this is your protruding langue-something or other muscle, and here's the velum, and ..." And my brain was just so confused, because I wanted to stay in the sensory learning. And even though I've already had the Latin and Greek, I've taught the Latin and Greek, my brain—it's just a different frame of mind. And I think that this teacher thought that by putting those labels in at the same time as the sensory thing, that people might connect them. When I was learning *both* at the same time, it didn't work.

If you're teaching a vocal pedagogy class and you're teaching other people the basics [of] anatomy, that's fabulous. Go for it. But I would separate that from the experiential learning of, "Here's how you do stuff in your body." Even when I'm seeing clients who have a medical diagnosis, I don't talk in complicated language to them. I will to their doctor, because it's shorthand. Often the doctors are using vernacular as well. But I'll only go into anatomical language in detail if someone actually asks me, "What did the doctor mean by this?" You know, so it's important to know the formal stuff, but still be able to think in concrete three-dimensional: how the thing actually operates.

It seems like you are saying that the vocal coach needs to be able to speak multiple languages.

Exactly right. You need to code-switch constantly. You might be thinking physiology, but what you're talking about is sensation: "Here's what it should feel like when you do this thing I'm teaching you to do."

I think there are times when, probably even more so for newer teachers, they want to just spout out anatomy names ...

... To prove that they've learned it. But they haven't figured out which parts of it are actually relevant and useful to the *student*. Again, there's a lot of knowledge that's important for the teacher but not important for the student, if they're a beginner. Master's level student, that's a whole other thing. That's where you need to start getting the two sides of your brain together and be able to analyze anatomical stuff and associate it immediately with, "Oh, yeah, that's this thing that I can feel" or "This is what's going wrong" or "Oh, that aching over here— oh, yeah, that's a sternocleidomastoid. Okay."

Now, in terms of the method that has the most detailed physiology? I would look at Estill. The Jo Estill system. Because she made a point of learning the science and then translating it into familiar gestures that people learn to fine-tune in great detail. Estill doesn't do very much with breathing at all. I happened to take the last seminar that she herself taught in 2004. And she said, "I don't think any of us understand breathing. So, I'm not going to teach it because I don't think any of us have it right yet." (laughs) This is somebody who'd been working and studying and teaching for fifty years. So, again, humility counts. She knew what she didn't know. And she wasn't prepared to go out on a limb and teach stuff that she wasn't sure of. The detailed pharyngeal adjustments she knew in great detail and could teach. So, that's a very useful system. And there are a couple of her gestures and exercises that I use all the time. All the time. They're accessible to my clients, most of whom don't know why they're in my office and what I do, and what in the world voice coaching or voice therapy is going to offer their life. So, we're starting with basics.

It seems like there is much more of a trend these days toward multimodal healing where, ideally, an otolaryngologist is very supportive and works with a speech and language pathologist. It's not so much, "Here's a medicine" or "Oh, let's do surgery on you" anymore.

Through their training, laryngologists have met speech pathologists who are doing voice care. They've met vocal coaches. They've got the concept of working as a team and referring out. And they are the least likely to want to do surgery on someone who's a "professional voice user." They're the most conservative in care because they understand, quite a bit more than the average doctor does, about the details of the vocal demands that an artist has. And what the risks can be. That's the new standard of care.

I wonder what your thoughts are around helping a voice coach understand how and when to refer a student or client to someone like you or a team of medical professionals?

The general rule is that most vocal coaches don't refer soon enough. Theatre coaches tend to have a better ear for it than singing coaches, who come from a different lineage and different culture. And old school folks often used to try to fix things for years before they would give up and say, "Okay, you really need to see a doctor." But there's actually a pretty good list of criteria … A version of this is in [my] book. And these come mostly from one of the elders in laryngology who's no longer with us, Dr. Hans Van Laden. So, this is mostly his list with some wisdom annotations from me:

A vocal coach should refer for medical care if any of the following things are true: If there is pain in the throat or pain with voice use, that's a red flag right away. If there is a sudden change in the voice, a voice goes out in the middle of a performance, you want to get to a doctor as soon as possible. If there is an acute illness—a normal cold or laryngitis—that doesn't resolve in the normal amount of time, just a week or two. This is one of mine: If there's a consistently distorted sound that your most obvious coaching methods don't seem to make a dent in. Or maybe they help a little bit. But if nothing's happening in a month or six weeks and you're doing your job and the person's doing their homework, and nothing is really changing, go ahead and refer, don't wait till the end of the semester. Certainly, don't wait until finals week when, you know, the person has been cast in a show and then they're really in trouble. So, when in doubt, refer early.

The other criteria that come from Dr. Van Laden is kind of related to that: If somebody doesn't make the progress that you expect in an appropriate amount of time. So, if a coach has been working for several years, and kind of knows, "Yeah, in the course of a semester or a ten-week coaching package, I sort of know how much progress to expect from people." And if someone goes through that ten weeks and they sound the same as they first did, there's probably something anatomically or physiologically going wrong. So, it's really a question of humility, number one.

Number two: know who the resources are in your community before you need them. And that means don't just know where the ear, nose, throat person is, but know what city you need to go to in order to find a specialty voice clinic that has laryngologists, voice-oriented speech therapists, and a good understanding of how to take care of a professional, elite vocal performer. If that clinic is a couple of hours away, it's worth getting acquainted with them and knowing who they are and how they operate so that you can be a really good resource and advocate for the people that come to you. And if that knowledge is in your Rolodex, so to speak, before you have a client in trouble, you're that much more ahead of the game.

Like a fire drill, right?

Yeah. And in a way, the same is true of having some mental health resources. Know who the trauma psychologists are in your area, or close enough. In case you start to suspect that there's something on that level getting in the way, or someone discloses to you. You know, having resources and saying "I think this other person could help you" doesn't diminish oneself as a coach. It really shows your professionalism and your care for the whole person. That you know what you can do and you know what you can't do. If you're willing to open up that team, trust me, the referrals will come back to you. And I'm not giving away business by doing that. The referrals will come back, your credibility with people will absolutely increase, and word will get around about that too.

A CONVERSATION WITH ANDREW KELTZ AND MICHAEL LERNER

As you embark on your career it will be important for you to connect with individuals like Joanna. And as Joanna advised, it will also be important for you to find local teams who can support you. Michael Lerner, MD, and Andrew Keltz, M., SCCC-SLP, at the Yale Voice Center in Greenwich, Connecticut, USA, are one such team. The Yale Voice Center at Greenwich Hospital is a multidisciplinary voice center that provides comprehensive assessment and intervention for voice, upper airway, and swallowing disorders. They serve a large array of individuals ranging from professional singers and actors, to public speakers, to school teachers, to everyday voice users who are experiencing a challenge with their vocal function. Dr. Michael Lerner's interest in working with professional voice users grew out of his desire to blend his passions of music and medicine. In his youth, he discovered his love for guitar, singing, and songwriting. As he pursued his rigorous medical and surgical training, he initially felt as though he would have to sacrifice his love of the arts and music, that is, until he discovered the field of laryngology. He brought Andrew Keltz on board to be part of his team. Prior to becoming a speech language pathologist (SLP), Andrew worked as a singer and actor for over a decade, performing in plays, musicals, and concerts in the US and abroad.

Dr. Lerner envisions the intersectionality of the laryngologist, speech language pathologist, and the voice coach. He believes that the three fields can support and amplify the client's overall vocal health. Recently I began working with The Yale Voice Center to provide baseline scoping for my students at SUNY Purchase College. As Dr. Lerner said, "Voice is so deeply connected to our sense of self and personal identity and the larynx is in such a concealed location that until you see it, it's really hard to appreciate all that it does for us on a day-to-day basis." This is just one example of how a voice coach can approach a team of medical specialists to empower students.

The following conversation is meant to provide you with an experience of sitting down with two supportive medical professionals. This is not meant to replace any medical advice, and if you ever have any questions or doubts about what you might be encountering with a student or client, it is imperative that you direct them to a medical professional and empower them to make informed decisions about their vocal health. My questions and comments will be in bold and you can follow along with Dr. Michael Lerner (ML) and Andrew Keltz, M.S., CCC-SLP, (AK), as if you were sitting down and having a coffee or tea with them. This is meant to be read as a conversation, not as a formal paper.

As the three of us sit down here together, I think it would be helpful for readers to understand what is important about working with medical professionals who are precisely trained to work with professional voice users.

ML: Sometimes there is a lack of clarity of what exactly voice medicine is, and what type of doctors are qualified to treat professional voice users. As a fellowship-trained laryngologist, I really look to partner with like-minded professionals to treat our patients comprehensively. I think it's so important that I work on a team with someone like Andrew, in that a voice-specialized speech pathologist with his performing arts background allows him to serve as a natural bridge to voice teachers and voice coaches. I think there is a shared common language, which sometimes a medical professional or medical doctor might actually lack.

That makes a lot of sense. I wonder if you could expand a bit to demystify the terms otolaryngologist, laryngologist, and ENT.

ML: Absolutely. I definitely appreciate that question. So, an ear, nose, and throat doctor (ENT) is the same thing as an otolaryngologist. An otolaryngologist is a doctor who, after medical school, completed a five-year residency training in what is now officially called "Otolaryngology – Head and Neck Surgery", which encompasses a lot of different disorders of the head and neck, so not just voice … Think sinusitis, cochlear implants, and head and neck cancers. After completion of that residency training, you are a "general otolaryngologist" and can treat the ears, nose, and throat and you have the basic tools to visualize the voice box or larynx. A laryngologist, on the other hand, is an otolaryngologist who subsequently underwent additional subspecialty training, called a "fellowship," to become an expert in the management of voice, swallowing, and airway disorders. It is this training in laryngology that prepares physicians to provide care to professional voice users. Laryngologists use more sophisticated video and audio equipment to accurately diagnose and treat voice issues. Laryngologists also tend to work in a multidisciplinary fashion with voice therapists to more holistically address vocal issues [in] the most comprehensive way.

Thank you, that's helpful. Andrew, how do you see the medical profession working with voice coaches?

AK: I see us, as Dr. Lerner said, as the bridge between healthcare and arts for facilitating the most effective human communication. Someone comes in with a voice complaint and we work to identify what's going on. Often the voice coach is the person who recognizes that someone is having a vocal problem that warrants medical assessment, and they can provide us with incredible insight into the nature of the problem. If we determine that someone needs some kind of intervention, whether it's voice therapy, medical or surgical treatment, or a combination of both, we guide them through that process step by step to achieve the best possible outcomes. We often think of our approach as vocal rehabilitation, bringing a person back to their baseline vocal function, and also identifying and remedying any factors that led to their problem so as to prevent future injury. Then once we're done and things are healed, and they're functioning at their optimal way, we need to pass the baton back to that voice coach or teacher for maintenance and further vocal growth. Voice therapy is typically short-term, around five to ten sessions over the course of a few months, unlike voice lessons or vocal coaching which can be ongoing over the course of years. For many patients, once we have achieved our goals in voice therapy, we recommend that they begin working with voice teachers or coaches if they don't already have one. As a team, we can help our patients and clients to sustain their vocal function for the long term and grow and evolve in a vocally healthy way. It can be a wonderfully collaborative relationship between laryngologists, voice therapists, voice teachers, and voice coaches, which is another reason I think I was drawn to this career coming from being a theatre artist. I love being a part of a voice team.

I think that some voice coaches view the larynx through an artistic and intuitive lens, and maybe not from as much of a scientific perspective. Having said that, these days there are many programs that actually bring in SLPs and laryngologists to teach voice coaches about voice science. So, I'd love for you both to weigh in: How much vocal science do you think voice coaches need to be versed in, and when would you advise them to bring in medical professionals to help with a student or client?

AK: I think it's really helpful for voice coaches to be knowledgeable about the anatomy and physiology of the vocal mechanism because it allows them to translate what is physically happening into something more intuitive or artistic. Also, as we all know, every patient/student/client is different, and there may be a person who responds best to a more scientific description or cue to help them achieve their target voice. The more knowledge that a vocal coach has at their disposal, the better they will be able to adapt to the particular needs of an individual. One of the skills that I think is crucial for all voice professionals is one that I would imagine most voice coaches are already pretty amazing at: being able to listen and assess a person's voice quality. Without having the ability to look at the larynx, as we do in a medical setting, your ears are your most crucial tool. So, being able to understand and think about what it is that you're listening to is super important. A scientific understanding of the vocal mechanism, how it works and functions, will help to guide you when something sounds out of balance or unusual. It's really helpful to be able to say, "Hmm, what I'm hearing suggests to me that something might be going on in my client's voice" and that's when it's probably time to refer to a voice center so the larynx can be visualized and the voice team can be expanded.

That makes a lot of sense. When I as the voice coach notice that my student loses their voice consistently after shows or is hoarse at the end of class, or my executive clients consistently have a creaky or scratchy voice, I can say something like, "Hey I'm hearing these particular things. It would make sense to have a laryngologist take a look at your instrument to get more clarity on what you are feeling and I am hearing."

ML: You have raised such an important point! If you notice a change in voice quality, we really must have a low threshold to visualize the vocal apparatus in order to eliminate the guesswork. It is better to recognize anatomic factors early rather than trying to "power through" or work around. An examination of the larynx and vocal folds is really not invasive and is quite brief. Watching and understanding the video recording of your vocal function together with your voice team and coach is as critical to a professional voice user as a slow motion video replay is for professional athletes. We really do use the sports or athletic analogy a lot in terms of explaining how we support professional voice users. I am like the orthopedic surgeon and

Andrew is like the physical therapist. Optimal results and long-term health is achieved through teamwork. As a medical voice team, we try to arm our patients and their voice coaches with information to ensure the individual's long-term vocal health and career longevity.

That's a really excellent analogy because you don't see the coach trying to do surgery on the field, right? Maybe you need to go see the physical therapist, the SLP, who can teach you some exercises or maybe it's a bigger problem that can only really be properly diagnosed with scoping.

ML: The basic rule of thumb for us is that a sudden change in voice necessitates a laryngeal examination. Also, any voice change that lasts for longer than two weeks should prompt the need for an evaluation of the larynx or vocal folds. It's important to remember that we all can become hoarse, or our voices can change, depending on demands or if we suffer from allergies or a cold. The key is that if it's prolonged or persistent, past the two-week mark, clinical practice guidelines suggest that an examination is indicated for us to visualize the vocal folds.

AK: And we're not only talking about how the voice sounds. The way it feels to produce voice is also an important factor. We often see patients who say, "Gosh, it's just uncomfortable when I use my voice." And voicing shouldn't be uncomfortable, right? It shouldn't be a hugely effortful action if things are working in a balanced way. If you or your client have doubts or concerns about what is going on with their voice, it can be validating and comforting to examine it from a medical perspective. It can also be demystifying. I want to encourage people not to be afraid about having a medical voice evaluation. It provides us with information that empowers individuals to take the appropriate steps to get their voices functioning in the best way possible.

So, let's talk about the fear factor. I think there are two elements there. One is from the voice coach's perspective: I know many voice coaches may never have experienced being scoped or have never experienced going to see a laryngologist or speech therapist. So, how should they prepare their client or student or actor for the experience when it may be a mystery to them?

ML: Vocal coaches should feel comfortable reaching out to establish those connections with regional voice centers. It makes sense to build those bridges and establish those pathways for communication early so that they will be accessible and familiar for you and clients when you need them most. Most laryngologists and speech pathologists would be very welcoming and could show you firsthand what an evaluation entails. The best way to prepare one's client or student is to convey that the evaluation is not painful or invasive. Your client or student will gain additional insights and will gain a visual understanding of the mechanics of their larynx to guide recovery, strengthening, or rehabilitation. The laryngeal exam is very brief, well-tolerated, and will be video-recorded for you to review with the team. We have numbing sprays available that can help make the examination even more comfortable, but many patients prefer to have the exam performed without any spray at all.

Yes, finding out who in your region specializes in the voice is important. Another thought that comes to mind is when students or clients come to the voice coach and either complain of "nodes" or have been told by someone that they have nodules. There is a huge fear around losing one's voice. What would you advise a voice coach to do in a situation like that?

ML: There are many different types of swellings that can form on the vocal folds and they go by many different names which often leads to confusion. Singers, vocalists, and other types of professional voice users are predisposed to forming some degree of swelling on the vocal folds … That can be okay and not necessarily problematic. I definitely would encourage people not to wait to seek evaluation, so that whatever swelling exists could be identified at a very early stage. The vast majority of swellings on the vocal folds, whether they be nodes, nodules, or polyps, are highly treatable without any surgery or procedure.

And what's the difference between nodes, nodules, and polyps?

ML: This gets to be very detail-oriented, but I think it's important. Nodes, nodules, and polyps are all considered benign swellings of the vocal folds which result from phonotrauma or the traumatic collisional forces of voice use. Nodules are bilateral, meaning they occur on both vocal cords and are often compared to calluses. Nodules are usually symmetric in size and by definition should not require surgery. Voice therapy alone is the gold standard for the treatment of vocal fold nodules. Nodes is a term that is used synonymously with nodules. A polyp, on the other hand, generally occurs on one vocal fold, but they can sometimes be present on both vocal folds. If a polyp is identified early enough when it is still small, voice therapy can often help improve pliability or its vibratory characteristics to help improve voice quality. Having said that, many patients with vocal fold polyps end up proceeding with some sort of procedure, especially if voice therapy does not yield an improvement in voice quality that is satisfactory to the patient. From a macro level, all of these names or terms we use to describe the various types of vocal fold swelling are used to help guide appropriate data-driven treatment options.

AK: Beyond thinking about what words medical providers use to name or describe a voice problem, it's important to think in terms of how your voice is functioning and what we can do to improve that function. Just because something looks a certain way, doesn't mean that it is impairing you at the equal level to what you think the name means. Does that make sense?

Yes. I love it, that idea of naming what you feel. What voice coaches try to do is help their clients tune in to their breath and their voices, sense their bodies in space, and then be able to talk about that and establish a language in which they can help their clients stay healthy. And then refer them on if they're concerned.

AK: Right. And if there is some sort of barrier vocally that someone is experiencing, then being able to get a video of it and analyze it allows us to take the steps that need to be taken to make sure that their voice functions better for them. More specifically, it guides us toward the most appropriate tools to target the particular vocal problem that we identify. And, yes, I can totally appreciate that it may be scary to imagine that we might find something that you didn't know about. But at the end of the day, knowledge is power and you're coming to a place where our goal is to set you up for vocal success.

Absolutely! Do you think it's important for professional voice users to have a baseline vocal evaluation?

AK: Yes. For people who rely on their voices for their living, having a baseline voice evaluation when someone is feeling vocally healthy can set them up for optimal vocal healthcare in the future, if needed. It gives us as the medical voice team a point of reference, which we can always compare to. By getting baseline measures, including videostroboscopy, while a voice user is not experiencing any voice problems or symptoms, we can identify any laryngeal abnormalities or unique laryngeal findings that aren't causing any problems. And if we know what it looks like when things are going vocally well, then in the future if they ever encounter a problem, we're eliminating the possibility of the new problem being blamed on something that was there the whole time. We usually see people for the first time when they're in some kind of vocal crisis. It would be really helpful if they came to our clinic with a video saying, "This is what my larynx looked like when it was feeling great." It gives us a broader picture of what might be going on. You can see why I am so supportive of baseline voice evaluations.

ML: When we have the opportunity to follow our patients over time, it is so helpful to look at video recordings side by side because this allows us to draw more accurate conclusions and to objectively assess efficacy of our therapeutic approach. And as far as how that relates to the nomenclature and naming of the different things that that we see, like nodules, polyps, cysts, or pseudocysts, we're really using those terms to help identify the best course of action and to expedite the process of recovery.

AK: As Dr. Lerner said, comparing videos and acoustic recordings over time allows us to make sure we're giving the best level of care. For voice users who tour or travel, it's really helpful to have a video of your baseline voice evaluation easily accessible in your smartphone. If it's on your phone and you end up at a voice clinic wherever you are touring, you can share the video with the voice team there.

ML: That is absolutely right. We all have patients that have been evaluated elsewhere in the country, or even outside the country, for that matter. Having a prior video for comparison really sharpens our ability to diagnose, prognosticate, and determine what the next best course of action should be.

It seems like sound advice for a voice coach might be to recommend a baseline vocal evaluation for their professional voice users. Because if you're an athlete, you get your bloodwork done, you get your heart rate monitored, you look at your VO2 max, and you compare them over time. So why wouldn't a voice coach work with a team to help prevent future problems and more efficiently treat them?

AK: Absolutely. Another benefit of a baseline voice evaluation is that you identify a multidisciplinary voice team *before* you have a voice problem. If you encounter a vocal challenge in the future, you don't have the added angst of searching for the right place to go for help. You already know where to go, or at least you know who to reach out to for recommendations. I strongly encourage voice coaches around the world to identify *who* in their community is providing multidisciplinary voice care and to connect with them. By building this bridge, you are setting up the systems to get your clients and students the right kind of voice care should the need arise in the future.

Yes, it seems that being in the room together and becoming a team for our students and clients is really important. And online or "telehealth" appointments have certainly made it easier to help people all over the world connect with medical professionals like the two of you. Do you have any additional recommendations for voice coaches to learn more about how we can work with laryngologists and speech therapists?

ML: To gain a better understanding of what a laryngologist is and what we do, I would direct voice coaches to the American Laryngological Association (ALA). The ALA website does a great job of explaining the specialty and there is even a newer patient education section which helps translate the medical jargon that clients might hear inside and outside the doctor's office (https://alahns.org).

AK: The Voice Foundation is a great organization that has a conference every year, which is a real melding of the minds: laryngology, speech pathology, vocal pedagogy, and education. I have also heard wonderful things about the Summer Vocology Institute, which is a six-week course [Sponsored by the University of Utah] open to a variety of voice professionals: laryngologists, speech-language pathologists, voice teachers, vocal coaches, anybody interested in voice habilitation.

Any tips or tricks for staying healthy that voice coaches can pass on to their clients?

AK: General tips for vocal health and hygiene definitely include staying well hydrated. That involves drinking plenty of water to hydrate systemically. It can also be valuable to hydrate the vocal folds superficially by breathing in steam or inhaling nebulized isotonic saline. There are personal steam inhaler devices and handheld saline nebulizers available that many professional voice users find helpful, especially if they use their voices in dry environments, like dusty theatres as an example. Maintaining a healthy lifestyle overall is important for vocal health as well. That includes eating well, getting adequate sleep, and exercising regularly. I certainly recommend avoiding any kind of smoking or vaping. Those kinds of habits can be very irritating to the vocal folds, not to mention the other health risks they pose. Try to avoid yelling and screaming. Avoid excessive throat clearing. Incorporate a gentle vocal warm-up into your pre-performance routine and a vocal cool-down afterward. If your voice feels tired, allow yourself time to rest it.

ML: With our professional voice users, we really emphasize the importance of vocal budgeting. The voice function, like any function of the body, is not an unlimited one. High-frequency traumatic collisions without rest will eventually lead to swelling or stiffness. Rest your voice when you can and be picky about when, how, and with whom you spend from your vocal budget outside of your professional vocal duties. Sometimes, that means making distinct choices about when to lean into digital, text messaging, or email communications as opposed to making a phone call. Other strategies include using confidential voice or arm's length voice and reducing competing background noises which all equates to reducing unnecessary voice overuse.

AK: One research area that I'm excited to pursue is vocal warm-up and rescue strategies. Many voice coaches and professional voice users have products or teas or tinctures that they swear by to either rescue their voice if it's feeling tired, or that they use regularly to keep their voices functioning well. However, many of these products haven't been thoroughly studied. It would be fantastic to have scientific data to help us make recommendations about which remedies and tricks are best for different kinds of vocal demands and challenges.

Great food for thought! Here's to partnering more with the triad of laryngologists, SLPs, and voice coaches!

AK: Yes! It's so exciting.

As you look to build a team of professionals to help you as a voice coach, it is important to find local resources who have an understanding of your clientele. The British Voice Association, populated by singing and spoken voice coaches alike, offers periodic multi-disciplinary events and seminars, both online and in the UK. The National Center for Voice and Speech is another resource; they host a summer vocology institute in the United States. The Performing Arts Medicine Association (PAMA) is another organization that offers conferences. Wherever you search, it will be important for you to find a go-to laryngologist and speech-language pathologist whom you can reach out to when necessary. In this way, you will be able to offer your students and clients the most comprehensive opportunities for keeping their voices strong and healthy, and ultimately empowering them as they move forward in their careers.

Section II

Introduction to Words of Wisdom

When I was asked to write this book, my first thought was that this is not just my book; it is a book by and for all voice coaches. My goal was to curate an inclusive and expansive survey of experts that would both inspire and inform the next generations of voice coaches. In order to do that, I reached out to roughly 100 professionals and was granted interviews with over fifty of them. Some of these luminaries, like Kristin Linklater and Fran Bennett, unfortunately did not live to see this book come to fruition, however their wisdom will inevitably provide you with invaluable insights. My interviews spanned from January 2020 to August 2022. The printed version of the Words of Wisdom section includes a selection of interviews conducted, while the Support Materials, available online to anyone who purchases this book include all of the interviews.

The goal was to capture the feeling of sitting down and having a heart-to-heart conversation with truly talented humans who have a passion for voice. While I edited out some fillers and repeated words, you will notice that I have included "(laughs)" in the interviews or indicated particular physical move-ments [she demonstrates breathing out] by the interviewee. These discussions are not meant to be scholarly recounts, but rather imperfect, vulnerable, and open conversations.

My original idea for this section was to conduct identical interviews and ask five questions that were exactly the same. I soon learned that a cookie-cutter approach would not elicit the most delicious responses, so I pivoted, and came up with about ten general questions. I sent these to each interviewee in advance and let them know that we would likely go down a variety of paths. Two of my

DOI: 10.4324/9781003006206-8

favorite questions were (1) How do you identify as a voice coach? and (2) What advice would you give your younger self? Both of these questions brought such a depth of wisdom, unique to each person. It was refreshing and a great delight to be in the presence of each person I interviewed. I only wish that, as I was starting my career, I had had the opportunity to be exposed to the generous guidance offered from such a collection of experienced professionals.

Most interviews lasted between sixty to ninety minutes. Each person is worthy of a book, so you can imagine how difficult it was to cut the interviews down to offer you bite-sized chunks of individual and improvisational insight. This section is organized in alphabetical order by first name, and any publications mentioned in the interviews will be cited at the end of the book. Now, I invite you to sit down with your favorite beverage and flip to the pages that call you as you peruse and digest these Words of Wisdom.

List of Interviewees

These interviews were conducted between January of 2020 and August of 2022. The names asterisked indicate those whose Words of Wisdom are included in the printed version of this publication. Many of the interviewees are quoted throughout the book. All interviewee conversations are included in this book's online Support Materials., with the exception of Andrew Keltz, Joanna Cazden and Michael Lerner, whose conversations are all featured extensively in the Vocal Health for the Voice Coach.

Amy Hume

Amy Stoller*

Andrea Caban

Andrea Haring*

Andrew Keltz, S. L. P.

Ann Skinner*

Antonio Ocampo-Guzman*

Barry Kur*

Ben Furey

Beth McGuire*

Betty Moulton

Bonnie Raphael*

Christina Shewell*

Cynthia Santos DeCure*

Daron Oram*

David Carey*

David Smukler*

Doug Honorof

Eric Armstrong

DOI: 10.4324/9781003006206-9

Erik Singer*

Fran Bennett*

Hilary Blair

Jan Gist

Jane Boston

Jenny Kent

Joanna Cazden, S.L.P.

João Henriques

Katerina Moraitis

Kristin Linklater*

Leith McPherson

Louis Colaianni*

Mary MacDonald

Micha Espinosa*

Michael Lerner, M.D.

Michael Morgan*

Nancy Houfek

Oscar Quiroz

Patsy Rodenburg*

Patty Raun

Paul Meier*

Rachel Coleman, S.L.P.

Rena Cook

Ros Steen*

Sara Matchett*

Scott Miller*

Shane-Ann Younts

Stan Brown*

Tola "Bimbo" Benson

Tom Burke, S. L. P.

Walton Wilson*

Words of Wisdom

Interviews with the Experts

AMY STOLLER

I don't think you can be a good dialect coach if you are not interested in sounds, language, and speech. But you can be interested yet not very curious. Curiosity is the desire to keep learning more. That need to take it to the next level is key.

How do you identify as a "voice coach"?

I don't consider myself a *voice* coach or voice teacher. I'm a *dialect designer*, and I'm also a *dramaturge*—which I pronounce with a "soft g" and spell with an e at the end because that's the English spelling.

How did you come to settle on using "dialect designer"?

I can't remember where I first heard the term—it may have been [fellow VASTA member] Eric Armstrong, but I'm not sure. It appealed to me because what I do *is* a design job. For a production, I have to research and select from a range of authentic speech patterns and/or devise new speech patterns to create a community or family sound for a full cast of characters; or sometimes for

DOI: 10.4324/9781003006206-10

individual speech identities for one or more characters, but not all. Then I have to tailor the speech pattern(s) to any specific needs the production may have, often including the abilities of the performers. In private practice, working with individual performers, I do the same thing, just on a smaller scale. Either way, it's comparable in responsibility and scope to, say, costume design.

You can also compare dialect design to choreography, which is another design field: choreography for the mouth. Either way, "dialect designer" is the credit I most often specify for theatre, because it best represents what I do.

And how did you become a dramaturge?

When I started doing dialect design, I found I wasn't satisfied with teaching actors how to pronounce things if I couldn't also help them understand what they (their characters) were talking about. So, I started providing a glossary. Over several years and successive productions, each show's glossary turned out longer. It evolved into what I call the "Glossary & Text Notes"—with topical and cultural notes as well as definitions. This could be anything from twenty to thirty pages in length. Being faced with too much unbroken text can be off-putting, so I started adding photos, drawings, all sorts of fun things to help people absorb whatever concept I was trying to make accessible. And then I began adding articles that expanded on some of the notes, and picture collections, and audio files, and videos.

I remember having a conversation about this with [fellow VASTA member] Lynn Watson at a VASTA conference, and she asked me if I was getting paid extra for all that. I said I wasn't. She said, "Are you at least getting credit for it?" I said, "No." She said, "Well, you should!" I owe her for that.

How do you navigate getting deep into the dramaturgy in productions that have a dramaturge?

I make sure to introduce myself to the show's official dramaturge as early as possible. I may say something like, "I normally do a glossary. Are you doing one? If you're not, would I be stepping on your toes if I do one?" Sometimes they *are* creating a glossary, which I can learn from. But I find I still have to do a certain amount of deeper research for myself. Even if I don't make it available directly to the company, it informs my work.

What was your path to now?

I feel the biggest decisions in my life have made *me*; I didn't make them. I was good at accents as a kid. I started doing them when I was three. When I was acting, I usually did my accent work all by myself. And I had, at that point, no formal training in it. What I *did* have was an innate facility … "the bloom of ignorance"[1] had not yet been touched, so I had a very strong ear-to-mouth connection. If I could hear it, I could do it—well enough to book and keep jobs. In all my acting career, I only worked with a dialect coach on a show twice.

What led you to dive into coaching full-time?

It was a sideline, then a part-time thing for about five years. But after September 11th [2001], when the economy bottomed out, and I lost my day job and couldn't find another one, I said to myself, "Well, what the heck? Why don't I just do this full-time?" Now, that's an *insane* thing to do, especially with no capitalization. But it's also insane to start out as a dialect coach with no training in it. It's a very good thing that nobody told me I couldn't do it that way.

These days it seems many people find their way into voice coaching through MFA programs.

I dropped out of undergrad to work in the theatre, so my path is a very different one: I got my degree from the School of Hard Knocks. I learned a lot of what I know on the job. My work benefits greatly from the knowledge and research of folks in academia, but I'm not an academic myself. I did eventually complete a bachelor's degree as an "adult student," but it's not in any of the fields I work in, and I went right back to working in showbiz.

What qualities do you think are necessary for a coach to cultivate?

Interest and curiosity. I don't think you can be a good dialect coach if you are not interested in sounds, language, and speech. But you can be interested yet not very curious. Curiosity is the desire to keep learning *more*. That need to take it to the next level is key. It can be very helpful to be curious not only about language and speech sounds, but also about cultural and social history. And assuming you want to work with performing artists, I'd add performing-arts training. You need to understand the community you want to serve.

What are your thoughts on the International Phonetic Alphabet and using that in your coaching?

I did all my accent and dialect work as an actor without any knowledge of it. I barely knew anything about IPA *or* phonetics when I first started coaching. I'd already been coaching for several years when I first learned, from [fellow VASTA member] Doug Honorof, how IPA charts work. Later, Knight-Thompson Speechwork brought me to an even deeper understanding of phonetics. So now I find IPA enormously valuable. I learned it when I was *ready* for it, which made it fairly easy to learn. But if you're not ready for it—and some people will never be—that doesn't mean you can't do accents and dialects. The IPA is a notation system, it's not the thing itself. It's like the relationship of musical notation to musicality. If it was an absolute necessity for musicians to be able to read notes on a staff, then Ray Charles would never have had a career. So, just as there is a difference between musical notation and musical talent, there is a difference between being able to notate accents using IPA, and being able to perform in accents other than your own. When I work with people who don't know the IPA, or have no phonetics training, I have to meet them where they are and help them using whatever tools work for them. "Fauxnetics", color-coding—whatever works.

What gives you joy in coaching?

When I can watch that little cartoon light bulb go on over a client's head. And when I can see a production or performance I've coached and feel I've achieved 85% of my original goal. Am I a hard grader of myself? Heck yes. I'm a recovering perfectionist; it took time to learn that reaching 85% of a goal was genuinely good.

One of the resources on your website is "So you want to be a dialect coach?" which I encourage readers to look at, but I'd love you to highlight the part about being realistic as you build your career.

It's very difficult to make a living as a dialect coach in the performing arts without at least one other string to your bow. You need another source of income, whether it's a job in academia, a job at a professional acting studio, a yoga practice, a sideline as a jewelry designer, an acting career (like *that's* easy!), *something*. You *will* need, at some point in your career if not throughout your entire career, another source of income. I don't think I know anybody in the field who doesn't have some other way of achieving financial security for lean years. Let's not gloss this over: *Nobody should be going into show business for the money*.

Do you have additional advice or thoughts for aspiring coaches?

It's a good idea to go back to class when you can. It not only will teach you/remind you of/expand your understanding of a skill set, or philosophy, or point of view about your work; it will also help you remember what it feels like to be someone who doesn't yet know what you know. That's a way of developing empathy; to put yourself in your client's or student's place. That's one of the things I like about VASTA conferences. When I was in the early years of my VASTA membership, seeing somebody like [master teacher] Rocco Dal Vera be completely willing to roll around on the floor and try something new, just as though he hadn't written books that were standard texts in many universities, was inspiring. That kind of openness and humility is very valuable. It's easy to rest on your laurels, but it isn't good for you.

ANDREA HARING

For me, voice work is not about a "lovely" sound—you have to hear the human being. Our human presence, the complex content of what we think and feel, can be revealed in a kind of transparency through the sounds of the words as we speak them. You need to bring the soul into the voice.

It seems that you came into voice coaching through a musical background.

I started as a singer, but when Kristin Linklater and Tina Packer started Shakespeare and Company in 1978, I had the privilege of being an actor in that company and it changed everything. Exploring the Bard's rich imagery and the structure of the verse spoke to me in a more satisfying way. The company trained together in movement, mask, stage combat, Alexander Technique, Voice and Text with Kristin, and Structure of the Verse with Tina or Neil Freeman or John Barton. Such exciting exploration. I worked with Shakespeare & Co. for almost twenty years.

And how did that lead to your teaching of Kristin's work?

Several company members trained as teachers with Kristin. I was designated as a Linklater teacher in 1982 and hired by Dartmouth College to teach voice. Later, I joined the faculty of Circle in the Square Theater School where I taught, directed the thesis plays, and also coached the shows. I've since taught at Yale, Columbia, The New School, and Fordham University.

You have coached actors and trained voice teachers, but is working with "professional voice users" also part of your practice?

Yes! I give workshops in public speaking at The Linklater Center for Voice and Language, NYC, and have enjoyed corporate coaching over the last twenty years teaching for the World Economic Forum Global Fellows, the Obama Foundation Scholars, and the Columbia Senior Executive Program, among others. It's so useful to bring the benefits of acting training into the professional world, and help them avoid looking and listening to themselves, to focus instead on their message. Not "How do I sound?" but "What am I saying and why does it matter?"

Do you see a difference in how you coach these areas, or would you identify your core process as similar?

I would say the process is similar in that we are loosening tensions, developing resonance, undoing jaw, tongue, and throat tensions that filter the message, opening up vocal range for expressive choices, and stimulating lively articulation. But primarily, you have to understand their focus and goals. For the most part, they're into the end product. "What's the strategy? Give me a bottom line." (laughs) And I respect that. I absolutely do. There's money riding on what they do and bosses who are expecting results. So, if my corporate people are a little stiff or self-conscious, I have to find ways to bring them out of themselves and every group is going to be different. It's good to give a purpose for the work and for them to know what they're going to get out of it.

Actors understand that developing a character and responding to the events of the play is a process. There may be moments when they don't know what's going on because they are investigating. It can take a while for corporate professionals to [understand] that experimentation can also have a purpose—that there's a reason behind what we're doing. And to learn: "Can I be okay in this moment with not knowing, feeling foolish, and still give it a go?" Whereas the first lesson for an actor is, "I'm going to say 'yes' to what's happening and trust I have everything I need to respond."

What has helped you communicate and coach effectively in the corporate world?

I try to be present with them and hear what it is that they want out of the session. And then I'll tailor my work to serve their needs with building skills and finding an authentic connection. I may simplify an exercise to open up their voice, or play a quick game to use more vocal range rather than going through the entire resonating ladder. I'll evaluate: How much time do we have? What do they feel they need to work on? What am I hearing in their voice? How can I come up with something that really works for them? It's about finding a natural progression so they can feel more alive in themselves. I want to give them a payoff—a takeaway.

You said in an interview with Nancy Saklad, "Voice begins with the human spirit and the authentic sense of oneself." How do you help uncover the human spirit and guide an individual to find their sense of self?

For myself, "being present" works best when I connect my state of being to my sensory world through my body. It's being aware of what I'm physically sensing as well as emotionally feeling, my state of mind. It helps to think of the incoming breath as a connection to thought, feeling, and my sense of myself right now. And the outgoing breath as a willing 'letting go' of what I'd like to express. It's a continual interplay between my private self and the world around me, and I'm constantly interacting between them. I appreciate Patsy Rodenberg's Second Circle work as a blueprint for this.

How much does a voice teacher or coach need to know about anatomy and movement?

I think if you are going to be a vocal coach, you should at least do Alexander Technique and Feldenkrais® work and know the basic structures in the mouth and throat. That's required for the Linklater trainees, as well as Experiential Anatomy: Body Mind Centering where you see how all the different body systems are interconnected. Would I bring all the technical talk into my coaching sessions? Not necessarily. I need to know how everything interrelates, but I simplify it for my students or clients.

What are the most important qualities for a voice coach to possess?

It's my job to support. My job is not to be right, but to go in and be flexible enough to take all of the knowledge that I've gathered and use that to accomplish whatever the task is at hand. I need to listen really well. It's good to have a plan and to be organized, and yet be flexible enough to let go of my ideas and work with whatever my clients feel they need. I have to meet *them*. Flexibility is really key.

There are times when I'll work with a cast and I can just tell they're really down. And I might introduce something playful, or something gentle and sweet, that just gets them being with each other. Or we might get very physically active to shift gears and to help the group find an ensemble dynamic. You're exchanging, you're doing something together, and that's where a group song can be great, or some verbal games. Especially if the project is a difficult or painful play, encouraging a different dynamic can alleviate the stress. It helps to know what you can draw from your own actor training. Which is why I like to take improv or acting classes to refresh what to draw from that can open the person.

If you could speak to your younger self at this point, what would your advice be?

I encourage my trainees to keep training and to get an MFA because it's difficult to find a teaching position without one now. I prefer acting training as opposed to just voice pedagogy, because many of the people you're going to be coaching are actors. You need the acting vocabulary. You need to know what the demands are for an actor. And as a vocal coach, you should feel what it's like to be in the hotspot—to be afraid. (laughs) You know? We all need an opportunity to feel nervous and then rise to the occasion.

Mary MacDonald said to me, "We're working to help give wings." I love that imagery, to help give wings to these larynxes, and to any human trying to find their voice. I think of it as midwifery, in a way. You're trying to help birth that voice.

It's the human being that is being revealed through the voice. That's the interesting thing. Not how loud or strong the voice is, although that might be useful. But if you don't hear the person then it's going to lack soul. You need to bring the soul into the voice. Voice work is also self-care. And when you breathe and hum, when you interconnect all these disparate parts of your body—it helps get you grounded. I talk with my students about resilience and the ability to recalibrate. Tough things are going to happen in life. That's just the way life is: a roller coaster. So, developing your belief in yourself, and a practice that encourages resilience and self-care, is something all of us need to take on.

ANN SKINNER

There's a place to go in every being where their voice sits. And there's a place beneath that which is where their humanity sits.

There isn't just one way to become a voice coach, is there?

There really isn't, no. I've talked to many of my colleagues, and it seems that to become a voice coach/teacher they haven't necessarily set out to do that. (Pamela laughs) They may have experience in acting, singing; perhaps like to write poetry, or build props; but not, "Oh, I'm going to be a voice coach," because they probably don't even know there is such a thing.

Your journey in voice coaching has so many components. From working and co-creating with the renowned clown teacher Richard Pochinko, to Canada's Stratford Shakespeare Festival, to working with Marion Woodman and Mary Hamilton in the creation of BodySoul Rhythms® ... I think there's space for your authentic voice within the world of the voice coach.

Yes. And here is certainly something to know as a teacher or coach: have colleagues in different disciplines i.e., a team. Over the years I've collaborated with many artists. When Marion and Mary and I created BodySoul Rhythms®; the hours we three would spend during the intensives; in the evening, over breakfast, over lunch, over dinner: "Well, what do you think we should do now?" "Well, I don't know. Do you have an idea?" It was [in] all that sharing that BodySoul Rhythms® evolved.

That was true for me working at The Stratford Festival as well and The National Theatre School. That is, voice coaches working with movement coaches is so enlightening and so important. I've worked with so many different movement coaches; and I've studied the Alexander Technique because the work we do is of the voice *and* the body. For the stage, the body and the voice are one. What I am saying for those who want to be voice coaches, is that there are many roads, some sharply deviating, to take you there; and one might say the more roads the better for the richness the journey can bring to the work.

What I hear you saying is that you didn't set out to say, "I'm going to make a living as a voice coach." You came at it from this pure place of Joseph Campbell's, "Follow your bliss" of listening to what's being presented to you and then feeling into it, and then following the "yes."

Yes, that's right. But not consciously. When the light went on, I would follow the light no matter how irrational. For instance, that light came from Richard Pochinko and guided me from stage management to becoming a clown through an extraordinary experience of mask-making to founding a theatre with Richard and on from there. Something in my not knowing, wanted *life,* really wanted *life. Yes,* "follow your bliss," or I would say: "follow the *red*, just follow the blood, the red, whatever it is. It was in a rehearsal that I learned what *red* meant to me.

Let me explain: A director asked me if I had any notes for the actors after a dress rehearsal. Initially we always find words to encourage, and I said, "Very good" and then I said, "However, I think something is missing." And he said "Well, what? Do you have a word?" And I said, "Yes, I do: *red*." And they all looked at me like I was … (laughs). One of the actors said, "I think she means R-E-D, not R-E-A-D." And I couldn't say anymore because I didn't know why I'd said it. But later I realized that *red* for me is *life force*. There was no *life force* because [the director] had total control and the actors were simply playing it out. In speaking of the theatre, we often use the word *live* with theatre….without life force i.e., oxygen in the work, there is only loss.

What are your thoughts on how teaching has evolved?

We are moving into a new world where we are attempting to recognize and welcome the wealth of our diversity; and then to write and tell stories from there. [James] Baldwin talked about vulnerability and fear, and the patriarchy, dominating. I would say to young coaches that there is a place to go in *every* being, where their voice sits. And there's a place beneath that, that is where their humanity sits.

For a teacher/coach, anything we can do to know ourselves deeply and wisely and learn deeply and surprisingly from the person we are teaching is more than ever essential in this new and exciting time. There will be "vulnerability and fear." Be prepared. Be grounded. Know yourself. And then, stay open and learn. As coaches, we are holding a safe place for the artists to bring their *life force* to make *live* theatre.

What is your advice to the voice coach when the coach may present differently from the humans being coached?

Listen and learn. Create a safe environment for the student. Breathe and take in, and wonder; and question your own fragility and the fragility in the artist or artists with whom you are coaching. Listen and learn from the unknown and the creativity will enter the room.

It's always been important to bring a sense of, "I'm the learner as well."

Yes. For the story is the most important thing. And everybody has a sense of story. I had a student from Iran once, and he did the most wonderful work on a monologue. I thought I was sitting in Persia many years ago when listening to the story. The monologue was the same for the next actor to tell. But the colors, the words, and the richness of the story were altered by the storyteller. We need to feel our connection to the words. And if the connection breaks down between the actor, audience, teacher, then we are back in, say, a patriarchal world or a world where the connection is broken and we cannot reach each other.

I just got this image of the coach as the facilitator of the storytelling.

Oh yes. For example: at the Stratford Festival there was an actor of considerable talent who played the leading roles. Audiences loved him, admired him;

however, during one season, there were audience complaints that they couldn't understand him, hear him, which was shocking because he was always incredibly clear. The stage manager came to me for help and I thought, "Well, I'd better go to see the show again," I hadn't seen it for a while. This was repertory: a long run.

I went to see the show three times and as I am sitting there, I am thinking, "I can't hear him. What the heck is going on? Because I could detect no problem with his voice. But we can't hear him." And then I remembered what I knew about his health. I went to see him in his dressing room later—he summoned me in—and he said, "You have some notes for me?" I had pages of notes of every line I couldn't hear. And I looked at this man who had had all these years of experience. I thought, "He doesn't need my notes."

I paused, looked at him, and I said,

I know you are having your hips replaced. I know they are incredibly painful. What appears to be happening is that you are looking at the stage floor most of the time. You are afraid that if you look up and out and if you move here or move there, or you have to go down the steps into the vom, or up to the balcony you will trip, fall. Your voice is being absorbed by the wood of the stage. I think that's it."

And he just looked at me and laughed. (laughs) From then on, he was of course completely audible.

So interesting. That's it, that's what you do. It's a kind of story clarification, right?

Yes, and we need to remain open to every option for clarification. Sit back and breathe in; and then say, "I don't know. I don't know what to do." Then maybe share the questions: you and the actors will work on it together. And/or discuss with the director, your colleagues: "Did you see this? What did you hear?"

We are coming into a new era of the story in theatre; stories involving race, nationality, roots, culture, and much more. It will be a fascinating time to be a voice coach. We will need to know there will be pressures and anxieties for ourselves as these new stories are written and heard. We will need to recognize the fragility of our students and ourselves as we bring our voices and our bodies and our humanity into full focus and expression.

It is such a delight to speak with you. I wonder if you have any other Canadians you might recommend as resources for aspiring voice coaches?

The Stratford Festival of Canada is now one of the few repertory companies left, I believe. That is, it is active over ten months of the year, producing ten shows, employing at this time 120 actors. The Festival employs ten voice coaches: a mix of Voice and Text coaches; Voice, Text, and Dialect Coaches; a Singing Coach; two Assistant Voice Coaches i.e, in training as well as one apprentice coach in training; and also three Movement Coaches.

Janine Pearson, Head of Voice and Coaching at The Festival for thirty years, and now Head of The Birmingham Conservatory for Classical Training, built this team over the years to carry out what she calls "The Work," i.e, voice, body, text, and dialect work for the actor. Janine is a remarkable teacher and organizer, as are the team … There are many roads into the World of live theatre and they may merge eventually into the road of the voice coach. There, "The Work" may evolve and lead into new roads all dedicated to connection, life, and story.

ANTONIO OCAMPO-GUZMAN

"Keep the sense of joy, the sense of exploration: there's no arrival. There's no such thing as, "My voice is now free, thank you very much, all good now, bye!"

I would love to understand more about your journey to what we're calling a "voice coach."

Growing up in a very exuberant family, "voice" was always present. There was always noise, sound, people having big arguments … My first love was music and, certainly, opera. What I fantasized about when I was eleven, twelve years old was to be an opera singer. What the heck was I thinking? Anyway, when I was eighteen, I went to New York and I lived there for six months. The New School for Social Research had [a] kind of Extension School, and there [I took] a class called "The Singing Self." I have this distinct memory of my body tingling, being led through a physical awareness exercise and then singing with my whole body. Like, "Wow, this is awesome!"

Then I went back to Colombia and started to train as an actor. The person that helped me navigate acting school was my voice teacher, Livia Esther Jiménez. In the second year, she asked me if I'd be interested in TA-ing for her. That's when she gave me *Freeing the Natural Voice* and I started translating. A year and a half after I graduated from the Conservatory, I came to the US to participate in the month-long intensive with Kristin at Shakespeare & Company. At the end of that I thought, "I need to learn how to teach this."

So, that's how it all started, basically. I knew early on that I did not want to be pigeonholed as "the voice teacher." This was the best piece of advice that Kristin ever gave to me: "Don't let yourself be pigeonholed as 'the voice teacher'." Because I wanted to teach acting, clown, and improv, and I wanted to direct. Certainly, teaching voice has been a huge pillar of who I am and what I do, but it's not *all* that I do.

One of the things that I learned about you early on was your connection with CEUVOZ.

Yes. Centro Estudios para el Uso de la Voz.

Through that, did you translate Kristin Linklater's book, *Freeing the Natural Voice*?

I started translating parts of Kristin's book even before I came to the US. When I was first given Kristin's book by my voice teacher in Colombia, she asked me to translate the introduction for the other students in the Conservatory. And after I had worked with Kristin, I began to loosely translate bits and pieces of it. When I started to teach *Freeing the Natural Voice* in Spanish, I realized that I needed to adapt it rather than translate it. Kristin's work and the way that she used language was so Anglo Saxon. Also, the way that one speaks Spanish in Mexico is very different from in Spain.

For this book to be helpful, I needed to use as simple a Spanish as possible—so that people in [both] Spain and Mexico can read it. That's why I said to Kristin, "I cannot translate it. This has to be a living adaptation of the work." And she got it, you know. One of the testaments of her great, great trust in me was that she allowed it to be an adaptation and not a translation, and for the book to have my name and not her name. Because it wasn't a complete translation. It was an adaptation that came from my own personal experience of teaching it in my first language and adapting it between Spain and Mexico.

As we think about working with voices across countries, genders, ethnicities, economic differences … I'm interested in how we make adaptations rather than direct translations.

The biggest pedagogical challenge for me was grappling with the concept of freedom. Kristin's work is called *Freeing the Natural Voice*. That presupposes that every voice can be free. It means that on some level the voice *can* be free, and that there's some universal access that we all have as humans, if we're all born with the same, let's say, health. That there's a primal ability to be free. However, the concept of freedom resonates very differently when you teach it in England or the US. Whereas when you teach it in Mexico or Colombia, it is very difficult for a culture that has been educated towards obedience to have a concept of freedom.

While I was adapting Kristin's work, I resorted back to Paulo Freire, whose work I had read when I was much younger. The Brazilian educator and philosopher talked about education toward oppression versus education toward liberty or freedom. There were a number of instances, mostly in Spain and Mexico, that taught me a lot about the difference of teaching this in a culture in which educational pedagogy is toward freedom versus toward obedience.

It's a powerful concept as we look at the big questions around decolonizing teaching and voice work. How do we use the discoveries that people like you have made in your cross-cultural, international work?

For me, the most current thinking is how I present myself in the room. I certainly was taught, and then trained to teach, by people who have inherited the notion that the teacher is the expert in the room and therefore, "I come into the room as the expert, I lead x, y, z exercises, and then I judge you on how you do them, and then you'll be fine." (laughs) But also, there's the notion that I don't have to make you "fine." I have to come in from the place where I *may* be able to teach you this thing rather than, "I am *going* to fix your jaw by releasing it, and you just have to release your jaw and your life is going to be better."

In my experience teaching at Northeastern University and in Spain and Mexico, the one aspect of theatre training that makes the most sense to me is clowning. It was through clowning that I was able to synergize all the things that I had learned as an actor, as a director, as a voice teacher. And therefore, for many years, I have attempted for my classes to be infused with the spirit of clowning: meaning not to take it too seriously, finding delight in the failures that we're going to explore. That the only thing you have to really do is show up.

There is something quintessentially joyful for me about voice, about feeling a full breath, feeling my voice resonating in my bones. That has always been an experience of joy for me. And I've always attempted to bring that into my teaching, specifically in voice but also in all the other things that I teach, which includes clowning and improv. And it's mostly because the people that I was working with in Spain and Mexico were coming from a very rigorous, have-no-fun way of training actors. It's like, sacred. "Don't you dare enjoy it. It's very important. Suffer!" That rigidity and a lot of ego in the teacher. So, I have always attempted to play the curmudgeon, the clown that ruffles things around. And that has worked well, as a teacher of voice, to keep that sense of joy and exploration happening. There's no arrival. There's no such thing as, "My voice is now free! Thank you very much. All good now. Bye!" (laughs)

What gives you the most joy in your teaching?

I get such a kick when I or anybody else is surprised by what they can do, "Oh my gosh, I had no idea I had that in me." As a teacher, director, and a trainer of actors, when I see an actor do that, those moments are priceless. I love a surprise—at least that's how I understand acting. Acting is a constant seeking of surprises. So, when it happens, especially when genuine, I find a lot of joy in that.

I do want to make a little caveat here: For me, there's a very clear difference between *fun* and *joy*. I hate fun. I cannot stand the notion of, "Oh, just have fun with it!" "Wouldn't it be fun if we do this?" Fun to me is trivial; joy is something very, very deep. And joy can be painful sometimes. There can be joy in a big cry; there can be joy in deep pain and grief. *Fun*, to me, trivializes everything.

Do you think learning anatomy is important for your clients, your students?

I think it is important to understand how it all works. I don't think it's important to know all the different names of things, but I personally have always enjoyed studying anatomy and understanding how the body actually operates. This is a difference that I've had with some colleagues in the past: the notion of guiding your students mostly through images. For me, anatomy is really important, also because it's fascinating. All the connections that are now being made so much more explicit through neuroscience about how the body actually operates … To me, those things are incredibly important to make sure that the student or client understands. But it's not an anatomy lesson per se, you know? Just to have a clear understanding of the process. I think it's important.

How would you advise somebody who says, "You know, I like this coaching thing. How can I make a living at it?"

Join VASTA. That's the first thing. VASTA, for me, has been useful and eye-opening. When I first came to the US and trained with Kristin, that's all I knew. VASTA has given me an opportunity to see many other different ways of training and understanding.

The first question that I would ask is, "Are you interested in training, in helping actors use their voice? Or are you interested in teaching other people to use their voice professionally?" Because they might be a little bit different in terms of how the profession might develop. And then, for those people who answer that they would like to work with actors, I would ask, "Are you interested in making a living as part of—as Nicole Brewer calls it—the Theatre Industrial Complex?" Meaning, working in academia and in regional theatres and whatnot. Those are two of the main sources of income and they come with certain complications.

So, when it comes to people who are interested in the academic route: make sure that you have a clear sense of what the institution you are employed at considers "tenurable." If that's the case, then how are you going to navigate those promotions and those commitments in the university? Is there a union for part-time faculty? Navigating the Academy is very complicated and what I've seen, for many colleagues, is that voice teachers and movement teachers tend to be at the bottom. So, I think it's really important to understand what you're getting yourself into and if you really want to get yourself into that. That's one thing.

The other thing to understand is that there are many ways [to train] a person's voice. It might be useful to consider taking a deep dive into a particular methodology. There are many other methodologies that may be in complete disagreement with the first one, but at the same time can augment your tools. One thing that I know for certain is that what I teach and how I teach helps, but it does not help everybody. Having more tools at my disposal to help a student is useful, rather than just relying on the one thing that I know. Lastly, one never finishes. One never finishes learning how to teach or how to train. It's a constant journey of discovery and exploration and, again, something like VASTA becomes very useful to continue to learn.

Is there a challenging moment you can recall that a voice teacher might face?

I would imagine that this is relatively common for voice teachers: when people begin to breathe freely and deeply, a lot of stuff gets stirred up, right? The body holds a lot of layers of mysterious things that are not understandable. I've had a couple of very challenging moments in which students go into these experiences, and I do not know how to bring them back to the reality of the room. For example, once I had a person who had a diagnosed personality disorder, and another personality took over.

Something that has helped me is trauma-informed pedagogy. Understanding that when you deal with breath and the body, there are traumas that can be unlocked, so how to bring it back to the reality of where you are. Those moments have been incredibly challenging, particularly when I was a young teacher. It was very scary when people would hyperventilate and disconnect from the reality of the room and the person there.

And how did you help them, or what helped you?

At that point, what helps is gravity. Bringing them to the floor; making sure they feel that they're supported by the floor so that they're not going to collapse;

paying attention to the rest of the class, so the whole group becomes the support system and not just me; making sure that the person makes eye contact and recognizes who everybody is and is able to name them; or just return to the reality of what's inside. Fortunately, that has always worked for me. The bigger challenge is then speaking about it to the rest of the class, integrating it into what we're doing, and making sure that everybody's willing to continue with the training and not be terrified of what happened. (laughs) Creating that container. The first step is always building the community of trust in the room.

BARRY KUR

Alignment informs breathing and breathing informs alignment, and there's that wonderful organic synergy that we can learn from. It's never stagnant.

You have had a rich and international career. What kind of qualities do you think a voice coach needs to possess?

I found as I was looking at my journey, and having the opportunity to review and adjudicate for others in their promotion and tenure track, that the individuals who had the strongest dossier and confidence were those who were immersed in a particular modality of training. I'm not saying that's absolute, but there was a time that individuals studied for *themselves*. They studied a particular way of working for themselves for creative development, and then took advantage of the next stage of training, which was how to teach it to others. You have a training on teaching the self and then expressing that to teach others, and that's an important transition. In fact, for the Lessac Institute, that's been my primary institutional job.

I coined this term called "the teacher within," and that is the primary source of, "What do I teach?" or, "How do I teach?" If you're practicing it yourself, then you have the answers within you. And that's how you develop your lesson plan, that's how you develop your instructional language. Because it works for you, there's a great trust because the students see it within you and then apply it to make it their own. I'm not talking about imitating, I'm talking about the essence of how much I enjoy the work, how much I make it a part of my own life, how I am optimized in the way I behave.

And as I'm getting older this is really important, so that I still have a good sense of health within me vocally, physically, movement wise. The first thing Arthur Lessac said to me when he sent me off to teach was, "Don't stop learning." He maintained a really intensive curiosity throughout his life. And so, I've studied with others and I've studied related movement and voice processes: Tai Chi, Yoga, singing …And I did have some Speech Pathology work in my early background as an undergrad. Make it a point to study whatever you feel is missing and would enhance your teaching, even if it's another training program.

I remember Walton Wilson using the term "teaching artist" when I was working for him. It was the first time I had ever heard that term.

I call it "the art of teaching." What's fascinating about teaching is that it has to be in the form of a verb. "As a result of this lesson, your students will be able to …" I mean, talk about objectives and tactics and strategies, and all the stuff that's so important to actor training! It also uses both sides of the brain. There is the side that deals with creativity and psychophysical awareness, how you ignite and keep it interesting, esthetic as opposed to anesthetic … And the way you do something and when you introduce something.

Sue Ann Park, when she mentored me, was brilliant at constantly fine-tuning the progression of events, that one event will lead to the other. It's a very important part of the Lessac training: you learn organically from familiar events so that you can self-teach. You move from a familiar event and that gives you confidence to move to a new event. That's become so important to me. You can look ahead and say, "Oh, I see something familiar in that, so I'll go toward that." It will build the bridge to the new event and you say, "Oh, now I have a new familiar event." It's a great process and it's called "'kinesensic learning."

Tell me a bit about how you are looking into voice and identity.

Well, it's in an early stage of development. First of all, we recognize that we probably made a lot of mistakes. We all did. We white folks all made mistakes. Acknowledge it, don't be defensive about it, listen, be present. And then allow the students to inform you, to teach you a little bit more. It's okay. Don't get defensive if that student says, "But then..." What's the difference? There's a fine line between the skill you may need for the task and the pain that might be felt from removing your identity from it. Be aware that if you're teaching today's students, you're going to work with students who voted, who protested and marched. *Not* folks who had their days planned by Mom and Dad for every little activity after school and beyond, but have self-initiated movement. Recognize it, honor it, and see what they bring to *you*.

What gives you the most joy in your teaching?

I love the first "ah-ha" moments. I still love, to this day, to teach an intro class or workshop. The moment of noting, "I didn't realize that." I was doing a little workshop for my wife's aunt's senior community. It was on movement, alignment, breath, balance, and easy walking without having to lean and waddle and give into injuries, aches and pains. How can you still maintain mobility, an anti-gravitational feel in your alignment? All you have to do is just float up. It was all new to them.

We were exploring this Lessac term known as "buoyancy": lightweight sense of release, relief of weight, and fatigue. Probably the oldest man in the group, in his mid or upper eighties, was just exploring with his arms, and I said, "Let the breath come in and your arms rise, and then you settle down and you float. It's very Tai Chi-like, if you know what that is, and if not, it doesn't matter." And he expressed what I always look for in my students, which is an "as if." "I feel as if." He said, "Ah! I feel like I'm conducting an orchestra!" I was practically in tears. Because, oh my God, even at his advanced age he had a curiosity and a playfulness, and he arrived at this ease for his own body through exploration.

That's the "ah-ha" moment. Those are those little beginning introductions that somebody didn't realize was within us. We can self-heal. We can relieve pain and stress. That's a really strong principle, a precept of the Lessac kinesensic work within us, that there are these pain relievers, stress relievers.

You brought up Tai Chi and movement work. It leads me to questions around anatomy and movement or energy training. What do you think is important for aspiring voice coaches? How much? What types?

There's never a limit to how much you can learn. Whether it's anatomy, physiology, speech science, therapies, or whether it's something related to how we behave with mindfulness such as Yoga, Tai Chi, Feldenkrais. All of that just enhances what you already know. It gives another sense of richness to it. Now, how much do we impart to others? Frankly, I don't speak very much in anatomical terminology. I have enough confidence in what I do and how the client or the student is going to feel as a result of the instruction I give them that I don't need to give it credibility by saying, "Now you're moving this particular muscle; this cartilage is engaged in blah, blah, blah." Because if you take a look at the vocal tract—if we're talking just about voice—there's so much of it that needs to be left alone. It needs to be in its reflexive condition.

If you talk to a speech pathologist, most of the time they are treating "hyperfunctions," which means somebody's working too hard in that area to either do what they think is going to help them produce sound, or they are set in a pattern that they learned in their life that's stressful and effortful. So, I'd rather work with those things that are controllable, no mystery, you can truly *feel* them. I want them to be confident that they can recall what I'm imparting to them and it will lead to whatever they need. That's what I loved about Lessac work when I first became aware of it, because it was specific and controllable. Not in the negative sense of control, but *awareness*.

It's that visceral connection with which you're working to connect to your clients or actors.

It's an organic way of teaching. You smell an object that's pleasurable to you. And then you take note of how it moves you and what condition your body is in, and you also learn all that you can about alignment and balance. And how do the two relate? One of my favorite events is this tiny little "organic instruction" event: After we do the pleasurable smelling of a flower, I say, "Slouch." And they try to smell the flower. The breath doesn't come in freely, it doesn't work.

You're aligning all the senses.

Alignment informs breathing and breathing informs alignment, and there's that wonderful organic synergy that we can learn from. It's never stagnant. I try to avoid the word "posture" because it means "set," as opposed to alignment or orientation.

You've been in academia for quite a long time and you've had to deal with student learning outcomes, rubrics, and grades. How do you measure these things?

I assess on self-reliance. I have three levels: The first level is, are they getting the procedure? Are they recalling it and giving it enough attention in their brain to at least know what to do? The second step is, are they applying it in some degree? That's really important to me. I've always stressed this in the work: they need to find a way not to do it just for the voice studio, but to integrate it into the whole sense of communication in reality, everyday life, and the demands of acting. And the third—or the highest level of self-reliance—would be total integration. If a teacher from another class, like the acting teacher, came into the room and saw a student applying the voice/speech training to an assignment I gave, they wouldn't know that the student was doing a "speech assignment" or "voice assignment." It was fully integrated, they were utilizing and exploiting the craft, but only to the point of truth, honesty, affecting the other, and so on. So that's the full-roundedness.

I wonder if there were any times when you were like, "If I had known then what I know now …"

With reviews for voice and speech work, if I don't get mentioned that's really good, because the time you get mentioned is usually when it's drawing attention to itself in a negative way. I always, if possible, try to work into the contract that I should be part of callback auditions. I compare it to tap dancing: you wouldn't hire an actor to tap dance in a show if they couldn't prove ahead of time that they can tap dance, because there's not enough time in the rehearsal period to teach them or to even know whether they have the aptitude. They don't even have to have the accent or the dialect or whatever it is, but an aptitude. And then I can work with them.

I do not have to talk in phonemes and IPA notation. In fact, as soon as I introduce a dialect to a company, I say, "Okay, let's just try some sentences and go off and do a little bit of your role and come back in." And most of the time, I'm talking about letting go and speaking the line with *point of view*, which actually makes the dialect better. I want it to be integrated in the whole, so it can be a whole part of the character. You don't notice it; it's like the wallpaper on the wall. That's why I make sure I can be part of the audition process.

What is your advice for somebody going into the field right now?

I often say first to young teachers: teach what you know and feel confident about. Over the years in training—whether it's through an MFA program or through some other way of training—establish a relationship with someone who can be your mentor. And then just keep learning. One of the things that I find, and it's unfortunate, but a lot of job descriptions tend to be so broad. The process of promotion and tenure—it's just too tough. Make sure you're a good fit for the job description, primarily in academia. Don't fake: "Oh, I can also teach theatre history." They're trying to get a lot out of a little bit of bucks here. Go for the job that you're *really* suited for and nobody could be better than you when you go into that interview. And when you get it, their expectations will be clearer. But don't fake it.

BETH MCGUIRE

My approach to the craft is to use tools that connect me with whomever I am coaching and to keep expanding upon my skill sets. I approach each project with humility, presence, and generosity of spirit.

How do you identify as a "voice coach"?

I identify as someone who is a liaison between the actor and the text. My craft consists of an understanding of phonology, dialects, and accents with all of the components of breath and resonance, the craft of acting, an understanding of Alexander Technique, and creative application of chakra work. More precisely, my role is to assist the actor in embodying text with ease and expression.

We've known each other for a long time. In fact, you hired me for my first job at the School for Film and Television in 1998. When did you get into the field?

I've been working in coaching and teaching multiple aspects of the performing arts since I was about twenty. I have been coaching/teaching in my current discipline since I was about thirty-five.

And, over that time, you have been involved in all areas of voice coaching. Is there anything new you're doing these days?

During the pandemic, I've been very active in coaching video games and radio plays. And for about six years, I have been working with my colleague Jane Guyer Fujita to create a teacher-training series for folks in our profession.

How did you find your way into the field?

My observation is that there are multiple paths into this profession. Some folks train specifically for it at institutions like Central School or ART. Other folks train to be actors/teachers, which is what I did. I've been acting since I was eight and teaching since I was twenty. I feel that my understanding of the craft of acting in my own body enhances my abilities as a vocal and dialect coach.

So, if an aspiring coach is moving from actor to voice coach, what would you advise?

I would suggest that they experiment with working with their acting skills through the particular lens of the vocal coach. The coach's toolbox is entirely in relation to their particular experience and is as rich and varied as their own curiosity and self-education.

What have been inspirations and tools that you have added to your toolbox over the years?

The techniques of Yoga, Alexander, Lloyd Richards, Catherine Fitzmaurice, Laban, Arthur Lessac, Roy Hart, etc. I listen to many genres and ethnicities of music, immerse myself in different cultures, create friendships with people from different cultures, and enrich my understanding through visual history by going to museums. I watch a lot of films and series and I read a lot.

I love that approach. So, what's your advice on what to do with the tools?

Something that Jane talks about, and I have conveniently stolen, is evaluating everything we work on as a project. Our first task is to identify the particular criteria for the project. A number of years ago, I found myself coaching a minister who wanted to be "more effective in communicating to their congregation." That was the project and it was up to me to figure out the *how* of that. I recognized that they were not experiencing language in their body; so, I asked them to sit on a therapy ball and speak through their pelvis into the ball. A very simple technique, but a game changer for them.

I always feel like it's especially rewarding when a non-actor finds that kind of connection.

In my experience, defining the project for every individual or production is the first step in that kind of connection and the *how* comes through an acute listening and then an application of one's toolbox.

How important is listening for voice coaches?

For me, listening on a full visceral level is what allows my creative imagination to best serve the actor or layperson I am coaching.

What is a "road in" that you've found to help people own their voices?

In my experience, what I find most effective is to be present with myself 100% in the embodiment of my listening and connection with the person.

Do you think there is a generational difference in the "how" of teaching?

Generationally, we bring skills that are innate because of our generation. We also bring skills that are learned that are out of our generational experience. What helps me is to educate myself generationally both behind and in front of me, but most importantly to educate myself in the present.

What other skills do you feel are important in the art of coaching?

I feel that adaptability and fluidity are the most important qualities for me in enabling a successful project.

What distinctions do you see between your work as a teaching artist and a professional voice coach?

In my experience, coaching is a more accelerated process than teaching. The projects are quite different in that when I'm teaching, I teach a more expansive process that allows the actor to develop their own agency independent of a coach. When I'm coaching, I'm doing a bit of that, but I'm also helping the actor with a product.

What gives you joy in teaching and coaching?

I have two primary joys. One is that the work is like a puzzle and I enjoy figuring it out, but my greatest joy is watching an actor who has integrated the work and is free of me.

Can you share a particular "ah-ha" moment in your coaching?

My chopstick moment: about twenty-five years ago, I was coaching an actor who was having a very difficult time with the proprioception of their tongue. I ran into the kitchen, grabbed a chopstick and had them look in the mirror and touch their tongue to the chopstick. Eureka! Proprioception accomplished.

Would you say that you follow a particular method of teaching?

I think being didactic is the death of art.

What is your advice to early career coaches in building a practice for themselves?

Gosh, that question humbles me. I would suggest that a young coach take stock in relation to each project they encounter and to recognize and lead from their strengths and not be afraid to ask questions. Curiosity has always been the key for me.

How about the question of making a livable wage as a coach?

I suppose the first question would be what the individual feels is a livable wage. Then they craft their choices around that and cultivate relationships with people in the field.

What about coaches who also want to work as actors?

As in everything else, it's a juggling act. If you're lucky, you're hired to do both if you're in a theatre production. That is fun.

Do you have any personal wisdom or advice for the next generation of coaches?

I feel sappy in saying this, but I can't imagine doing this work unless you love it. I would say to revel in the tools that you have and to pay attention to each project and how it expands your skillset. And as I mentioned, flexibility, humility, and humor go a long way.

BONNIE RAPHAEL

It's a shock when you realize that your perception of the Universe is not universal.

How do you identify as a voice coach?

Right now, I'm identifying as a retired voice coach. In my last twenty-five years of professional work, I trained graduate acting students in vocal performance, I coached an (Actors') Equity theatre company, and I worked with private clients.

You have had such a journey. What got you on that path?

I was still living at home when I went to college; I was the first person in my family to go to college. My parents were smart, but they had no higher education. So, for them, I majored in speech education and minored in theatre—in retrospect, a good choice. I took courses in anatomy and physiology, speech disorders, audiology, phonetics, clinical practice; I even taught as a student. I still got to take some theatre courses.

Fascinating. Did you end up doing some acting right out of college?

I didn't. I got a master's degree in theatre. And when I decided to get a PhD, my parents didn't even know what that was. They thought you went to college and then you went to work. I could have gotten a PhD in either voice pathology or in theatre. Michigan State University was the only school at that time that would allow me to combine the two. I wrote my dissertation on a scientific subject that related to actors' voices. The reason I sought a PhD is that it was very hard for women to obtain tenure or promotion in a university without one.

I'm thinking of all these conflicting voices: "You should do this." "You should do that." "Coach here." "Do volunteer work." "Don't do anything unless you get paid for it." How do you stay on track and keep listening to your own voice?

It's a constant challenge, especially for women. I don't call myself a feminist, but being taken seriously is something I take very seriously.

I love that.

There were years in academia where male colleagues were appointed to personnel or syllabus committees while I was in charge of the tea for the incoming graduate students—ordering cookies and making sure that there were enough ice cubes. I hated that but I considered it part of the dues I had to pay. Another example: When job searching, I learned that a letter in my dossier was not flattering. I read it and decided to keep it in my file because this is who I am. The letter described me as stepping on toes and not being sufficiently respectful to my elders or to men in general. I decided that either I could pretend to be different, or I could let a potential employer know who I am.

What has given you the most joy teaching and coaching?

I really loved my career. I wasn't getting paid what I was worth. (Pamela laughs) Ever. Ever. I just love the work. I love what I learned, even if some of my knowledge was acquired the hard way. It's less about teaching voice and speech and more about helping your student or client grow as a human being, whether that person ends up acting on stage or making movies or running for office—helping a person take a few steps they might not have taken without your encouragement. There's no such thing as too much encouragement when it comes to the insecurity that actors or other public speakers may have.

When you think about making a livable wage, what would your advice be to someone starting out?

At first, I did some work gratis: I let myself teach a masterclass or coach a show. And then, I chose not to do that anymore. I didn't want to spend my whole life in debt, paying off student loans or depending on my parents or whatever. However, to this day, if a project interests me enough, I'll take it on whether or not it pays. But if somebody calls me and says, "We need someone to come in during tech and fix a few problems …" I don't need the money that badly. Invitations like that compromise my idea of respect for the work.

Did you find it different working with executives versus actors?

It's the same stuff. You're helping your client to find a different door into the same room—by making better choices, by not cannibalizing the voice in the process of doing your job. It's the same stuff, but it has to be presented differently depending on the receiver.

What helps you find the language to connect with people in positions of great influence?

Listening is very important, as well as not coming in with an agenda that can't be scrapped at the last minute. I think it was Eisenhower who said, "Planning is indispensable; plans are useless."

That's a wonderful point and an important reminder not to have such an agenda of, "Let me show you all I know."

Or, "I have a plan that works for everybody." because there is no such thing.

That's such a wake-up moment, isn't it? (laughs)

It is. It's a shock when you realize that your perception of the Universe is not universal. I don't think I ever got over that realization.

What qualities do you think are really important for a voice coach to cultivate for a positive career trajectory?

You have got to be an excellent listener. Don't waste time advertising yourself. Impart knowledge that is practical and useful. When I begin to work with a new client, I start with one or two "quick fixes": something they can hear or feel and that they can do almost immediately, rather than get buried in lots of instructions or hand-outs. And once they figure out that I'm on their side, I can take bigger chances and invite them to do the same. Even if I think I know the 'way in', I like to say, "If I were a fairy godmother with a magic wand, and could do something right now to help you, what would that be?"

Great question.

And realizing that their perception of what they need does not often include their speaking voice. "Lower the pitch of my voice? I'm a woman, I don't want to sound like a man." So many women have been trained not to make waves. When I work on a musical, some of the women who are breath-taking sopranos talk like sopranos as well. Their singing voice is fabulous, but their speaking voice may sound insipid. Often, they have spent years in singing training and no time at all training their speaking voice. Also, many people don't realize that what feels like a giant change to them may not even get noticed by a listener. It's like when a guy shaves off his mustache and nobody notices, he feels practically naked and nobody says anything.

What words of advice do you have for the aspiring voice coach?

I wrote an article called "Dancing on Shifting Ground." I got that expression from Cicely Berry. (I steal from only the best.) She basically says the director has their way of working. The actor has their way of working. And if you're joining this team, somebody's got to adjust. So, instead of assuming that the director will change modalities to suit you or that an actor will change their way of working, it's got to be the coach. You've got to learn to dance on shifting ground. How does one do this? How does one get results without stepping on the director's or actor's toes? The coach has to join the dance without really knowing where the ground is going to be!

I remember working with the CEO of a billion-dollar international business company: I went in for our first session, and he was having his hair cut. He had worked me into his day, but he believed that he could listen and even talk with me at the same time his hair was being cut. I could have just said, "This is not the way I work." and left. But instead, I adapted and then said, "Next time we see one another, if there is a next time, I need to have your total attention." He thought that working me into his schedule was the only thing necessary. He didn't reply, but he did schedule another session. The next time we met, it was just the two of us. I said, "I will do my best to make every minute of this session worth your time."

If you could go back and give your younger self some words of advice, what would you say?

I would have far more respect for how insecure some actors and public speakers are. I took for granted for too long that I had something good to offer, and if they just listened to me and did what I told them, my students and clients would improve. But even when I worked with some extremely talented and famous people, I underestimated how a shake of my head or my sitting where they could see me taking notes was very difficult for some people. I never considered the possibility that just my presence might feel threatening to them or interfere with their creative process. So, I've learned just how sensitive actors and other public speakers might be to implied criticism. When I was younger, I might have said, "Oh come on. Don't take yourself so seriously." I no longer do that.

CHRISTINA SHEWELL

I talk about PBs: we're complex Precious Beings and we're working with complex Precious Beings.

How do you identify as a voice coach?

I suppose my role nowadays is mending and extending voices. I definitely see my role as being a healer, you know, mending broken voices. But also, every variety of person comes and says, "I need to sound different." So, there's both those aspects. I never say I'm a speech and language therapist or pathologist. I say, "I work in voice therapy, mending voices. And I work with people who want to develop their voice or extend it in some way."

What qualities are important for a voice teacher to possess?

First of all, curiosity. I [tell] my students the two questions to always think of: *Who* have we here? And *what* have we here? The *what* is the voice, obviously, and the *who* is just as important. And within that curiosity about the person, a complete openness, no discrimination … Carl Rogers talks about "unconditional positive regard" with everyone you meet. And that is so important. No matter who they are, what they look like, what they smell like, what they sound like, you're willing to work with anybody. Now, along with that, you have to have an understanding of the science aspects—what I call in my book "voice foundations"—the physical foundations for voice.

I've taught basic counseling skills for years, and I teach it at the Royal Central School of Speech and Drama each year. I want people to realize that, actually, emotional stuff comes up in our work and, just as we have skills in terms of being a voice coach, we need skills in managing people. So, curiosity, foundational knowledge, emotional skills, humor, and an energy to improvise. We all know when you first start working in the field and you plan everything out with a class, and you go in there and actually, you do other things. There has to be that flexibility around a core sense of what you're doing. So that you respect the work—you respect people, obviously—but you also respect the moment and being able to respond in the moment to the individual.

Another quality is willingness to link with other colleagues. I've learned so much not just from my clients but from my colleagues. And to go on learning and doing workshops with them. And to know that the older you get, the more you know that you don't know. That's part of my meditation practice: all we have is this present moment. And into that comes all sorts of things that we've learned. But then there is the magic of that moment.

What was your road into voice work?

I always wanted to act as a teenager. And I didn't have the confidence, really, even to go for drama school. I was very self-conscious and very self-critical. One of my peers in my school year was doing speech therapy, as it was called. I went along and watched a clinic. I mistakenly thought that it was going to be a bit to do with poetry and drama. I had no idea it was so medical. It's a really interesting thing: I've had to, over the years, come to terms with the fact that it's okay to have a science brain as well as an arts brain. So, I did speech therapy, but I worked with people who had lost their speech after a stroke. And I did a master's in linguistics because I was very interested in language, and then went on working and became head of the department in Cambridge.

And then a personal crisis when I was in my early thirties precipitated a professional change. I thought, "I'm going to go back and be a student, and I'm going to train as a voice coach." And so, I did the Central School course—I think it was in its third year. I was really lucky in that I met Ann Skinner. She's extraordinary. She and I and two other women went to the Roy Hart Theatre and that changed my life, because I suddenly understood the depth that voice work can take you to and the magical aspects of that. Anyway, so then I went to work with Patsy Rodenburg. I was on the staff of The Guildhall for nine years, but I was doing other things as well, as we all do as voice coaches.

Somebody said to me, "Your handouts are so long, why don't you put them in a book?" And I thought, well, there were such good books around—Kristin Linklater's book was the most important book for me. But then I thought, "I've never read a book that actually talks about voice in common with singing teachers, voice coaches, and therapists. I wonder whether I could do that." As you know, Pamela, when you embark on something, there is an energy that comes in and keeps you going. And I now look at that book, and I honestly don't know the woman who wrote that book. I've no idea how I wrote that book. There are so many words. (laughs)

How much anatomy do you think a voice coach needs to know, and how are you finding an effective way to translate that information to your students/clients?

Katherine Verdolini, one of the top American speech pathologists, talks very clearly in *The Vocal Vision* about how mechanistic knowledge may be important to *us*—and it is important, so we don't do harm—but that, actually, it can be unhelpful to our students. What's relevant is that when you add up the twenty-seven laryngeal muscles, there are fifteen extrinsic and twelve intrinsic. And when you say that to clients, they invariably go, "Wow!" And then you say, "Well, that's why the voice is so emotionally expressive. But things can go wrong with those twenty-seven muscles." Voice coaches need to know the underlying structure and function, but they certainly don't need to give all that knowledge to their clients.

In terms of movement and energy, Alexander Technique. But I think there are other movement methods that are really relevant. Pilates have a lot to help with in terms of the core. Feldenkrais, certainly. But also dance—not formalized dance, but free dancing. To a number of my clients, I've suggested—because they're so tight, particularly young actors—I say, "Put some music on in the kitchen and dance, and then let some voice come out, because that will loosen you up." Free movement, I think, is really important. And in terms of energy training, that's a very specific term. I think that lots of us are drawn to particular areas. We may do Reiki, we may do a healing course, we may do bioenergetics, somatic work. We need to integrate that into our practice, not lecture our clients on it.

How do we measure if a person's more resonant, more communicative, more connected?

You can invent scales of client satisfaction, because after all, I still think the most important thing is the client's view of their own voice. There's a lovely story of one of the top American ENT surgeons years ago. He came over [to the UK] and it was in the very early days of what's now the British Voice Association; it was called the Voice Research Society. He stood up and he said, "Ladies and gentlemen" in his lovely American voice, "I'm really glad to be here because I am the world expert …" And you could just feel people going, "Oh, God, arrogant American." He said, "… I am the world expert on the sound of my own voice." And it really stayed with me, that. He then went on to say, "If a singer says there's something wrong, there's something wrong." The ultimate judge needs to be the person whose voice it is.

It sounds like a concept called "un-grading," which is not about the teacher grading or rating the voice, but rather the client learning how to hear and feel and sense themselves.

Yes. And become more in tune with themselves. Mindful attention to the inside of the body is incredibly important for our clients. It's only part of it; I'm really careful when I say this. You can have too much mindfulness and it gets in the way of you dancing in a musical. But actually, when you're trying to solve something, to really know what you're feeling in terms of your physical body, whether it's emotionally or whether it's, "Wait a minute, what does happen when you as a voice coach say I'm constricting, what does that actually feel like?" It's essential the person feels that, because then they'll be talking to someone in a bar and they'll suddenly go, "Oh, wait a minute, *that's* what I'm doing." That recognition of physical and emotional feeling is incredibly important.

Is there an "ah-ha" moment that you want to share?

First of all, when you first start teaching groups as a voice coach, it's terrifying. Be gentle with yourself. Yes, you have to plan everything, but it's quite normal that (A) it doesn't work, or (B) you find yourself doing something much better. My first job was working with Patsy Rodenburg, whom I saw as having great self-confidence in her voice work, whereas I was really scared! So, it was a demanding first term, but it gets easier and you just keep going, and you accept you make mistakes, and some classes don't work and most will begin to work as you gain experience and confidence.

Another difficult or challenging moment was when I moved into working in the corporate world—that's another world, as you know. It's very different to working with actors. And you really need a different mindset and different tools. (laughs) You need to dress differently sometimes. You talked about learning outcomes and measures: the corporate world quite likes that, and you may need to have that. So, that was a challenge for me.

As you stand in this moment of your life, if you could give your younger self any words of wisdom, what would you say to her?

Well … (laughs) that's a huge question. On an emotional level, I would say, "Don't be so afraid, so anxious, so self-critical, and so self-conscious." But saying "don't" to anybody isn't the right thing. I think the loving kindness meditation—the mindfulness approach—had I learned that earlier, it would have benefited me but also my clients. Also, the honoring of working from who we are, that we are complex. When I'm teaching, students laugh at me sometimes because I talk about PBs: we're complex Precious Beings and we're working with complex Precious Beings. I have learned so much through working with people.

There's one other thing I'd say: don't neglect your own voice. Yes, you're in service to someone else. But actually, you have your own fire as well. It's really important to take care of yourself, whether you're the president of VASTA or not. Actually, make that time not to be afraid of being on one's own, to understand the nature of truly taking care of yourself. And body work. Body work is an absolute vehicle for traveling, for oneself and for others. What's that saying? "Take care of your body. It's the only place you live."

CYNTHIA SANTOS-DECURE

Know your strengths, know your limitations, and ask yourself: Do you have the cultural competency to work on this particular production, to work with this particular actor?

When you hear, "Cynthia is a voice coach," how do you identify?

Well, I like to think of myself as a hybrid because I started my training as an actor. I'm an actor, a vocal coach, a dialect coach, but I coach from my own intersectional position as a woman and as a Latina. So, I call myself an actor/dialect coach/vocal coach that specializes in accents of culture. I don't want to say just accents of Spanish, which is something that I very specifically specialize in, but I want to say *culture*, because there's a lot of nuance when we look at it from that perspective.

So, if a professional actor was working on a dialect of the Spanish language, you would be able to coach them?

Yes. In fact, I was going to talk about working with a Spanish-speaking actor wanting to change from one accent of Spanish to another and how that transpired. That was a challenging moment. I was first approached to work with this particular actor, an Academy Award-nominated actor. That person was working on a TV series. And the TV series was full of dialects because the majority of the actors were from either Australia or England or Europe. And so, there were a lot of dialect coaches on set. This particular actor's character was from [a] South American country that was different from their own, and they had dialogue in Spanish. This [was] the first time in the script that the dialogue was happening in Spanish.

I was first approached by the head of casting saying, "Are you available to work with this person? Is this something you do? We were told you do this." And I said, "Yeah, absolutely. It'd be great to work with this person." Didn't hear anything whatsoever. Then I [got] a call a couple of months later from the same person saying, "We need you to work with this person on post [production] because it was very upsetting, what happened. We hired this other coach, and this coach—a non-Latinx coach—did not do a good job and really traumatized the actor." That's what it really turned out to be: the actor complained and it was a big deal.

So, I worked in post-production to try to, mostly, empower this actor. They were able to understand where their own linguistic vocal tract posture was different from this other accent; we worked with the prosody in Spanish; we really worked with thinking to picture, with making sure that they felt the fluency; really working with a confidence that they *own* this, and it wasn't so far away from their own personal sound, but also from their own ability to be able to transform.

Often, I am hired to fix things or to come in at the point where they believe the actor is no longer able to maneuver on their own, because often they expect

Latinx actors—Spanish-speaking actors—just because you speak one accent of Spanish, or you own one sound of Spanish, that you can automatically transform into everything else. There's this thought that, just because I speak Spanish or I'm a Latinx actor, I have already, inherently, the ability to transform to all of the accents of Spanish by the virtue that I speak Spanish.

Just because you're American, doesn't mean you can do all the accents of the US, or because you're British, all the accents of the UK and the subtleties of each culture, right?

Exactly! It's that same expectation of an English-speaking actor, which we know is unrealistic.

What I hear you say is that you need to know your limitations as a coach. Know your strengths but know your limitations.

Right. Know your strengths, know your limitations, and ask yourself: Do you have the cultural competency to work on this particular production, to work with this particular actor? I think it's one of the skills that a dialect coach and a vocal coach ought to have. Really look at twenty-first century cultural competency: anti-racist, anti-oppressive methodologies that show up in our work, that are inherent in voice and speech already, historically. [Know] how to unpack that and how to be able to maneuver, to be able to work with the person in front of you.

I'm of the opinion right now that BIPOC dialect coaches have not been given the opportunity to compete to coach accents that they already have access to. [Not] in the same manner that primarily white, English-speaking dialect coaches have had access to, to coach accents across the globe. So, know when to step aside and find someone who's really more adept at working on that. Or work in conjunction, right? Share the job, bring someone else in.

What do you think stops people from making that choice, saying "Hey, why don't we team up?" Why aren't people doing that?

I think we operate in a business of scarcity. We always think there's not enough work to go around. The majority of my work has come from referrals: from people who have gotten to know me, directors that I've worked with, other dialect coaches, actors that I've worked with, producers—people that know my work. And I think goodwill begets goodwill, you know? There's a flow. Generosity begets generosity, and there's a flow in our business. It's a small world; it's a really small group of folks who do this kind of work. We're all interconnected, we know each other. If we don't know each other personally, we know someone whom you've trained or worked with. There's one degree of separation. So, the more we continue to think that there's not enough to go around—that we have to power hoard—the harder it's going to be for all of us. We need to proliferate this work. We need to make sure that we are in every facet and fabric of theatre, film, television, private coaching, corporate, and that our work is seen as professional work. And in order to do that, the best person for the job needs to be performing that job.

Being culturally sensitive is so deeply important for teachers and coaches. What are other characteristics that you think a coach ought to cultivate?

A curiosity. Deep curiosity for sounds and for *diversity* of sound. Not just one aesthetic or one thing, but a myriad. Open your listening palate out to the globe. First and foremost, [have] a passion for what you're doing. If you're just doing it for the money, guess what? It's gonna become prescriptive, robotic, canned, and one-size-fits-all. I think you definitely should have some training in phonetics, IPA, somatic trainings. It's really important because we need to know the bodies that we're working with. The voice doesn't live in absentia from the body. Sounds are corporal, they come *from* the body. We have to understand how the body operates, and how trauma also lives in the body and can sabotage the voice and the speech, and confidence.

How do you take care of your own voice and body with your packed teaching and coaching life?

You know, I'm just gonna say … San Pellegrino. (laughs) Constantly hydrating. All the time. Drinking coconut water, knowing my telltale signs of when my voice and body is exhausted, and knowing when I need to take a break and not push myself. I used to work and speak through exhaustion, and then I learned how to support my voice correctly and how to use my body and know what the limitations are. I used to have complete and utter laryngitis, I mean, no voice whatsoever. And when I learned how to take care of myself with greater accuracy and generosity, I stopped getting that, and I have not had laryngitis since 2011. I mean, [if] I feel a little scratchy I just go, "Okay, I know what's going on." I try not to clear my throat. If anything, I vibrate, hum and try to drink liquids and all sorts of things. And just rest.

A few words of advice for those building their careers?

I would say that each job is an opportunity to perfect what you do. It's okay if you start small but, you know, quality over quantity. Any day. Because that quality of the depth in which you work on that particular show, even though you're working on one thing, is going to become the blueprint for something else you do later on, and you can repeat that one over and over again. Plus, it's going to establish your own strength and your own confidence as an early career teacher.

Let's say you're covering for somebody who is on leave so you have to fill a syllabus. What are your thoughts on finding your voice within a set syllabus?

Find your way; teach from who *you* are. Not only teach what you know, but teach from who you are, from your strength and your own point of view. The students are going to really appreciate it, and not only that, you're going to be more confident as a teacher and as a coach, because you're teaching from something you know, which is *you*. Your own personal strength. For the early career coach, especially in younger generations of dialect coaches, they're gonna find that their impulse comes from responding to their generation and their own lived experience, which is certainly different than ours.

What are your suggestions to help create a framework for success, growth, and eye-opening awareness for the organism of the classroom?

There's this whole concept right now on intent versus impact: "My intent was not to *fill in the blank*, but the impact was *such and such*." We're really not talking about the intent of what you said, but the impact that it had. So, amends are about the impact and it takes away this whole sense of defensiveness … There's an opportunity to begin dialogue because the impact was deep or was felt. If it's in a classroom situation, one of the things we have an opportunity to do in the very beginning of the semester is to really set a tone; create some precepts; [establish] your classroom agreements, things that you know we're going to live by. Those agreements are fluid, always; they're always there, we have an opportunity to add to them, delete, things like that. Everybody is a participant in crafting the agreement so that we have a common vocabulary and we establish a culture of safety, [so] that the teaching and learning is lateral as opposed to top-down.

Well, voice is not just the larynx, it's not just the vibration. It's one's voice in the world. It is a layered, deep, generational, cultural identity. Sometimes I think of the vocal coach as an alchemist, and I think of the word "curandera."

Wow. Yeah. We do have the healing power. I agree, the "curandera" power. We are em*power*ing folks to access and step into their own voices, right? Their metaphoric and literal voices. For any speaker in any medium, we are empowering folks to step into their own vocal, linguistic, literal, and metaphoric power. And we have to treat that with incredible care.

As you stand here in this place, if you could see young Cynthia, how would you encourage her on her journey?

I say it to myself every day: Be authentic to yourself. Let your own sound come through because your uniqueness and your sound is your imprint—is your DNA. Your authenticity and the way that you present yourself gives other folks an opportunity to be authentic themselves. So, just continue to be who *you* are.

DARON ORAM

Our homes are different, and we do find different homes in this work.

How do you identify as a voice coach?

Well, for me, there's a difference between coaching and teaching. Coaching, for me, is supporting someone who's had some training to do the job, whereas teaching is training somebody *how* they're going to go about doing that. I've reached a point now where I see myself primarily as a teacher of voice, and that's teaching actors and also teachers of voice.

What kinds of classes are you exploring with your RCSSD MA/MFA Voice Studies students?

Where I'm focusing now, and this is as a result of the research I've been doing, is on theories and strategies around anti-oppressive pedagogy. The main areas are working with neurodivergent students and working in ways [of teaching] that are anti-racist and anti-classist.

How do you define neurodivergent?

That, in its broadest sense, covers any neurodiversity. It could be dyslexia, dyspraxia, it could include autism, Asperger's, all of those diagnoses. My research focused predominantly on dyslexia and dyspraxia, so that's where I have most knowledge.

How might you suggest we educate ourselves in anti-racism, anti-classism, and neurodiversity?

They're all enormous areas. One of the things that was really apparent when I was doing that work [was that] there was very little research, very little knowledge. You could find information about neurodiversity in high school education, in early years education, and within Math and English, but within actor training there was very little. One of the problems is that a lot of the knowledge is in academic journals, and so that's difficult for people outside of academia to get hold of. But all of the work on neurodiversity is held within the three journals that VASTA gives members free access to. So, VASTA is a great gateway into that information.

There are limited resources, but it really is worth investing time to find out about neurodiversity because, on average, within every actor training cohort there's double the average number of neurodiverse students than there is on, say, Math or English degrees. That's because, particularly with dyslexia and dyspraxia, there's a whole heap of creative advantages that come with an alternative way of processing information. As soon as you step away from a literal, linear model of thinking, suddenly you start to have all of those creative skills [that] we really want in theatre-making. It's no surprise: theatre, architecture, art, music—there are many more neurodivergent people in those fields. So, if you're working as a voice coach, you *will* be working with dyslexic, dyspraxic actors.

Thanks for the VASTA plug, by the way. (laughs)

I could do that over and over again. (laughs) In terms of race and class, obviously there is more discussion and, in the last few years, that discussion has grown in volume, and that's been a very necessary and important thing. With that work, there [are] two sides to it. About the anti-racism work, we need to educate ourselves around race. And when I say "we," I'm talking about particularly the dominant white majority within the voice world. Well, actually, everybody. We need to educate ourselves about race and to understand how racism works, and how white supremacy works, and how that filters through structures and systems. And to understand that racism is not about overt interpersonal racism. Yes, that's the tip of the iceberg, but there's so much more that happens which we are unconscious of, which we're not aware of in the way that society works, the way education works, the way the theatre works.

I know we both sit on different sides of the pond here, but I think there's a lot of cultural overlap, you know, because of British colonialism and American colonization.

That relates a little bit to what I'm doing when I'm training teachers. One of the things is to set a context, to say, "This is very complicated." (laughs) Usually, if I'm in a room with people when I'm doing this work I have "it's complicated" [written] on a board, and when we start to get stuck, I will go back and just say, "Let's just remember that it's complicated." The thing about things like microaggressions [is that] it's not about the intent behind those, it's how they're received by people. And so, how I begin when I'm starting these discussions is to share stories from students as to how they've received what have been well-intended interventions from teachers, but have landed in a way that could be perceived as racism. It's starting from the perspective of the person that is receiving that.

Within that, I will always share stories of when I have done things in the past that now I look back [at] and see from a different perspective. So, it's also about sharing my culpability in this, and what I've changed, and to say that I'm still on the journey. We can attempt to deal with racism, but we live in structures that are racist. And so, it's a constant questioning and a constant looking at that. But I think it is through those personal stories and experiences that people start to engage with us. If you start from an ideological perspective or from a theoretical perspective, people can argue back against that. But if somebody is sharing a story of a personal experience that has been traumatizing for them, then hopefully, with an empathic teacher, that begins to open them up to see things from a different perspective. That's what I think is important: that we tell stories, hear stories—and that's something that we're good at doing—that we listen with empathy, tell stories with empathy, in a way which is challenging but not re-traumatizing.

How much is in-depth anatomy important for you when you teach actors?

I don't introduce anatomy at all at the beginning. I work in a very somatic way of getting the experience into the body using hands-on partner work, really getting people to *feel* what's going on. Once a student has a physical experience that they can anchor into, *then* I will bring in anatomy as a way of clarifying the experience. It helps to deepen the experience:

> I felt all of this going on. Ah, now I can *see* what's happening underneath the ribs, I can *see* the diaphragm, I can *see* an animation of that. Now I can take what I've seen visually, and rather than that being something that needs translation, I've got a physical experience that I can link that to.

So, I will bring anatomy in, but as a way of deepening a physical experience rather than teaching the theory beforehand.

One of the key bits of information that I picked up in my research is this idea of the narrative and experiencing brains, and that we have two modes of being self-aware. Research that I've drawn on has shown through MRI scans that when we focus on the narrative, the somatic knowledge goes away, and when we focus on the somatic, the narrative goes away. They're inversely proportional. You can't hold in your head loads of information *and* feel what your breathing is doing. And if you're teaching through the anatomy first, that's a lot of narrative information, which actually becomes a block to being able to feel, because your mind is trying to remember the detail. So, it's trying to bring the student into the sensory, somatic place as much as possible.

Could you share some thoughts on how to make a living as a voice teacher?

I think people will find what works for them. I just said "yes" to everything at the beginning. I came into this work in my mind going, "I'm never going to teach accents and dialects. I was terrible at them as an actor, I'm not going to do that." And then I ended up with a job which was predominantly doing speech, accents, and dialect work. (laughs) But actually, in doing that job, I realized that I *could* teach that, and that having been bad at it as an actor was really helpful because it gave me great empathy with my students! (laughs)

Isn't it funny when you look back at what you were doing in the early part of your career and you're like, "How the heck did I juggle all that?" (laughs)

I have no idea how I did it. But what that enabled me to do was to go, "Okay, *that* school is a good fit for me. *This* school is not a good fit for me at all." It was really helpful in terms of working out where I fit, because our homes are different and we do find different homes in this work. So, that was my journey, to just keep saying "yes" and then holding on to the things that were working for me and letting the other things drop to the wayside.

Is there a challenging moment that jumps out for you?

A challenging moment [was] when I had a large group of neurodiverse students and my teaching wasn't working. It was the kickstart to all of the research. It wasn't an "ah-ha" moment in terms of, "Oh, I found a solution to that," but it was the beginning of a four-year process that led to many "ah-ha" moments. The big change in that was, rather than going, "How do I help these neurodivergent students access my teaching?", it was the realization that my teaching was discriminating against those students and not allowing them to access the learning. So, it wasn't about helping them to access my teaching, it was about changing my teaching so that everybody could access it equitably. If there's an "ah-ha" moment that has gone across all of my teaching, that's the one. If there's a problem for a student, the first port of call is, "What's wrong with the way that I'm delivering the teaching?" Not, "What's wrong [with] that student?"

It's a pedagogical shift: if you're taught a certain way, learning to flip it—to change your teaching style.

Yeah. As teachers of voice, and across the board for teachers of acting and movement as well, we have a lineage of training and we're taught to train in the way that our teachers taught. It's only in recent years that people have started to question those modes of training. It's not the value of the work at the heart of it, but the philosophy around it or the language of teaching that. The approach to voice training that I have as the core of my work comes from Kristin Linklater, but I've really interrogated, questioned, and changed the language of that and the philosophy of that on the basis of research.

You know, I had a very good conversation with her about that just before she died, and she was really supportive of people doing that kind of work because she saw the value of it. So, it is time to really question. We receive work and often we believe, "Well, this is the truth of this work," but sometimes it turns out that that's actually a myth and that it's not a truth, it's just the way it's always been done. And if we take that truth away, the work doesn't fall apart, it just becomes more available for people.

What would your advice be to a new or aspiring voice coach?

If you are able to, go and work with as many different teachers as you can. Go and meet the people rather than just read the books, if you can. That's difficult because that costs money. But if you can make it work, just try to form an opinion through the experience rather than the idea of people's work.

DAVID CAREY

It's wonderful to be able to just give. Give of oneself … to give of the skills that one has and the ability that one has developed.

What was your path into this field?

I like to say my journey started at my mother's knee because of listening to her reciting poetry and reading stories to me. But also, my father was an actor. So, as I got older, I would often hear his lines and pick up from him the way of the dialogue and the dialect of a character, just instinctively. It wasn't until I got to drama school that I realized all my strengths lay in this area of voice. I was lucky enough to find a job fairly early as a full-time voice teacher in Edinburgh working with drama students. And from there, [I was] extremely lucky to have Cicely Berry take me on as an assistant. It was like a mentorship; I described it as being like a PhD in voice and text work.

That set me up to move to [Royal Central School of Speech and Drama] training voice teachers, for seventeen years. And from there to [Royal Academy of Dramatic Art] training actors again. And then moving to Oregon. My first contact with Oregon was back in the early 90s: Two of my students from Central days, Scott Kaiser and Nancy Benjamin, were the first full-time vocal coaches here. They invited me to come out and do a couple of workshops. And I just fell in love with the town and the theatre, and hoped that maybe someday I would get to come back. And, as luck would have it, I was able to do that in conjunction with my wife, Rebecca. So, we've been resident voice and text coaches here for years now.

What are some of the qualities you think are really important for an aspiring voice coach to possess?

Oh, there are so many … There needs to be an openness to where people are and what their needs might be. That requires a perceptiveness about where somebody is [on] their journey. You need to be passionate about your work. You need to also have a sense of rigor about your work. You need to be sensitive in how you address people's needs. Working with professionals in all sorts of different fields, you need to be diplomatic. You need to be clear in what your needs might be. You need to be specific.

What gives you the most joy in coaching and teaching?

Ultimately, it's about seeing people fulfil their potential. In a training program, you get to see somebody develop over three years and you know that you've helped them with that. In Oregon, we've got a resident company and so you get to know the actors well, and you learn what they need in different areas and how to help them. Also, you get to work with actors who are coming into the profession for the first time, and you get to contribute to their professional development.

At the same time, there's the joy of teaching itself. If I'm working with a student or an actor on a piece of text or a dialect, I think, "What is it that this text or dialect specifically is asking of this actor?" It's the act of investigating. "How are my skills going to be used on this occasion?" That's the excitement of teaching. So, it's wonderful to be able to see somebody take what I've given them and develop. But it's also wonderful to be able to just *give*. Give of oneself … to give of the skills that one has, and the ability that one has developed.

What are some of the ways your coaching has shifted over the years?

When I first started doing warm-ups with actors, I'd often do a lot of floor work, breathing work, and leave it there. I remember doing that once, and a couple of actors [said], "We wish we could have done more energetic work." That was my "ah-ha" moment. I needed to adjust my vocal warm-ups toward something which left people energized: not scattered, energized in a focused way. Ever since, I've worked toward developing a vocal warm-up that is releasing and opens the body and voice, but is also energetic. In order to do that, I engage [with] a lot of T'ai Chi-based work. I found, in my experience of working with T'ai Chi, it leaves me immensely energized in a very focused way. And so, using those techniques and applying vocal exercises to them I find most beneficial.

How much anatomy, movement, and energy training do you think are important?

All of that is essential for a voice coach. There's no question about that. [There] needs to be a deep knowledge of vocal anatomy. You need to have at least that level of awareness of what's functioning and what may be disrupting that functioning of the voice. You cannot identify what is clinically wrong with a voice; that is the job of a laryngologist or a speech pathologist. But you can identify that there is something worrying there. I also think having a knowledge of one's own physical life, as it were, to have trained physically in some form or other and to have that training geared toward energy as opposed to relaxation, is vital.

What is your advice for finding work as a voice coach?

It's about being clear about what your strengths are and what kind of work you want to do. Where's your passion? One of the pieces of advice I gave my voice teaching students was to be prepared to build a portfolio of work over the first two to five years [after] graduating. You're not going to walk straight into a full-time job. But build up a client base, use your connections. Connect with LinkedIn and other professional networks; use your friends and your parents' friends. Also, be prepared to have a part-time job that has nothing to do with your profession. But use it to forward your other skills in building up your business acumen. There are so many skills you need to acquire in the professional world. You can build those skills when you're not being a voice teacher.

Is there a moment early in your career where you've thought back and said, "I wish I would have had someone prepare me by telling me this or that"?

Something I came up against several times in working with actors of considerable experience within the Royal Shakespeare Company [was] understanding their sense of their own process. To be respectful of, "I know that you're an experienced actor. I'm not coming in here to tell you anything new [or] change you. I'm here to act as a resource for you to bounce off."

One time, we had a very experienced actor but he hadn't worked in the Barbican Theatre before, which is a tricky space to find the vocal needs of. I was taking this very experienced actor in there, and I thought I was helping him by pointing out some of the challenges of the space. But, for whatever reason, he chose to see this as me patronizing him. That certainly was not my intention. But it was a key learning moment for me. You have to be extremely sensitive about how you [work] with experienced actors. Recognize that actors *are* vulnerable. And that vulnerability can pop up in the most unusual circumstances.

What are your words of advice for the aspiring voice coach?

One of the key things I learned from Cicely Berry [is] it's not about you. It's about the work. The work is what is central. And it's about the person in front of you. I also think it's helpful to befriend a speech pathologist, to have an ally in that respect. Somebody [to whom] you can say, "Hey, I've got this student and I really don't know what the problem is. Could you give me some advice?"

The final thing is to be very clear about professional boundaries. You are a voice coach or a voice teacher. You are not an acting coach or director, and you are not a speech therapist. You are not a psychological therapist. You are a voice teacher. Text work, if you're lucky to be doing that, can often overlap with a director's requirements. But you need to be diplomatic in that respect. You're in service of the director's vision and the actor's intentions, what the writer has given the character to say and do. It's not about you. It's about what's in front of you.

DAVID SMUKLER

It is very important that I am actually practicing the work as I am leading the work.

How did you become a "voice coach"?

I grew up at the Cleveland Playhouse, founded by the first three graduates of Carnegie Tech Drama School. Saw my first play there at age two. Those were war years and my mother worked in the box office. There were no babysitters; my mother plopped us in the back row. I grew up at the Cleveland Playhouse. Age sixteen, the director said to me, "You're going to Tech, aren't you?" Destiny.

Carnegie Tech was wonderful and overwhelming. The voice and speech work was Edith Skinner, at her heyday. A tin ear and trying to shift from my Eastern European version of Americana to "Good American Speech." Edith changed my name from David "Sm-oo-klerrr" to "Smuklah" with the "schwa" ending … It was a struggle. I wisely did not take the class with Edith in my second year, but in the third year, I took both the second year and the third-year courses and I flew. I had figured out how to work. I ran out of money and started teaching at the John Robert Powers Modeling School in downtown Pittsburgh.

Edith sent me to Teacher's College at Columbia University to study with a major phonetician. But, she had retired and instead, Magdalene Kramer, the *doyenne* of "oral interpretation of forms of literature," became my advisor. I did a range of pathology and rhetoric courses to balance my theatre and phonetic background. Just twenty-one, I completed my master's. I taught at Evander Childs High School in the Bronx for three years, and paid off all my student debts.

In 1964, the days of charter flights, I went to Europe and saw theatre in London and Stratford. Then on to the Netherlands. I bought a motorbike in the Hague. During a rainstorm in the south of Germany, I took refuge under a tree with a cow. The cow and I had a conversation. The cow made some beautiful noises at me and I had to find a voice that she would respond to. A penny dropped: "I have worked so hard to create proper theatrical voice and speech that I have a vocal facade." I found myself making sounds with this lovely cow that were coming from a place in me I didn't recognize. Instantly, I knew that when I went back to New York, I had to find somebody who would help me— and I actually said—"free" my voice.

After a year back in New York, after three years teaching both day and evening high school, I couldn't do it anymore. I resigned and faced the unknown. Two weeks later, a letter came from Carnegie Tech telling me about a grant to train Voice Teachers for the American Theatre; was I interested? I responded immediately. A few weeks later, I received a letter with an audition time from a woman by the name of Kristin Linklater. Kristin asked us to prepare a sonnet for the audition, and as I stood up to speak, I did something I had never done before: I put my hand on my belly to make sure I was breathing. Two months later we began the first Linklater training.

I think someone would look at your career and go, "Really? *He* had that experience?" To me, that in itself is inspirational.

When I finally found my core—the connection of thought, feeling, and the need to communicate—it wasn't in the studio. Every morning I walked from 86th and Broadway through Central Park to the studio. Six or eight weeks in, I'm sitting in the park at eight in the morning. I'm starting to do some simple voice work and I realize that the birds haven't moved. The birds are still there, even though I'm making human sounds. "I think I'm beginning to understand something, but I don't know what it is. I sense I'm beginning to be present through my voice."

Eventually, I went to auditions in New York and experienced the pleasure of playing in the spaces. Often at auditions, they brought in another actor to read with me. I knew I connected, gut to gut. Not mouth to mouth, but gut to gut. I am very lucky: I had four years teaching alongside Kristin at NYU and two years alongside her at Stratford, Ontario Shakespeare Festival, before I became the coach at Stratford.

It's an interesting pulse check in authenticity when creatures are willing to be present to you.

When I met my wife, coloratura mezzo-soprano, Patricia Kern, her eight-year-old dog was used to going into the studio with Patricia. With each succeeding dog, it was very important that once they were old enough to enjoy "crazy voice things" we tested the dog's response to people's voices. We would sometimes have to point out, "I don't know what you're worrying about. The dog is sleeping there. They're safe with you. And you're not safe with your own voice." or, "You notice how the dog perks up every time you say that word? What is it? What's going on?"

How did you adapt your teaching of the IPA system or the Skinner book?

The Skinner work primarily goes from brain to mouth. For me (Iris Warren through Kristin): the thought needs to be rooted in the *gut*. The Celiac nerve ganglia is the primary emotional core of the body. The vagus nerve, which passes the message from the brain to the vocal cords, travels straight down the left side of the torso to the very bottom of the pelvis, connects with the celiac nerve ganglia—our primary nerve ganglia—and then sends the thought up the right side to the vocal cords.

It's fascinating to get scientific verification of a felt knowledge.

I established the Voice Intensive in Vancouver to aid the film industry with openness, vulnerability, and truth on camera. At York University, I established the Voice Teacher Diploma program to meet the need for teachers of acting and voice (camera and stage) with access to the gut connection as the source of language and voice. A priority of the program is extensive work in vocal anatomy and physiology. We need to ask; "How does this actor work? How does this language work? How does this character process the experience? What is the neurological experience? What is their language story?

Preparing a role for the actor is a process of examining the physical, emotional, and intellectual experiences of the character. Always a balance: What is the physiological? What is the emotional? What are the instincts? And what are the habits to be observed? What is the neurological patterning? Am I living in the moment or putting constructs on it? How does the character breathe? What are their intellectual, physical, emotional habits and how do these affect their voices? What is useful at this moment?

What qualities are important for aspiring voice coaches?

Being present in their physical, emotional, historical, present living body. They need to understand the body choices that have evolved for them. What are their familial, historical, or cultural patterns, choices? Today, it is crucial we examine and support cultural voices. Then, "How do I observe human interaction? How do I process the information? What knowledge is there of the physiological body? Is it an intellectual process or can I link body knowledge with cellular experience?" As a teacher: "If I'm going to take a group of people on a journey, how do I lead the journey and protect them at the same time? How do I make sure they're safe on the journey?" I know I must practice the work in order to lead the work.

I hear you say that it's extremely important to "know thyself" completely in order to show up completely in a room, and to be able to then support and hold space, authentically, for your students, actors, or clients.

"To know" is an intellectual process. Avoid that word … "Have knowledge of"; "to feel"; "to experience." A *cellular* experience. The actor's job is to create experiences for their audience.

As you sit here now, with such success in your career, do you have any words of advice to say to your younger self?

Oddly, no. Because I had to construct, or deconstruct, the world that had been created. I had to plough the field, do the planting and the nurturing. Trees: An important metaphor for me. I owned a tree farm here in Ontario for twenty years; I planted and nurtured trees. When it became too much for me, I turned it over to another tree person. Now, I have a property further north where the British Navy did not cut the forest. These trees are original and ancient. We can see the roots from one tree family interweave with others. When a tree dies, we can actually see the other trees withdraw their roots from the roots of the dying tree as well as extend roots over to the new saplings.

As actor trainers, our task is to aid the actor in a process of rooting the script in the character's life or rooting the character and their voice in the particular world. I would never use the word "planted." It's, "Where are the roots?" As you work on a character, what & where are the *roots?* What's in the roots that causes that experience? How do you, the actor, uncover the roots for the character? We are trained to create the history of the characters we play. My maternal grandmother was Romanian, and I got a chance to play Dracula in summer stock. I found a retired Romanian theatre director who actually read to me in my grandmother's Transylvanian, allowing me to approximate a dialect that Dracula might have used. That emotional connection allowed me to go into the dark side. It's absolutely crucial that we explore the physiological, auditory, linguistic world of each character.

Is it your belief that every living organism has a voice?

Based on my experience with trees, every living organism has a voice. My small Toronto back garden is dominated by a very mature walnut tree and a middle-aged maple. The conversations that go on back there are incredibly loud. When we sit in the garden, we are aware of the conversation. The walnut dominates; she has many friends, a whole neighborhood of walnut trees.

They're a noisy bunch? (laughs)

Especially at the end of the summer, when the walnuts drop.

I would love it if you have any additional words of advice or inspiration for an aspiring coach.

It never decreases: the fear, the anxiety, the pressure of being on-the-spot. After fifty years of coaching, the primal fears are still there. Trust them, because, as actors, we use them daily. Six, eight rounds of therapy … I'm still raw. But I know *how* to play with the raw places: "Okay, it's raw. Breathe the moment. Make it a present breath" and then let it out "on voice."

You see it, you name it, you breathe through it. And in that way, it becomes part of your toolset.

A mature actor does not run from the unexpected.

It seems like the *cow* gave you that message at that moment, having been taught by one of the greatest in terms of creating *the field* of voice and articulation, Edith Skinner. A protégé of hers, you were able to, at that point in time, say, "It's got to come from a *felt* place."

From a German forestry report: "The trees in the new forests we planted are not talking to each other. We planted imported trees instead of indigenous ones." My task is to do a voice journey, to guide others on their voice journey. The actor's job is to guide the audience on a journey. Tap into our voices, nurture them. Do not hide them in preconceptions or ancient history.

ERIK SINGER

Ceaselessly and with unending curiosity, striving to be the best coach or teacher you can be is perhaps the best way to go about building a career in an area where there is no set path.

What was your path to becoming a voice coach?

I started out as an actor. And then in 2007, 2008, I had been doing a fair amount of coaching on the side: acting coaching, audition coaching, grad school audition coaching, for about eight years or so. And then I went and trained and certified with Catherine as a Fitzmaurice voice teacher. In the second year of that training, there is a week with a focus on speech and a week with a focus on text. That's when I met Phil [Thompson] first, during speech week, and then Dudley [Knight] came in for text week …

When I encountered Dudley and Phil's work, Knight-Thompson Speechwork, it was like the heavens opened and clouds parted and a pillow descended from on high with a magic key on it: "Oh! This is how I do what I do when I do accents, and this is what we are actually doing, and therefore these are the tools. This is how you can communicate it, and how you can come at it, and how you can teach it." I told Catherine almost immediately, "*This* is what I want to do." And then, either right then or the next day, she asked me if I'd like to work at Rutgers (laughs) teaching in the MFA program, which was a job that was opening, and somebody had asked Catherine if she knew anybody. And so, I went straight from finishing Catherine's training to teaching speech and accents in the MFA program at Rutgers and then, not long afterwards, started teaching Knight-Thompson Speechwork workshops with Phil and with Andrea Caban after Dudley died.

In the interim, I did a lot of development work with KTS: I was the Associate Editor of the Pronunciation Phonetics Linguistic Dialect and Accent Studies section—I think was its title—of the *Voice and Speech Review*. Dudley was the editor for a couple of years and asked me to do that, so I was the Associate Editor of that for a while. And then I taught workshops in Knight-Thompson Speechwork, training other teachers and coaches, and then started doing a balance of teaching: teaching at Rutgers, at HB Studio in Greenwich Village, and Knight-Thompson Speechwork workshops. Then I gradually shifted and was doing more film and TV production coaching. And then around 2015, I think, I started doing only that and had to step back. I was still teaching Knight-Thompson Speechwork workshops all the way through 2017, but now I'm just doing full-time production coaching for film and TV.

Did you have a plan or a solid goal to become a voice coach for professional actors?

I'd say all of those transitions—and even my transition from most of my income coming from acting to most of my income coming from teaching and coaching—every single one of those transitions was gradual. My main income for many years was voiceover income. Mostly commercial, some audiobooks.

And obviously, like everything else in our profession, that fluctuates. It sort of goes up and down. So, there were great years, and there were terrible years, and there were medium years in between. (Pamela laughs) It's one of the reasons why I started teaching and coaching in the first place, to try to even things out a little bit. And then KTS came into the mix, teaching KTS workshops and also developing that work, you know, the intellectual labor.

You worked with Dudley and Phil prior to the publication of *Speaking with Skill,* right?

Yes. But I wouldn't say I was contributing to the forward development of the structure of the work, and what we were teaching and how we were teaching it, until after Dudley died in 2013. At that point, KTS was me and Phil and Andrea Caban. *Speaking with Skill,* Dudley's book, is a first-year MFA speech book. And so, the follow-up is about accents. The work that we taught and that KTS is still teaching, that is the follow-up from that, is the accent work.

Those transitions were all gradual, and I transitioned into doing more production coaching when those jobs came along. I think I left Rutgers to teach at HB Studio in the city. They had a conservatory program. Did that for a few years. In 2015, I got a job production coaching a Gus Van Sant [and] Jenji Kohan HBO pilot about the Salem Witch Trials, which was quite brilliant and very beautiful, and had some amazing performances and writing, and did not for whatever reason see the light of day. It did not get end up going to series. That was when I decided I needed to be doing more production coaching because it was fun and interesting and inspiring and challenging and was new.

What would be a path to consider for a person who's interested in being a voice coach?

I mean, it's not like there's a direct pathway … But the Royal Central School of Speech and Drama is *the* pathway for doing something in voice in the UK. The way that I got the first bunch of high-level production jobs that I got almost all came because I was recommended to the producers by other coaches. There are numerous colleagues and coaches who've recommended me more than once. It wasn't just one relationship or one person. I think my "way in" was to try to get as good as I could possibly get at doing what I did, to cultivate relationships with colleagues, and to be involved in training teachers and coaches. And I was fortunate enough to make some connections and to establish a bit of a reputation as being somebody who knew what they were doing.

I would call that "authentic networking." It's not *trying* to get jobs, it's just building relationships, right?

Maybe it's that. But it's interesting because there are not that many dialect coaches working in major films and TV. So, everybody knows everybody, or at least knows who everybody is. And if you're on a job, you can't do another job simultaneously. So, you're going to recommend somebody else. That is, maybe one way that you can build up a career: get really good at what you're doing and cultivate: go to VASTA conferences, cultivate relationships with colleagues, collaborate with them and make friends. And you may be in a position to be recommended for jobs when other people can't do them.

What is your advice to help aspiring coaches build a career?

I put a lot into trying to go very deep in my understanding and really develop, as much as I could, the skills of voice and accent coaching. And understanding as much as I could—and I continue to do this—about the physical. The physicality of how these processes work, how language works itself, then the actual practice of working on that with actors. Ceaselessly and with unending curiosity, striving to be the best coach or teacher you can be is perhaps the best way to go about building a career in an area where there *is* no set path.

Are you mostly doing dialect coaching?

I still will do voice work on a film set sometimes. It's hard to have time, and room, and permission when you are a dialect coach and you're there on set to coach an accent. But I do consider myself still as a voice teacher and a voice coach. And so, when and where that is useful and possible, it is still very much part of what I do, although most of what I'm doing obviously is accents and languages.

Also, when you're on set, on a movie or on a TV show, the dialogue is usually very fluid, very subject to change. You're going to get new lines on the morning of. The actor may be like, "I don't want to say it this way, I would like to say it *this* way," and you're going to get new lines in rehearsal. And so, if you are coaching the lead actor and the lead actor is playing a character from Liverpool and they're American, then you are going to need to be as familiar as you possibly can be with everything about that dialect or that language variety so that you can weigh in on that, and hopefully you'll be recognized (laughs) as the person who has the authority there.

Is there a typical day on set as a dialect coach?

Every set is different. Wildly different. A lot flows from the director. There are directors that hate dialect coaches. (Pamela laughs) Perhaps, to give them the benefit of the doubt, they've had bad experiences with not very professional dialect coaches. The absolute imperative is not to cost the production money. Every minute on set in a big-budget movie is worth something like $10,000. And so, if you are taking an extra minute giving a note to an actor when everybody else is ready and the director is ready for a take, that costs the production $10,000. You don't want to do that. That is an absolute no-no. So, there is a whole other layer of things you have to get good at very fast as a coach on productions like that, which is understanding the flow and rhythm of the set; having eyes in the back of your head; making sure you don't block the way when equipment is coming through; knowing what the things that they yell are—when they yell, "Points, points!" you have to get out of the way.

Do you think it is important for voice coaches, dialect coaches, to have an actor training background?

God, yes. Absolutely. There are two things that I say to people when they ask me, "How do you become a dialect coach? I'm interested in doing what you do.

What is the pathway?" I say, "There isn't one." (laughs) But here are the things you need: You need a really good, specific, scientific, descriptive understanding of articulatory phonetics and as much phonology and sociolinguistics as you can get: the areas of linguistics that directly inform what we do. And we want to be able to stay current on things as well, because there is an enormous amount of knowledge, techniques, practices, and understanding of language variation that we have to learn from the field of linguistics. The articulatory phonetics stuff is vitally essential, and understanding things about how language varieties work is also incredibly important to be able to do what we do sensitively.

But, you know, we are also acting coaches. And I say that with a little bit of trepidation over who might read that because, obviously, directors don't want us to be directing the actors nor coaching them in the acting. That's not what we've been hired to do. I would never dream of dictating a performance to an actor or even suggesting, "Well, I think this is probably the better way to go" unless they really want to know and we have that relationship. But we are acting in a support role for the actor in this particular version of storytelling, this particular way of telling stories. You've got to understand how that storytelling works. And you've got to understand how actors work in order to be able to support them. So, you have to be able to hear their concerns, give them notes, see the way they take those notes, see the way they retain those things over time in ways that are sensitive to that process, that support it and don't get in the way of it. And I think that's immensely complex. So, you have to know as much as you can and understand, really deeply, from inside your bones, how acting works and the different ways that acting can work for different actors.

Would you consider yourself a "dialect designer" in film and TV or is it that, really, you feel like a coach?

I think it's entirely appropriate, for sure, because it's always a design. No matter what the accent is, or how long or short you have to coach it, or how extensively you design it out, it's always a design. It's always a result of choices. There's certainly no one single English accent or American accent. There's no one single RP accent. There's no one single New York accent. There's no one single African American, Brooklyn, in-her-thirties accent. So, you're always, always, always making choices. And all of those are design choices. It's a design process.

FRAN BENNETT

If you are working with somebody who is not of your ethnicity and who is not of your class, you need to learn something about them. Or otherwise you're just going to teach them from your own perspective without looking at them.

How do you define yourself as a voice coach?

I've always said, "I'm Fran Bennett and I'm a Linklater voice teacher."

Could you give me an example of what coaching looks like for you?

I've had cases in my L.A. stay where named actresses have come to me because some outdoor theatre is doing Shakespeare and they haven't done Shakespeare since they were in college thirty, forty years ago. And they come to me maybe two weeks before the show opens. what do you do in situations like that? I try to go back and say,

> Okay, how much do you remember from what you learned when you went? Just try to find that, put yourself back in wherever that class was, and see what sort of hits you. Not just your brain, but your brain including your guts. See the teacher. What part did you like, what part stayed with you?

And then I go from there, because everybody will find some part. I go from there to work with them. I call that coaching. There are some people who come to me, also actors, who graduated from some school, who say, "What I learned is not working, is not helping me, as an actor. I've tried to use it. I can't use it. What do I do?" That's voice *classes*.

What do you notice really makes a good voice coach or voice teacher?

I have run into some people who are not in the moment, and maybe they're looking at you, but you know darn well they're not paying any attention to anything you say. I think it's terribly important that you are *in* the moment. And being in the moment means you've got good eyes, you're looking. It means you're really seeing, not just looking but really *seeing*, and that you're really hearing. Both of those, I think, puts you in the moment in the room with whomever it is in front of you.

When you think of this interesting time period we're living in—we have a huge resurgence in Equity, Diversity, and Inclusion with #BlackLivesMatter and LGBTQIA+, and the complexities of becoming a teacher at this point—what advice would you like to offer the next generations of teachers?

I think I would offer the same advice that I've given to other people, before the pandemic, before #BlackLivesMatter: If you are working with somebody who is not of your ethnicity and who is not of your class, you need to learn something about *them*. Or otherwise, you're just going to teach them from your own perspective without looking at them. I think that you have to get out of your own safe place and have to look at another ethnicity. Now, it might be somebody who's white but Jewish. Learn something about the Jewish culture. And I think you can learn it from the person you're teaching by listening: "Hmm, what are you doing with your tongue? What are you doing with your jaw? What are you doing with your top lip, or not doing with any of these things?" And then you might have to figure out, is that a cultural thing? My thing when I first meet somebody is, "Where are you from?" Before, "Why do you want to take voice?" I'm getting [to know] how you were brought up, something about your first speaking before you even got into any knowledge of voice. And I think that's very important for a voice coach.

It's about empathy. And it's also about knowledge. And that again means what's beyond yourself, your life, your religion. We get stuck with that. I mean, we get stuck with so many things, which is a lack of knowledge. I've had people who were teaching acting classes, who've said to me, "Fran, give me some Black plays with some good parts in them." Go fuckin' look for yourself! Yes, I got a lot in my library. I had a couple of professors say that to me at CalArts. I said, "You're perfectly welcome to come sit on my floor in my living room and look through my library. But I'm not going to tell you the name of a play." Educate yourself.

You've worn hats of a teacher and a coach, but how did you get here? What was your path?

I was born in the South in Malvern, Arkansas. And of course, I went to church all the time. My mother was a singer in the senior choir. I was a singer in the junior choir. There was no training to sing. I could not read the notes. They would play it and you would hear it and you would imitate what you heard from the piano, which is how I learned to do those songs, okay? Now, I remember walking, I'm coming from high school one day. And I hear as I'm passing the local YWCA, these voices. Something grabs me in my gut. I walk up the steps. I stand outside, I listen. I'm hearing only female voices. And they're doing poetry. This is like, "Whoa, this is great. This is better than singing. This is lovely." So, I sit there and wait till they finish. And all these Black women walk out, right? And I think "Oh God, I gotta be a part of this."

So, I go into the room and there's a white woman who is running this, right? And I say, "My name is Fran Bennett and I would like to be a part of this." And she said, "But this is not a teenage choir. It's an adult choir." I said, "Yeah, I know, I know, but can I do this? I want to do this." I mean, I was practically on my knees begging this woman. And she finally said, "All right. Okay. Are you free after school? Then come back tomorrow." I went back tomorrow. She came in and she gave me a poem to read. And I read it. I didn't know that was an audition. But that was my audition. And she said, "Okay, you can do it." So, I joined a voice verse choir.

I soon became one of the soloists and did all sorts of things. That got me very much into, "Oh. Expression, emotion from your gut, breath. Wow." All of that stuff. And, so then I went on to college —acting, directing.

What led you to Kristin Linklater's work?

I'm in New York. I see in the *New York Times* news on the Rialto: 'Voice teachers, actors being looked for by the Minnesota Theatre Company to train with a woman by the name of Kristin Linklater. Prepare an audition of a sonnet.' I'm late in doing it because I had to have a surgery. Finally, I send a postcard because, darling, there were no cell phones, right? And I sent them a Western Union …

… A telegram!

That was the fastest you could get there. The message was, "You need to see me, stop. Sorry I've been busy, stop. You need to see me, stop …" I think I repeated this three times. I finally got a card from Peter Zeisler saying that they would see me, and the time, darling, was eight in the morning … This woman called Kristin Linklater said to me, "You were late! So, I have to put you before all the other people that I have to see because Peter wanted me to see you." In that tone. Kristin took me into the program. I went off to the hospital, had my little surgery. We started training, I had a big bandage on me, and I'm doing all this movement and stuff, and broke the stitches—but I was fine, darling. And so, we were trained. And now I'm into the voice field.

How do you know what to say "yes" to?

Ah, how does it hit me in my gut? Will I learn something from it? Will I grow from it? Is it going to make me a fuller person? I look at that in making the decision to do something.

When you look at advising an aspiring voice coach as to what kind of anatomy training is necessary, what are your suggestions?

I think if you're going to be a voice coach, you really need to know a little bit about anatomy—the anatomy of the body and the anatomy of the voice. And I put it that way because your voice is in your body, so you've got to start with your body first. I think you also have to have done some sort of physical work to arrive at some kind of an awareness of your own body, because you're giving out so much when you're coaching and teaching, that if your head is gonna go forward like *this* (demonstrates) and you're gonna talk … your voice, it's gonna get all strangled in your body because you particularly don't have any awareness of what you're doing physically.

Why is it important to understand anatomy in terms of teaching?

Because sometimes, I've had in a class some students where imagery works fine. Some students who want and need, for their growth, a little more of a scientific knowledge. Now, with those persons, I will use the terms, I will bring in my *Grey's Anatomy*, I will show them pictures of it. I also have video tapes and that kind of stuff. I can show all of that stuff to them. Because that's the way they learn. But I also want to get them back to the inspiration and the imagination. Because I don't think you can act the science. But you can act, "That image, what does it feel like, that inspiration …" And I also think that's what you teach from.

I don't think you coach from the science. At least I wouldn't want a coach who's always talking only about the science. Because that might not be me. That's then you putting *you* ahead of me.

KRISTIN LINKLATER

My work has a form, a methodology, so that it actually goes with an organic logic through the process of releasing a voice from tension into its full potential. The form is what allows the content to be delivered.

How do you identify as a voice coach?

I'm a voice teacher. I don't consider myself a voice *coach*. I don't like that word.

Do you see a difference between "teacher" and "trainer"?

I think voice "trainer" sounds more as if you're saying it needs to be—it's more [of a] result emphasis.

How much anatomy does a voice coach need to know?

Well, you've got to have the anatomy. The trouble is, you have to *know* the vocal anatomy, but not teach it. You're not teaching what you know, as a voice teacher. "I'm going to teach you everything I know." Well, that won't work. But you *have* to be accurate in your understanding of how the voice works. The thing that I think people need to pay more attention to is the neuroanatomy, because it's what sets the voice in motion. It's rewiring the brain to connect with the body through a different way, through very subtle anatomical pathways. But you'd better be able to visualize those pathways clearly and make some choices.

One of the paradoxes is that you can know that the voice is made in the larynx in your throat, but if you think about it, it ruins the whole thing. If you focus on, "Oh, my voice is made here in my throat," then your voice doesn't work very well. So, there's vocal anatomy and then there's knowing which parts of the vocal anatomy are counter-productive.

It's about understanding what you need to know and what you need to teach, right?

Absolutely. What I just said grew out of your question, which was, "What does a young vocal coach or voice teacher need to know? Do they need to know vocal anatomy?" Yes, but not so that they teach it.

What kind of training, or experience, do you think helps younger coaches, as you've observed many of your mentees move forward?

They should know what acting is. I think, even if they say, "Oh, I want to coach public speakers in the corporate world," I don't think anybody enters this profession—I hope they don't—saying, "I am entering this profession because I want to make a load of money coaching corporate heads." That would be sad. However, that's a way where you can make money. But, what you're bringing to the corporate world and to the executive thinking is to be creative and imaginative, and then that's what lights up the voice. That's what feeds the voice: it's your creativity, your personal commitment, and your imagination. And that comes, really, from one's experience, I would say, as an actor.

Now, I can't be proscriptive about that. I do have people, always, who go through my teacher training who have not necessarily been on stage from the beginning to the end of a play. But I recommend it. I recommend it as something that tells you a *huge* amount about how to access yourself as the engine for your voice. So that's one thing. Then, there are the obvious things: Alexander Technique, Feldenkrais, which are about physical techniques or physical experiences that work on the same basic principle as mine, which is that we are restoring the brain to its best function. It's how the brain actually perceives the body and the voice that is going to make the deep change. And that's what happens with Alexander, what happens with Feldenkrais, and others: Body Mind Centering, somatic work. All of that's to do with the rearrangement of your psychophysical self. That's a terrific background.

I beg all my teacher trainees to do therapy: they should know themselves before they presume to understand others. Well, we never *know* ourselves completely, but they should be very interested. (Pamela laughs) And that will go on for the rest of their lives, right? So, therapy, psychophysical—what does it mean? What are the various psychological factors that can hinge upon the voice? Be adventurous. When I was in America, I went to every workshop, every "discover yourself" workshop on offer. Almost everyone. I was rebirthing, I was doing past lives, all of that. Getting oneself turned inside out. I don't know what the current offers are. It's very different in the UK from the USA. Although, the UK is catching up in interesting ways, in their interest in the psychological and emotional side of things.

So, from the point of view of preparation: go to the theatre a lot. Theatre is the [basis]. You can watch films, but you don't get the same information as you do when you're in the presence of the naked voice, unmediated. And tuning your body and your mind to: why does that work? What's working here? What's the actor accessing in himself?

You mentioned neuroanatomy, any recommendations there?

I think there are a lot of very accessible books, or books that make the subject matter accessible, such as *The Gut Brain*. At the moment I'm reading *The Brain that Changes Itself*.

I loved that book!

Really interesting. I'm always looking for new language anyway, in my own teaching, so that I don't get jargon-y. It's a very complex scenario, how the voice works. How can one simplify it? [To] simplify the language around it as much as possible is what I'm always looking for. The whole idea—which is much more current than it ever was before—of the brain in the body and the brain in the head, in constant two-way communication, is now getting to be familiar to people, and one can really benefit from that in teaching … Just constantly saying, "This is repetition because you are rewiring the synaptic connection between neurons. We can't address that directly, but we'll address it from the body and then the body will start training the brain."

The other thing that is a tricky thing to play with is the language within which we teach that makes the difference between how it's being thought. I mean, the very simple language in breathing, instead of "inhale and exhale"—which [are] active verbs—to say, "Feed in the impulse for a sigh of relief; allow the breath to come in; relax for the breath to come in; release for it to come out." You know? That it's not active verbs. Because the deepest way that the breathing works is on the involuntary mechanisms of the brain and the body. So, how are we going to access those? The secret language of our bodies is what we're trying to listen in to and change the vocabulary of.

Do you think part of your work is about empowering humans to *allow* a breath versus to *take* a breath? Noticing the energetic experience: *taking* versus *allowing* or *inviting*.

Why do you use the word, "empower"?

From my perspective, it's giving the power back to the person—the power of their voice, *owning* their voice, as opposed to feeling like they don't have any ownership. That's it's sort of like, "Whatever the voice is I have, it's what I have and if I sound this way, I sound this way."

Yeah. I mean, all of those things, once you break it down, are inarguable. For me, the word "empowerment" sort of suggests *more*. It's getting to know your voice, It's understanding your voice, It's enjoying your voice.

Befriending, perhaps?

(laughs) Well, I can say *owning.* Did I say that already? Really owning, "It's *my* voice." I think I change the language all the time, and actually "empowerment" is not in my vocabulary.

How do you stay delighted? Because you're still doing this work. (Kristin laughs)

People coming to me and wanting something, and I discover, "Oh, I think I can enter into a conversation about that." It's what comes *to* me and then, the kind of humbling realization that I know a lot of stuff! (Pamela laughs) So, that's why I think the word "empowerment" doesn't sit with me. I don't feel *empowered* by what I know. I feel *humbled* by what I know. (laughs) And I do know an awful lot. And I'm amazed at it. Particularly if I've had a good night's sleep, how much I can come up with that helps people! (Pamela laughs) I sometimes hear myself saying things, and I sometimes say, "Did you hear what I just said? Write that down!"

"That was good!" (laughs)

You say delighted? I think I'm just astonished by what my ancient brain, the 86 billion—have I made you cry?

Yeah, a little bit. (laughs)

(laughs) Oh, good, that's good. Yeah, it's the stuff that's stored in *here*. (points to her head) It is delightful.

Well, is there anything else you wanted to share or anything that I didn't touch on?

Because this is called a "toolkit," I just want to underline that my work has a form, a methodology, so that it actually goes with an organic logic through the process of releasing a voice from tension into its full potential. The form is what allows the content to be delivered. Any young teacher who has a job, for instance, in an institution or in a university, they really need to develop their form. So, knowing what it is they're aiming for. "How am I going to get here, logical step by logical step?" There's an awful lot of generalized experiential teaching. You know, "Let's have this nice voice experience. And let's now plunge into this lovely—" And it doesn't do the job as far as what the standards demand. That's all, really.

Our students and clients need a structure or a scaffolding to support them as actors or professional voice users.

Absolutely. Well, I'm rather touched that I've reduced you to tears. (Pamela laughs) Well, not reduced, but *released* you into tears. That's really nice.

You released me, for sure. Laughter and tears. It's been a fabulous conversation.

LOUIS COLAIANNI

Joy makes time slow down … This one, to me, is the flip side of "Time flies when you're having fun." When something is profoundly joyous, time presents only an illusion. The joy can keep you slow and steady in your process.

Do you see a difference between a coach and a teacher?

Oh, yes.

Tell me what that means to you.

Well, it means to me that as a coach, I may teach. And as a teacher, I may coach.

Long ago, when I did more coaching—when I really started coaching professionally on a regular basis—was when I joined the faculty at University of Missouri Kansas City and became the resident coach at Missouri Rep and Kansas City Rep, and did that for sixteen years. So, I was coaching regularly. The reason I mention that is because when I started coaching Shakespeare there, I went to Kristin Linklater, who in those days was truly and actively my mentor.

I said to her, "I'm doing a rep production of *Richard III*. So, I want your advice on how to do that." Kristin never gave me much advice about coaching. She said, "Well, the text is very straightforward for a coach." And then her second piece of advice was, "But it's not in the coaching where you'll really make a difference. It's teaching in the classroom." That was her perspective at that time—that would have been 1990.

And so, I took it on in that way, just to see what I [could] get done. The first professional coaching that I did would be Trinity Rep in 1987. I happened to be at Trinity Rep the year that Anne Bogart was the artistic director. And so, there were all sorts of interesting productions, interesting playwrights, interesting directors, actors. It was a great year to be there. And coaching was just part of the day. You'd plop down in the theatre between classes and see what was going on and who needed what. So, those were my early relationships with coaching.

Even with your extensive coaching, it feels like there was an affinity to teaching.

With Kristin's advice, the classroom is most important, and [to] do what you can in coaching. I was just getting ready to go out to Kansas City, and I was actually packing up from Trinity Rep. I was on a train from Rhode Island to Manhattan and I had a double seat. And there were no other double seats in the car, and an older woman and younger man—her assistant, it seemed—got on the train and asked me to switch seats, so I did. And they bought me a drink and I thought they were very nice.

We got talking and the woman said, "What do you do?" And I said, "Well, I've just left Trinity Rep and I'm headed out to Missouri Rep, and I'll be coaching shows there." And she said, "I'm in the theatre. What are you coaching?" I said, "Well, the first thing I'll coach is *Our Town*." And she said, "Oh, yes, I created the role of Emily in 1939." It was Martha Scott! And I thought, "Well, what a profound coincidence."

I was so eager because I was figuring, "Well, I'll coach this accent." So, I said, "Please tell me your approach to the accent." She said, "Oh, Thornton told us not to worry about the accent." on the eve of coaching *Our Town*, I got that advice from Martha Scott. So, I arrived in Kansas City and had my first meeting with George [the director]. And he said, "So what about this accent?" And I said, "Well, Martha Scott told me that you don't worry about the accent in *Our Town*."

What an auspicious way to start.

Yes, it just seemed like fate was on my side in some way. So, that was sort of affirming, I thought. That this coaching is about something layered—maybe even a little bit mystical. And so, I puzzled over coaching for a while. As a young man, I did not feel right, sitting at that folding table next to this designer and that manager, and having my notebooks and things spread out and many sharpened pencils. I sat there rather self-consciously as a young coach. And really, no one prepared me to coach in the theatre. No one prepared me really to coach anywhere. Kristin was the person who launched me into the world of voice and speech, and she would talk about coaching tactics. But they were really how you launch into coaching from exercises and things like that. So, I didn't know what the rehearsal room was all about [...] I had no experience.

There were no vocal pedagogy programs. That's a relatively new thing.

Yes. And so consequently, I'm wary of them. Because I went in not with the highest confidence, and not exactly sure what to do and how to do it. And I found my own way. I think because of that I very much became, without a better way to put it, my own coach—found my own way of doing it.

What would you say to a relatively new or aspiring vocal coach coming to you and asking you, "What kinds of qualities and skills are really important and valuable in terms of having a career or building a career with longevity?"

My best advice is, you'll find your way. I doubt anyone's going to coach the way I do. There'll be overlap, I'm sure, between all of us. But every production is so new, even to remount something, I have found. It's so new that what applied in another production really usually doesn't hold.

So, flexibility is super important in terms of a quality or skill.

Furthermore, even when coaching in the director's mind is of high priority, it seldom finds its way into high priority in the schedule. So, there's that to deal with. And it can vary from production to production. If I can get meetings with actors, then the coaching becomes very individualized.

And that allows you to personalize your approach?

Yes. Actors may have certain ways of doing things that they prefer, or they may feel they're in kind of an unfamiliar, created experience. So, the first conversations I think are helpful. And then to talk with the director for their impressions, but our impressions seldom agree. I find that time after time. You know, there may be something someone's doing in rehearsal, and I think it's just where it ought to go. *Seldom* does the director agree.

So, it isn't about me coming in with some kind of know-how. That is a commodity. It's not about that. It's not about tailoring it in some way. It's just about being there in a kind of dialogue. I wouldn't even say being a conduit with the director. Directors often tell me what they want or need in vague terms or expedient terms. They have a coach so that they don't have to think about it, in a way. Sometimes they say, "Just do what you always do."

Do you have some tips or tricks for dealing with coaching when a director thinks a microphone will "fix" the vocal challenges an actor might be encountering?

What people expect of microphones is not possible. So, microphones can't enhance intelligibility, actually. They can enhance how loudly you are intelligible or unintelligible.

They can't make the sounds for you. And I think I've heard often enough, "Well, the mics will take care of it." No, the mics will *find* you. But you have to be *found*. *You* have to be found.

How do you help the actor be "found"?

Well, that's where the art of coaching lives. And I don't think there's a tip about that. It's very individual.

What are some ways you use voice coaching in your practice?

Well, sometimes it goes right back to the breath. It's about getting them to let in the text deeply, or let images live in their bodies more. Other times it may be about getting them more on their voices, if that's something of interest to them. But I think in this case, it has to be something of interest to them to do these things. You know, I can give them some kind of quick exercise that seems like that would be the one to help them: maybe something with their jaw, maybe their tongue, maybe undoing certain habits in the body briefly. And then if they are craving more of that, I'll soon know that, and then I might even be able to give them a full class about something that will support their work. There are other people who are rather hands-off and so I do what little I can with them, and we take it from there.

How would you encourage an early career voice coach to take it slow and steady, and not assume you can digest it all and teach it all and know it all after three years of training?

Here's a little saying that I crafted and liked it better and better afterward. I just wanted to see what I could say in five diphthongs that had something worth saying in it. And so, this actually is a bit of a credo for how to work and what to strive for, in the explorations of rehearsal or class: "Joy makes time slow down." This one, to me, is the flip side of "Time flies when you're having fun." When something is profoundly joyous, time presents only an illusion. The joy can keep you slow and steady in your process.

MICHA ESPINOSA

I study voice every day. For me, for others, because for me it's more of a spiritual practice now. I can easily say that. I've seen the impact on the human spirit. I've seen the impact of what words can do to heal. I've seen how the voice can be a catalyst for change.

How do you identify as a voice coach?

I embrace the complexity of my identity. With that, I think of myself as a coach of voice, text, and acting and as a dialect designer. I am also a senior-level teacher of Fitzmaurice Voicework©. What brings all of my work together is that I approach and engage my practice, pedagogy, and creative research as vehicles for social change. My identity as an artist and an activist (*artivist*) would be the driving force for my work.

Would you say being an "artivist" is something that you bring into your work, whether with actors and professional voice users or your work as a professor?

Absolutely. Developing one's voice and telling one's stories are practical skills that empower. That empowerment makes people stronger on the inside. Then, these people can go forth to make a difference in the world, whether through telling stories in general or telling their own stories specifically, that is, speaking up for themselves personally and politically.

You're bringing in this idea of storytelling in the voice, how the voice is fundamental to storytelling. Can you tell me more about that?

As soon as you open your mouth, we know a lot about you, right? (laughs) We know how you are wired; we might know how you take care of yourself; we might know where you're from. In developing that story, whether or not it's telling your own story, you have to ask, "Does it reflect who you are?" And then, if you're telling somebody else's story, the questions become, "How is that synergy happening? How are you making that text come alive?" You're making that union, that relationship between you and the text.

Do you bring your story into your work?

I do. Awareness of one's identity is one of the most important aspects of my work. Understanding my origin story made me a better coach. If you know your situated perspective, then you understand your relationship with the "other." As a coach, you are helping people understand the world. And so, when you understand *your* world a little bit more, it's certainly helpful for world-making and transforming. Each situation differs: coaching in a theatre company, coaching a student, coaching an executive, or coaching somebody who might be in the midst of grand transformation.

So, those early imprints can be great information for yourself. It also helps in understanding "How did this character come to be?" In my telling of my own story, absolutely: my bicultural identity, my dual-language identity, my Spanglish identity; plus where I come from; the Southwest, my border consciousness. My Mexican-American identity has absolutely helped me understand the worlds I live in, the places I am from, and my pride in where I am from. So, I strive to bring those aspects of my identity to the stories that I am telling and helping others tell.

What are some of the most important areas for an aspiring voice coach to focus on?

Breath. Understanding breath is the foundation for everything that I do. An understanding of how the breath moves through the body so that we can illuminate the human experience. For me, that is the understanding between tension and release. In other words, having a relationship with tension and release, being able to guide students to understand the possibility for liberation and power in their bodies.

The study of shaping sound, whether through the International Phonetic Alphabet or Kinesensics, is useful to have. I have seen a difference from my training to what is now considered a "good voice." It is different from when I first entered the field. Then, there was a lot more concern with the *beautiful* voice. Now, I hear a lot more variety in voices and I am doing a lot more work in new media, gaming, and voice over. I think staying abreast of trends is essential. For example, audiences demand much more specificity when it comes to accents and dialects. This specificity is especially true for honoring voices from the Latinx diaspora.

If somebody feels a calling to become a voice coach, how would you advise them to explore finding work when they're first starting out and/or building a client base so they can make a livable wage in the field?

The voice is endlessly interesting. I've taught communication/litigation skills to lawyers. I've helped people transitioning from male to female. I have really found joy in teaching bilingual workshops, in reclaiming language, and in working on Latinx plays and Latinx stories because therein lies my passion.

And, so, I would add, "Find your passion in the field." It could be through theatre, it could be through books. I know people who are coaches for audio narration for books, for voice overs, for cartoon voices. There are many ways to enter the field, so I would say to find what brings you the most bliss. I love teaching; I found that out a long time ago. So that is where my focus lies, in teaching and coaching in the theatre and universities, primarily.

Another passion of mine is women's empowerment. I am proud to say that I am a feminist, and I have focused on coaching women. I am incredibly proud of a project called Mujeres Poderosas. I brought many of my loves together; I traveled to South America to work with female artists, empowering them to find their voices and develop their artistry. That endeavor came out of my passions, and it was incredibly satisfying. So, I repeat: "Follow your passion."

What do you think an aspiring coach needs to master?

There is no mastery. There is only learning. You are learning how to learn. You as a coach continue to work on yourself and your development of your teaching and the development of your core, your spine, your voice, so that you can be in a place to guide and listen and share. Yes, there are programs, but what works for one person might not work for another person. So, I think mastering means understanding the infinite capacity to express, then finding that way to do it. The methodologies fold into each other; they each help. But whether you study Fitzmaurice, Alexander, Feldenkrais, or Somatic Experiencing, the method has to matter to *you*. Because you're going to be taking that language and then filtering it through your work. The key is to continue in your own practice. Thus, you learn every day.

What led you to become a voice coach?

I lost my voice several times between the ages of eighteen and twenty-one. Something unspeakable had happened to me. Consequently, I didn't have a relationship with my voice. I didn't have a relationship with my body at that age. And the crazy thing was not that I had nodules. I was not able to phonate. There was no sound, but my vocal folds were fine when they scoped me. My body had gone into "startle." And the muscles spasmed between my hyoid and my larynx so that the vocal folds could not come together completely. Imagine a massive spasm around the neck, shoulders, and throat areas. That is what life had given me at that moment. I had to relearn everything I had known if I wanted to continue telling stories, if I wanted to have a career.

As I journeyed into this understanding, I went to graduate school where Mary Corrigan was my teacher. She was compassionate and sensitive and helped me on my journey. She introduced me to a whole other world, the world of voice. The voice is fascinating. It's this place where the head and the heart meet, right? So here I was, in this mental state, and my heart was broken so that, literally, my throat chakra was not able to function the way it needed to.

So, in that journey of losing my voice and then finding out why I had lost my voice, I had to learn how to let go. I had to learn how to let go of *so* many things. I had to learn to let go of my past. I had to learn to be more present in the moment. I had to learn not to be afraid of the future. So, I ended up going on this incredible journey where I met my greatest teacher, Catherine Fitzmaurice, and I studied Feldenkrais, and I studied with Patsy Rodenberg in London. Then somebody asked, "Can you teach a voice class?" And I said, "Sure, why not?" (laughs) I called people and asked, "How do I do this?" And then I began to follow their advice. I fell in love with teaching voice. And I fell in love with this being my calling for the rest of my life.

I study voice every day, for me and for others. because, for me, it's more of a spiritual practice now. I can easily say that. I've seen the impact on the human spirit. I've seen the impact of what words can do to heal. I've seen how the voice can be a catalyst for change. I've seen how it can build conscious relationships with me and others on all levels of society. So, I'm in this field to the end. This is what I want to do. I want to encourage people to get into the field. It has lots of opportunities. It's a field that makes a huge difference. It's made a huge difference for me.

What would your advice be to your younger self?

I wish I had been less afraid earlier in my life. I wish I had been more of a fool earlier in my life. I wish I had been willing to make more mistakes, I wish I were open to uncertainty earlier. I think that is the number one thing that I come against and that I see my students come against over and over again: The fear of sounding foolish, the fear of making a mistake, and maybe just making bigger mistakes. (laughs) I wish that I'd been patient with myself.

I like to work really hard and I like to get things right, and I don't want to look foolish. I think that a lot of us are like that. And, yet, when we jump into the unknown and take that risk, even with a simple sound, "Ahhhhhhh," just being able to make that sound. It always breaks my heart when I invite somebody to make a sound with me but they say they can't or they're afraid to or they don't know how. So, to see that little scared part of yourself and to not be so afraid, to be brave, were vital lessons for me, one I try to pass on to my clients and students.

Being brave goes with the business aspect of being a coach, too. There were times in my life when, if I had not been afraid, I could have done things earlier in my career. I'm pretty bold (laughs), yet I have learned that to conquer, I must be even bolder! "I'm going to go work with attorneys," or "I am going to reach out to that corporation," or "I am going to develop this program in this way." My resistance was my fear: my fear that I wouldn't be good at it, my fear that I didn't have enough knowledge of it. I have wonderful friends whom I can reach out to and share with, and I live in communities that I can gain and gather knowledge from, that is, collective wisdom. I've learned that the only thing holding me back was not believing in myself. So, I would say to myself, "it is okay to be afraid." I want to be an example for others. It is possible to reframe one's narrative by acknowledging fear and yet still finding the spine, dropping the breath down into the belly, expanding the ribs, releasing the tongue, and moving forward. Adelante!

MICHAEL MORGAN

You start by listening, not imposing. You start by gathering information, staying open to what and where people are, who they are.

How do you identify as a voice coach?

Most of my career has been in academia. I started off very young and have continued that. And I've done professional coaching in theatres as well.

How important would you think equity, diversity, and inclusion training is for aspiring voice coaches? How would you help a young voice teacher understand how to approach that world today?

We're at a really extraordinary point where we are reexamining the field in terms of the status quo and how it can grow. It's about time. And at the same time, I really do respect the past, the legacies. I just want more inclusion. Because there are other legacies, and other stories, and other voices, and other standards. So, I just think it needs to open up. This is a very exciting moment, not only in speech and accents but also in voice, to say, "What are the different kinds of paradigms and models and experiences that can be part of the conversation?"

I think you really have to be hungry and committed. Otherwise, it doesn't work. I don't think one should impose any kind of agenda on oneself about "I have to do this EDI thing in my classroom." But at the same time, I think the world is changing. (laughs) I might be delusional, but hopefully things shift and open up and this impacts the industries, which are also pretty closed off in terms of other voices coming into the mix. The new people, not me—they're pioneers. They have the energy, the commitment, and there's so much work they can do with excavating the old but also acknowledging that there's a wealth within other cultures, sounds, voices, speech sounds, other phonetics that can actually sit at the table with the more established ones.

It's deeply personal and this work is really hard. So, I would say you have to have a lot of courage and determination. Because you're coming up against something so reinforced in terms of: What is the norm? Or, what is the "ideal" in terms of how people should speak and sound? It's pretty much pervasive. Start to say, "Well, wait a minute, listen to these other sounds" or, "Bring in this other kind of music" and let it sit in equal rather than in a marginal, "Oh, that's interesting. That's exotic." Really see these different voices and speech sounds as inclusive. I think that's a lot of work.

I hear you loud and clear. I wonder what your advice would be for teachers and coaches: how do you walk into a room today with a, hopefully, diverse group of humans in front of you and approach that with integrity and authenticity?

You start by listening, not imposing. You start by gathering information, staying open to what and where people are, who they are. I would definitely start with some sort of conversation, or discussion, or a circle, or something that allows people to feel like they're coming to a place where they have agency. It turns over that traditional paradigm of the teacher as the expert and the student as someone who's absorbing all this expertise. It becomes, like, the student is the expert because they actually *know*, they have that experience of their story, their lives. And within that, their voices and imaginations, etc. No matter what the distinctions are in terms of race, gender, class, color, etc., those are the entries that would be more welcoming than starting off with, "Here's my curriculum. This is what we're going to do today." (laughs)

I think a lot of teaching is often driven by, "I'm your teacher and I want you to do this." But I think that it's important to open that up so it becomes more of, "What do *you* want to do? How do *you* see yourself in this world? What do *you* want for your voice? What do *you* want in terms of your expressiveness?" Not, "I want you to do this exercise" or, "I want you to lift your head" or whatever. But, "Can you find your own way? What's your way?" And then, obviously, there's a lot of interfaces so that you're giving guidance, feedback, you know. Those become discussions that are negotiations rather than positions.

And you know, honestly, you have to learn your audience, just the same way you have to learn your class. When I was starting out, and even now coming to classrooms, not everybody looks like me. In fact, most people *don't* look like me. And so, what I've done is immersed myself and learned, to the extent that I can, who these people are and what that culture is. It's being fluid, balanced, and going back and forth between your own personal identity, where you come from, and making space for other people's identities and where they come from, and finding out what you want to teach, together.

It sounds like you see the voice coach as a facilitator of information for the client or student.

I love that word. That's the word I often use. I certainly use it in my social justice projects: facilitator; I don't even use the word "teacher." I mean, I sometimes have to when I apply for grants. But even then I tend to lean towards—I think of myself as—a facilitator. I think that also in my conservatory work as well. There is, perhaps, a different kind of agenda because I'm inheriting that agenda to do our curriculum, to some extent. There's a requirement: these students have to learn *this*. I'm not saying that that doesn't occur in other situations. But in some of the projects that I'm doing, as I'm writing or imagining what this class or workshop can be, I'm thinking in terms of possibility, inclusion, and stuff which has to do with what *they* want, rather than my employer saying, "Well, they need to know the IPA by this date." (laughs) In those situations, it's fascinating to figure out, "How do I meet those qualifications and requirements and still keep a feeling of humanity going so that I'm not excluding other possibilities within learning?"

I would say that it's also about self-reflection, your evolution, and paying attention to yourself in relationship to others. And enjoying, hopefully—because otherwise, why are you doing this?—enjoying that process of evolution. That still means that there's joy in claiming your space. There is this foundation of, "I'm good at this" or, "I love this and I want to share it with other people." I think the way you continue—and the way I certainly feel about myself—is that I'm not comfortable, in the sense that I have to constantly challenge myself if I *am*. If I become this sort of sitting-on-the-law kind of guy, then I think it's the death of my work. I always need to stay hungry, stay passionate, to challenge myself. I think that's something that often comes baked into the situation if you're new. And I think that's something you have to strive to keep alive as you have more experience doing it. I don't think it's something that any teacher at any level can relinquish.

At this juncture in your career, what gives you the most joy in teaching and coaching?

What really gives me the most joy is seeing other people discovering themselves, discovering their potential through the work, and realizing that they can own it. It's just thrilling to see that. And it's even more thrilling to see them sustain it, because sometimes there's an "ah-ha" moment but it goes away. Part of my job is to support people in sustaining it. Very often, I think, a lot of that sustaining does come from discipline, responsibility, a sense of trust in oneself, and those, sometimes, you can't really teach.

I've noticed a throughline of almost insatiable curiosity in people who are in this field.

I've kept looking and digging for other parts that I felt were growing *me*. Pieces of the field of life, I should say, that were growing *me* and came out of a hunger and a quest. To me, that's what learning and teaching is: a hunger and a quest. So, I found that if I pulled from other sources, it would not only rejuvenate my thinking, but sometimes I'd be able to bring some of that into the classroom. I mean, I studied Chinese medicine, Qi Gong, acupressure, and all those things. And some of that I was able to actually bring into the classroom. I had to be discerning because I wasn't teaching, you know, acting students how to stick needles in people, for example. (laughs)

What kinds of movement and energy training have you found complementary to your work?

I started off with Alexander Technique. I studied Feldenkrais, which I thought was wonderful. Suddenly my body became an acting body; it felt like the connection between what was happening in my body and what was happening in the text or the scene became clear. And, of course, how you relax and open your body for breath and voice is useful. I studied Tai Chi and I also studied Qi Gong, both of which deal with energy, both of which taught me a lot about not only centering but also about economy of effort in terms of movement and being precise in the body.

How do you assess people fairly? What does that look like?

Yeah, that's a really good question. I look for outcomes of the ability to efficiently convey your interior through your voice with economy of effort, as well as with a clarity of connection between what you're feeling and thinking and what you're saying. And a physiological understanding of how your body works in varying circumstances, demanding circumstances of emotional context, as well as complexity of language. But then, I still have to take into account to some extent where the person is starting and the amount of effort and work that they're putting into it. Not effort like tension, but thoughtful discipline: going home and doing the work, exercising, making it their own, and then coming to a place where they experience growth and alteration. And they achieve more efficiency, more clarity, more ability to express the inner truth within their communication.

Hard, isn't it?

Yeah, it's really hard. When I went to school it was pass/fail.

If you could, standing where you are now in your career, speak to your younger self and give him some guidance that would help him thrive on his journey, what would you say to him?

I guess what I would say to him is, "Don't worry." Because if I look back, honestly, there aren't really big regrets. I mean, I might wish that the world had been different or I was a different astrological sign. (laughs) I still could say, "I really wish *this* would have happened." But honestly, if at the end of the day I still feel healthy and alive and productive, and everything I did was for a good purpose, even if at the time I couldn't see it … And maybe that's part of being who I was. Some people are more confident; I don't think I had a lot of confidence. So, that might be something I could have said to myself. But even that is part of my evolution. You know, I don't really know what I would have said, except relax a little bit more about things.

Are there any other words of advice or inspiration for aspiring coaches that you might have?

Stay hungry. It's so important to be passionate about your work. Keep growing, keep learning. If you're a BIPOC person, I would say persevere and keep opening doors and keep challenging old paradigms. I think that's really important. And I would say that to anybody who feels othered. Those voices are so important to have at the table; they have a place and they're part of our culture. They, however, have been marginalized voices: people living with disabilities, older people, elders, youth, various kinds of voices, I want them there. I think they should have agency, they should own their property. And so, I would say if you're a voice person, if you can support somebody in having that agency and owning, then that's wonderful. That's a great gift, that you're supporting and giving.

PATSY RODENBURG

We have to be simple before we become profound, and the thing that we have to know how to do with everyone we work with is how to embody the work.

What would you like to say to aspiring voice coaches?

The thing that I want to say to people all the time is there are many doors into the same room. This division on the planet … We have to teach in the time we live in. And we have incredible skills as voice people that are so required on the planet. We only have a short time to save the planet. And we have to bridge the divide; we have to find stories that matter to everyone; we have to learn to debate without rancor and rage and heckling. *We* have the skills. We have to change—we could be so relevant. We could be *so* relevant, or we could be so *ir*relevant. We become *ir*relevant when we start spatting with each other, saying, "This is the only way to do it." Because that is not true.

I've been teaching for forty-five years. There are things that I taught when I was young I know now were wrong and are not appropriate anymore, and really are not the source of what we do. We have to go back to the source. It's so easy to live in a sort of cosmetic world where we change a voice, we do this, rather than understanding the profoundness of what we do. We have to be simple before we become profound, and the thing that we have to know how to do with everyone we work with is how to embody the work. I meet a lot of voice people who are good at *explaining* the work, but you have to *embody* it. You have to teach people how to embody it. And that's called "craft" and, I don't know, that word has become a filthy word for whatever reason. It is not. A chef is allowed "craft." A musician, a dancer, is allowed "craft." A hairdresser has a craft. And yet, when actors talk about "craft"—not all, not all the great ones, and, my God, I've been lucky enough to be in the room with all of those people, just about—they don't hiss at the word "craft." Because it's about knowing how to work sequentially and simply in order to produce profound experience. So that's where I am in some ways: embodiment.

When you think of embodiment and how the teaching of that craft has shifted, what do you think is really the place that's crying out for attention?

What I think happened—and, you know, that's the great advantage of having lived through certain phases of these things, you know, if you hang around long enough, you start to see patterns—it's the most expensive part of a training. So, the quickest thing to make your budget balance is to take away the craft training. Now, if I'm honest and if you're honest, we know that we cannot train a voice, particularly a voice that has been bombarded by Western technology and the way that we live, so that humans are now not using their breath, not using their body, are communicating on tiny little instruments which disconnect and disconnect and disconnect. So, it takes a lot of time and money. On one level, on the practical level, heads of department just cut the craft training. But we cannot expect to train a voice that has been riddled with habits that have blocked it. The voice is blocked. Now, I have been lucky enough to work on certain parts of the planet, in certain places, where that doesn't happen and their voices are still there. When I first worked in Soweto with the Zulus, I found their voices absolutely and completely free, because nobody's blocked.

You know, I don't think Shakespeare's actors were blocked vocally. Although he did train his actors, think the fundamental instrument was there because they walked. You know, the average person walked fifteen miles a day. They were in their bodies. They weren't walking on flat, hard surfaces. They were walking on rough ground, so they're keeping balance: their body, their feet, their knees are fluid, they're moving. This is why so many people feel present when they're out in the country-side. They're suddenly walking on rough ground and they re-enter their body. They reembody themselves. Until you enter your body, you can't breathe. And if you can't breathe, you can't use your voice, or think, or feel, or power yourself. So, on one level, I think it started with incredible cost-cutting. I remember in the 80s people writing to me saying, "Can you write to my dean to say that this work is essential?"

You can't do it in a semester, right?

No, you can't do it two hours a week. But the other thing that I think has plagued us upon the age of reason, and this is why it's connected to conservation and saving the planet, is that education has become so left-brained. It's just about data. The humanities …

Rubrics, right? But how can you "rubri-cise" a voice?

But a human being? How can you not have the imagination, and the freedom, and the chaos, and the metaphor, and all those things that have been knocked out of education? I've been lucky enough to work with Dr. Ian MacGilchrist, author of the seminal, *The Master and His Emissary* which is about left and right brain. We got together because he said, "You can embody the work. I can explain it." But the practitioner, the craftsperson, has been mocked for the last thirty years.

And then of course, the need for ensemble, which is another word for community. We need community. I mean, remind my students that the word "civilization," what it deeply means is that the individual is important, but the group is more important. So, in leadership now, we have to teach people to serve the community. To serve the planet, not themselves.

Do you see voice coaching and teaching as the same?

Teaching is different to coaching. Teaching is a long-term journey. Now I've spent my life doing everything. I realized a while ago that I coached in some of the biggest companies for twenty-seven years or so. And that included the Royal Shakespeare Company, The National, where I set up the department, all these places. And on average, over those years, I opened forty-five shows a year.

How do you advise teaching and coaching, when it feels uncomfortable?

Well, it is uncomfortable. Number one, let's just admit that it's uncomfortable. And let's just admit that we have to hold a safe space. Nothing profound or nothing dangerous can happen until the space is safe. Whether it's completely ever safe … But somebody has to be in control. But what happens organically after a while, and this is what happens in ensembles and teams, the sports teams that I work with, that they feel safe enough for the group to control themselves. I mean, in the 70s when I was at Webber Douglas, it was the first drama school in the UK that actually taught Black actors to be classically trained actors. The first thing I say to all my actors, and I would say this differently to non-actors: "I will treat you, I am going to train you, as a lead actor. End of issue. If you don't want to be a lead actor, then I won't push you. I will raise the bar. Because I would be immoral not to treat you as a lead actor. Then it is your decision … Between us in the group, I'm going to treat you as a lead actor."

I love that. That's a really wonderful opening.

"These are the rules that I work with because I need to keep the safe space and I *will* keep the safe space. And if I feel that one of you is making it unsafe, I will stop immediately." What I teach in teaching is, as soon as something is wrong in the group, you have to stop it there and then. I made a huge mistake in my early teaching. I used to think to myself, "I'll give them three 'go's." And that's wrong. I think is it critical, and I do it [with] the top corporate people, is that if something is making others [uncomfortable], even if it's a roll of the eye, I'll say something. A top CEO the other week just said something so awful to one of his colleagues, and I said, "What did you say?" He said, "What's the matter?" I said, "You said something awful to that person." And I repeated what he said, and the person whom he said it to said, "Yes, it was awful." I said, "You can't do that." "Why not?" "Because it makes everyone [uncomfortable]." The thing that teachers have to understand is that, if you ignore it, they know that you've ignored it. So, you've given permission.

In classes, before we do anything complex, difficult, we have to make the place safe. And the place is only safe when everyone is fully present. They cannot be on their phone. They cannot be fidgeting in their bags. They can't be reading their speech when somebody is reading theirs. You have to keep a safe space. And until you do that, you can do superficial work, but you cannot do the necessary work that we need on the planet now. The safe space that I [create]: "The first thing you all have to do is to admit—you have to tell a story when you were wrong." Everyone in the room.

What a fabulous exercise.

I've set it up. And then I have to talk about when I'm wrong, and I often tell stories about when I got it *really* wrong. Then, each of them [has] to tell a moment when they had their mind changed. We cannot begin a debate unless you are prepared to admit that you could be wrong and that you might have your mind changed.

What do you think about the phrase, "perfectly imperfect?"

I like that. Because perfection doesn't exist. A great dancer once said to me, "I once did a perfect pirouette, but it was in class and nobody saw it." (Pamela laughs) There's a sort of lack of humility to think we can be perfect. And I don't mean that in a harsh way. I mean, it's just work. We just do the work.

This kind of circles back to where we started, talking about the journey. Failures are part of the journey, and successes, and moments of perceived perfection, whatever they may be. It's a quite metaphysical, beautiful gift to do what we do.

It *is* a gift to do what we do. It is. I mean, how lucky are we? How lucky are we? And I remind my students that in Shakespeare's time, "happy" didn't mean anything that you could ever sustain. It meant "lucky." "How happy some o'er other some can be!" This idea that we thought that we can have sustained happiness. No, we can be lucky. Every now and then we can be lucky. I don't want to go into too much of stoicism but, you know. (Pamela laughs)

Standing in the place that you are now with the experience that you've had, if there was something you could tell the young Patsy, whisper in her ear when she was twenty or something, what would you say to her?

Oh, God, there's too many things, I think ... I had a habit, and probably it's still there, that I don't have an opinion unless I've done a lot of work on it. I think very, very deeply and I prepare very deeply. But it has often come over as arrogance. In my youth, I think people are quite surprised that I've never asked for a job. I've just done the work and I've worked very hard. I mean, I still do huge numbers of hours, but the first twelve years of my [working] life, I was probably doing eighty hours of teaching a week to learn my craft. But I think I could have handled that better. Instead of saying "No, that's not right, because I've actually read a lot on that." I do admit when I am wrong, but I think that that was me having an unfortunate energy of thinking, actually, they haven't read the book ... So, I think that's what I would talk to myself about. I would say, "Look, you don't need to do that." I think a lot of my knowledge has come self-taught. And later in my life, I met extraordinary minds who got me, who absolutely got me. But I had to figure a lot out on my own and that does sometimes give an energy that is not particularly pleasant.

What a journey it is, right?

And it's still going on, I hope. I've got a lot to do. I still feel I've got a lot to do.

You have great vibrance ... I look at all that you've done and it's so impressive.

It doesn't happen by magic, does it? You get up and do it. You talk to any writer and they just say, "Whatever you do, you gotta get up and do it." And if you're lucky, the Muse visits.

Those days are wonderful.

The Muse has a little visitation. And, of course, it gets harder. It gets harder as you know more. It's easier when you know less.

PAUL MEIER

Rhetoric, in its broadest sense, is what we're all about. Perhaps without even knowing it, we are engaging in rhetorical strategies for more effective, memorable, and vivid communication.

How would you define a voice coach and what does that mean to you?

Well, I suppose it's important to notice that there is voice that we start with, and then there is speech. Voice and speech are uniquely, perhaps, human activity. The spoken word is hugely important and what the spoken word adds to text is immeasurable, as we know. So, gosh, it's such a big question for me. I like to dabble in all of it. Accents and dialects for actors are hugely important, more than a surface to the acting, but part of the storytelling and narrative and character definition —so, a hugely important ingredient in the art of storytelling and of theatre. I suppose that I would have to put that at the top of my personal list for things that I do. I also specialize, as you do, in heightened text. Getting to know ancient verse literature, that's an important part of it for me. Rhetoric, versification and meter are hugely important.

Rhetoric is one of those things that a voice coach, no matter who they are coaching, would benefit from a deeper understanding of.

Yeah, I mean, rhetoric's got a very limited and rather negative connotation in today's society. Mere rhetoric we dismiss. But, classically, rhetoric is the art of communication in its noblest, fullest sense. That's got to be of benefit to anyone in the entertainment business or to anyone who speaks in life or for a living. So yes, rhetoric in its broadest sense is what we're all about. Perhaps without even knowing it, we are engaging in rhetorical strategies for more effective, memorable, and vivid communication.

When I think of somebody new to the field of voice coaching, I wonder, how much of the nuts and bolts of things like rhetoric or IPA do you think a teacher needs to know?

Less than 1% of my clients know IPA; perhaps even fewer know the classical tropes of rhetoric. But I was certainly liberated by knowing them, and so to that extent I feel like it's a good idea to pass them on. One needs a little bit of science, I think, and it doesn't take more than a few hours to master the nuts of bolts and IPA so you have something scientific. But one can become entrapped in those disciplines because they are so demanding and so engaging and so very interesting that you can kind of get lost in that forest. You don't need to know the hundreds of names for all those forms, but simply to recognize that they're happening. To notice that there's a list of three, and that lists often go in three, and the second is more important than the first, and the third is more important than the second. That cumulative growth of enumerating the attributes of a particular thing that you're recommending … To recognize repetition and its many different rhetorical tropes is, I think, very liberating and enriching to your own skill.

How did you become Paul Meier the "IDEA" [International Dialects of English Archive] Dialect guy? Did you set out with this intention?

I had a wonderful phonetics teacher in drama school, Rose Bruford, back in London. Greta Stevens. I'm forever indebted to her: she turned me on to phonetics, and I took it all the way through drama school. It was an optional extra, but I took every option I could and realized that there was a scientific basis for my class clowning and for my irreverent mimicry. The scholastic justification of all that was nested within phonetics, I found. And so, it's been at the core of my speech work for fifty years now.

Did you set out to become a professional voice coach?

I was, very early on, given the opportunity to do some moonlighting, evening classes, drama school stuff. I never sought it, but it came to me and I found it very congenial. And it's been part of the matrix of my work forever. Sometimes I'll do more acting or directing, but teaching and coaching is at the core. There was a wonderful philosophy at Rose Bruford: you're a better teacher if you know how to act, you're a better actor if you know how to teach, so by the exercise of all of those skills you reinforce every other aspect of your skill.

There were people who saw the coach in you before you did and helped you see that potential in yourself.

Undoubtedly. Greta Stevens was someone who gave me one of the keys… she was a fabulous teacher. There was an English teacher in high school who [comes] to mind. And the lesson I learned from him … One day he made a mistake in class. And I think it was I or one of my classmates who pointed out this error to Mr. Armstrong, and he considered the point we'd made. And he said, "You are right! And I am wrong! Splendid!" So, his absolute humility and his delight that we had found an error, and could point it out, pointed to the fact that you can't bring ego to the classroom. You can't bring the guru to the classroom. You've got to take delight in the students. That's the lesson that I learned from Mr. Armstrong.

What is the knowledge that we acquire as voice coaches in service?

We're storytellers. The art of storytelling is important, and whether we're talking about an actor or whether we're talking about an executive giving a presentation in a video conference, that oral communication is how we reveal our humanity and how we appeal to the humanity in others. How we make things vivid and memorable. How we make things stick. So that's what we're in service of. Making more effective, memorable, vivid, honest, and authentic human communication. Mostly, in our business, on the oral level. Overcoming the tyranny of literacy and re-embracing orality.

Do you think storytelling will always be important?

It's never ceased to be, as far as we can delve back into our own species' history. It has never failed to be important. And I think we can get side-tracked in thinking that special effects or whatever are important, but at the core of it all is vivid storytelling and vivid rhetoric. Effective, memorable, vivid communication. "Sparkle," as you call it. (laughs)

Are you still teaching in an institution?

No, I am retired. I'm a Professor Emeritus at the University of Kansas where I gave twenty-nine years, but all through those years I was in private practice also, which is one of the very nice things about working at a research university. You're expected to form an international and national reputation and to publish. So, from the start I found that very congenial, to establish private practice and to establish IDEA all those years ago. I don't think I could've done it without the security of an academic affiliation. No more formal academic affiliation since retirement, but plenty in private practice. I work with 60% performers and 40% professional voice users.

What is some of the advice you would give a new voice coach starting a career?

The more a beginning coach understands that they are a one-person company and that they are the CEO, they're research and development, they're everything to do with their own business until they get that personal assistant that will take a lot of that off of them … But even then, you've got to think of yourself as a one-person company fulfilling all of those different roles within that company. The business end of it should not be dismissed as any less creative than the so-called "art and craft" of what it is that you do.

Can you recall a challenging moment in your career?

I tell you what comes to mind immediately: finally meeting John Barton at his flat around the corner from Broadcasting House in London. I'd been a fan of his ever since those London weekend television Shakespeare seminars [*Playing Shakespeare*]. For years and years, I was this avid disciple from afar, and I had a sabbatical and I finally got to meet John Barton. And there I was at the feet of the master, expecting to hear him corroborate and emphasize all of his teaching that I had absorbed, only to find out that he had moved on and he was disavowing much of what had become my gospel. That was hugely disappointing, briefly, but liberating, ultimately. To know that there isn't one right way of doing anything or thinking about anything. Just as any doctrine can become dogma and die a slow or speedy death. If I ever find myself guilty of hardening my thinking into some kind of dogma, then I'll remind myself of the John Barton moment.

What are your thoughts on keeping a connection to the past but also being aware of the present climate of teaching and coaching voice?

We must always be aware of the second generation of students who hardened the masters' teaching into dogma and carved out territory and professional power-houses for themselves. That's one of the reasons I've never become a franchisee of any of the main systems of voice and speech. I value my independence and borrowing and stealing from all of them. You know, there's inevitably some territoriality in *any* system that's developed, and you've just got to not succumb to that religiosity.

Can you say more about the apprentice model, its impact on your evolution as a coach, and how you are passing on to the next generations?

Clearly, the tradition of master-apprentice is an important one. I'm actually a believer—in fact I'm a bit of a blasphemer in this—I believe in line readings. I've gotten into trouble over that, but I think at the essence there's nothing wrong with doing a respectful exact impersonation of the way your teacher did something. And that's the way it happened back in Shakespeare's company. You were hired to do a particular job *this* particular way, and when you'd mastered it, then you made it your own and then you could change it, and then you could teach that to the next generation. There's nothing wrong with learning how to play a concerto the way *this* particular artist did. I think there's today too much lip service to the "authentic freedom that I essentially have." Well, you know, when you're eighteen years old you don't have very much authentic freedom because you haven't *lived* very much. So, learn the discipline, learn the skills, imitate your teachers, imitate the experts. When you are proficient at that, *then* you will be an expert in your own right, and you can change the tradition. But absorb the tradition first, I think.

How would you advise a new voice coach to continue building their knowledge base?

I would say, don't be a dilettante, don't be a tourist. Don't just go around skimming off the cream of this system or that system. Certainly, embrace one system, one method, for a while until you understand it. But don't shut the door to walking into other studios, where perhaps a diametrically opposed system is being preached. Find out what's going in there. You'll steal from all sources, I would say.

Do you approach how you coach actors or professional voice users differently?

You know, essentially, I think it's the same job. You want to be an effective communicator. You want the words to seem fresh and freshly inspired. Almost anybody who speaks professionally for a living needs to give it that "in the moment" spontaneity and every actor needs that, of course. So, looking for the things that are fundamentally the same in voice coaching, I think, will keep you healthy. Look for the things in common.

ROS STEEN

We have to confront ourselves and all the things that hold us back, or we deflect,
or where we're not going or afraid to go. You have to negotiate in yourself because
that's the only way you can negotiate with someone else, or provide that space
for them to negotiate and to understand what it is that's going on in the moment.

How do you create a career in voice?

Well, I've never built a business; my experience is not like that. I don't have a
website. It's all word of mouth. It's all reputation. I think initially it finds you,
but it's what you do with the opening it presents and the relationship you're
able to forge and build on, slowly and creatively, with whomever asked you
in. Whether it's directors—sometimes it's actors, actually—I've come into it
because actors have asked. But relationships aren't built overnight. They're
built very slowly. They're about reciprocity. It's not just, "What are you doing
for the director?" But, "What is the director doing for you?" It's about the
conversation; education is a conversation between two generations about what
is important. But if I'm not working with somebody who recognizes that I am
a creative artist in my own right, then I'm only going to get so far. You know?
You are making a creative contribution to the production. We are creative
artists. We work from our own creativity. And we contribute creatively to
production in the same way that the lighting person is a creative contributor,
costume makers, you know?

What do you recommend for practitioners for holistic listening—not just hearing,
but listening?

To me, the technique through Nadine George voice work. We're not just working on our voices, we're working on that level of being open as a generous
human being. You see something in the cells of the body, in the muscles of the
face, you stay alert to tiny changes just before they happen, or you intuit what
might happen and you might suggest somebody go on a note or whatever. It's
not about what you want for somebody else, that they should be doing *this*. If
you haven't confronted yourself—and that's what an artist is—if you haven't
confronted everything you need to confront in yourself, you are not going
to help anybody else that way. You know? Because you will come up against
the limitations of yourself the whole time. You have to work on yourself all
the time.

It's not about doing refresher courses in that sense. But all of us who teach
the work *do* the work. We stand with the student, we put ourselves through
it, and we have to confront what it throws up for us. We have to confront
ourselves and all the things that hold us back, or we deflect, or where we're
not going or afraid to go. You have to negotiate in yourself because that's
the only way you can negotiate with someone else, or provide that space for
them to negotiate and to understand what it is that's going on in the moment.

What are qualities that are important to possess in this field? I hear you say a deep, holistic listening and a building of trust in relationships.

Yes, absolutely. And the ability to keep confronting yourself and working on yourself. Your voice and yourself. I mean your *life* when I say "yourself"; you have to work on life. That is the whole essence of Nadine's work. Yes, you can use it just for vocal technique to get some more notes in your voice or some nonsense. It's not about that. It's about the connection between your voice and your life, and how they both develop together. You have to look fearlessly at yourself and you have to work with your resistances. If you don't go on working on yourself, not just working on your creativity but on *yourself*, you will come to a point when you can't take somebody any further because you'll come to your *own* limitations within them. If you're not centered in yourself, you won't center other people.

Yes, we can learn about muscles. Yes, we can learn about phonetics. But if you haven't worked on yourself, *none* of these things will work, deep down, when you teach. The reason that people gravitate towards this work, or have fears about it, is because that's what it's saying at the root. The work comes from Alfred Wolfson, it comes from the First World War, it comes from the voices of dying soldiers. Yes, it's used for artistic practice, but it comes from our common humanity. "How do we live as a human being and how does the voice work?" If your life and your voice are not connected, it doesn't matter how many voice exercises you do, in my view. Yes, you can make a sound. Yes, you can make the sound more balanced, resonant, and richer. But is that doing anything for that person? Have they been connected with who they are, what they are, what they work with in themselves?

I'm interested in what you said: you can't authentically teach or coach unless you face your own walls or blocks.

You have to learn how to stand in yourself. As a person who wants to please, or wants everything to be alright, stand your ground: "This is it, this is me, this is who I am, this is what I have. And if other people don't like it or don't want it, there we are. But I'm not going to make myself smaller." It takes a long time to stand in yourself, not be swayed by other people's opinions, not be made to feel, "I've done something wrong." In a rehearsal, I have learnt that if it's wrong, it's *fine*. Because it will lead that actor to what's right. It will lead that director to ratify something. Whereas most people have been—paradoxically—silenced for a long time. And often.

There was something about the beginning when I met Nadine, when I saw the work. It made sense. It made so much sense, not just to my head. It made sense in my body, my heart, my soul. It just made total sense on all levels. For years, all the time I was learning things, I never came out feeling bigger. I always came out feeling smaller. Even if people were the nicest people. (laughs) And it's not a lack of giving other people their due respect, if they've earned it. It's not a lack of recognizing that other people's level is greater than your own. It's hard to explain this, but I came out feeling smaller. My acid test now is, "Am I having to make myself smaller in some way? Do I feel smaller with this? Or do I feel *in* myself? Can I accept myself? Can I respect myself?"

It seems to me that you pretty quickly go into helping people, head on, look at fear, whatever that fear is that lies underneath for them. Whether it's the sound of their voice or the ultimate fear of death. And in some ways, that is the human journey. That is the journey of our characters, often: addressing, overcoming, facing, running from fear.

I negotiate fear all the time. With anything artistic or creative there will always be something saying, "You're not good enough, not smart enough, not clever enough." It doesn't matter how successful you are; actually, sometimes the more successful, the more fear you have. There's always a moment when you want to move forward and something's holding you back. And if you don't negotiate that space, you'll never be great. (laughs) It's not going to go away. It's how you work with it and how you come to recognize, "Oh, here's the old demon coming back in." What happens when you work practically in making these sounds is you'll come about the moment of fear. You can see the brain go, "This is too high, my voice is going to crack and break, I can't make this sound." Taking that away in the moment and just saying, "Whatever it is that you do, do it! Yes, you can!" Bang, and they're through it. So, actually, through the voice they're negotiating fear.

What gives you the most joy in teaching?

Working with ex-students in their professional life, seeing where they've got to. I have actors that come and continually research the process. Also, getting to watch someone for the first time consciously realize just how powerful they are. Because they hear it in the voice that comes out of them that they didn't think they could make. And then the question is, "Why do I not feel like this in real life? Why do I not feel like this all the time?" And that can begin to open up their life. This is huge. When these sounds come out of them, they realize just how powerful they are, what their life force is, and when they question, it has implications: "Why am I not feeling like this in real life? This is how I would want to feel."

How would you name what you do?

The terminology is difficult and it depends on where you are. I tend to use "voice specialist" because it's not necessarily theatre-specific. If it's in more of a theatre performance context, I really will always try and take the word "coach" out. I mean, some companies will just do it because that's what they do in their program notes. But, truly, when they send it to me I always say, "I don't call myself a 'coach'." Why do we find the words "voice director" so hard? Open any program: "movement director." They could be doing one dance, they could be doing the whole show, no problem.

Or "Fight director." It's not called "fight coach."

Why are we diminished by that? Partly because, maybe, women did it to begin with. It's old fashioned.

In the US, "vocal designer" is what we're starting to see now. Like a scenic designer or costume designer.

I understand why that is, but I don't think it's up to me to design it. It then puts me in the wrong creative place. "Voice direction," which is what one is doing when working on a deep level with text and voice, is one thing. I wouldn't use that unless I'm doing a specific level of work within a show. Otherwise, I just have "Voice: Ros Steen" or "Voice and Dialect: Ros Steen." Something like that. We have to get to "voice director." We have to get there somehow.

The resistance is in the directors in a way that it's not with movement. And that's traditional. That's got long, long roots, because *they're* supposed to know about the text and voice and everything. And they don't want voice people—some of them, thank God I don't work with them—interfering with their actors and giving them ways of saying things or, I don't know, acting suggestions that might be something the director hasn't thought of, sometimes doesn't want. I always say when I work with directors, "If I say anything that is not right or not useful in the end, put it in the bin. I'm not wedded to all these suggestions, but I will give a proposition because a concrete proposition will always get you to the right place, even if it's the wrong proposition."

Is there any advice you have for the aspiring voice "specialist" or anything you might have done differently, looking back on your career?

Is there anything I would have done differently? No. It's only through this sustained work that I stand in myself and have a measure of my life experience. If you could have done it differently, you would have. That's what I think. You don't know where you're being led. You might think you know where you're *going*, but you don't know where you're being *led*. My advice is the person who has the voice is the one who deep down, on an unconscious level, knows what they need. *Your* job is to have the right conversation with them that enables them to teach you.

SARA MATCHETT

Feel what it feels like for you in your body and in your spirit, really feel, before you venture out to experiment with other bodies.

How do you identify as a voice coach?

I teach at the Centre for Theatre, Dance & Performance Studies at the University of Cape Town, probably the oldest theatre school in the country attached to a university. It has a beautiful mixture between following a conservatoire model and an academy model. This ensures an ongoing conversation between practice and research. My main area of pedagogy is voice. In the past couple of years, particularly since 2016 following the #RhodesMustFall and #FeesMustFall movements in South Africa, there has been a rigorous shift to decolonizing the curriculum.

Could you share more about decolonizing curriculum?

We used to teach and assess voice, movement, and acting, for example, separately. They each had their own course code. What we have done at the Centre for Theatre, Dance & Performance Studies is to collapse all of these course codes and, instead, follow a studio model. For example, in the acting studio, voice and movement and acting form part of that studio, which has one course code. This means that assessments are no longer separate. The decision was primarily inspired by the context in which we locate. In Africa, performance is not delineated into these different categories. Performance is inclusive of movement, dance, song, voice, acting, and storytelling.

I think that integration can be a common challenge.

One of the challenges we faced was getting students to think about performance as inclusive of acting, voice, and movement, rather than seeing them as separate stand-alone courses. Students tended to box these and could not apply what they were learning in movement to the voice class, voice to the movement class, or movement and voice to acting. Further to this change, we looked at the kinds of texts we were teaching. For example, our second year acting stream focuses on heightened texts, where traditionally the focus would have been on Shakespeare and Greek Tragedy. One of the things we did was to include West African Dramatic texts into the curriculum. These texts are written in English; however, the metaphors and the imagery in the texts are embedded in the African continent. I observed a sense of kinship with the material on the part of the students.

Another thing we have done is to work with professional translators to translate Shakespearean texts into different South African languages. I don't think it's something the students can necessarily do on their own, hence the need to work with translators. It has been and continues to be an exciting exercise. We've also started to work translingually by combining different languages that are spoken in South Africa. A recent example of this is how students worked in Afrikaans and isiXhosa, two of the eleven official languages spoken in South Africa, to make a work based on *Hamlet*.

As a department, we have always tended to focus on choral work. Africa has a rich tradition of choral work and singing. What we have done is to work more intentionally with this. We have also started to rigorously engage students in processes of adapting texts from the Global North. What this does is enable them to find their own way into these seemingly foreign texts.

Do you co-create those in the class with your cohort?

Yes, the students become co-creators. The idea of collaboration, co-creation, co-meaning making, co-sensing, is key to the way I work. As the teacher, I am part of this collaboration. The other thing we do in the Centre, and have been doing for a long time, is to teach acting and theatre-making in different languages, namely English, isiXhosa, and Afrikaans. These languages are the dominant languages of the Western Cape, where the university is located.

The university's primary language of instruction is English, which means that the students have to do the English component of acting or theatre-making. They also have a choice of doing acting or theatre-making in either isiXhosa or Afrikaans. This means that students also get to learn and work in their mother tongues. In the theatre-making stream, students are given the opportunity to make their own work and tell their own stories. This, in itself, is a decolonial practice. It allows them to locate themselves in the world through their work.

How are you approaching generational trauma with your students?

It's not only about trauma held in the body. It's also about the trauma in the spaces the students are learning in. For example, we are based at a satellite campus that was the original university campus. Before that, it was a place for holding slaves, for the buying and selling of slaves. This history is embedded in the buildings; this colonial history which encompasses deep pain and trauma is embedded in the walls and the floors of the buildings.

That gives me goosebumps.

Many conversations are around how to grapple with our bodies that hold generational trauma. Additionally, in South Africa, the levels of violence are excessive. Particularly violence against women. We have some of the highest rape statistics in the world, if not the highest. As a result, particularly Black women and queer students' bodies are armored. This, in my understanding, leads to a disconnect between body, heart, and mind.

One of the big eye openers for me was doing Fitzmaurice Voicework with first-year students. It appeared to be too much for them because the work asks you to feel deeply in your body. This was a traumatic experience for some of the students. Consequently, I have had to adapt how I teach the work. One of the changes I have made is to start teaching it in the 3rd year, when students seem more equipped to manage what comes up for them in their bodies. Another challenge has been the combination of students who come from very disparate contexts in the same class. Some students come from rural, very poor contexts, violent contexts, and other students come from opulence and privilege. This comes with its own set of complexities. How I navigate working with bodies that hold trauma, tension, generational trauma, generational memories—whatever you want to call it—in their bodies, has presented significant challenges. What I have learnt is that there is no prescribed way of dealing with this.

Every class is different, and every year is different. As a teacher, I have learnt to become responsive from moment to moment. I have learnt to hold space for whatever presents itself in the moment. A major learning for me has been around how I hold space without imposing my privilege. Being a white South African means that I constantly need to check my privilege. There is no space for making assumptions. The way I pitch the work is critical. For me, being utterly present in myself to allow for my own intuition to lead how and what I teach, as well as the material I teach, has been vital. This has been the only way, really, because there is no textbook. (laughs) There is no textbook for this. It's something that I think, as teachers, we're all constantly grappling with.

What gives you the most joy in teaching and coaching these days?

Those moments when something clicks in the students' bodies, where there's an embodied understanding. Sometimes this happens in the classroom, and sometimes it happens many years later, after the students have graduated. The other day, a student I taught eight years ago WhatsApp messaged me to say, "Sara, Vipassana!" At first, I wasn't sure where he was going with the message and then he said, "I did Vipassana and all I could hear was your voice in the voice class, and it all suddenly made sense. What you were telling us suddenly made sense!" I have had students come back to me after they have graduated to say, "Oh my gosh! I *now* know where my transverse abdominis is!" "It now makes sense, now we get you." "We thought you were mad …" (laughs). One of the biggest lessons has been to trust that the work will find its way and click when needed.

What would you say are qualities that a voice coach should cultivate?

Deep listening with the entire body so that you have that ability to respond in the moment to whatever presents itself. I've found that cultivating a daily practice for myself has facilitated an openness in my own being. It enables me to be present somatically, entirely present in every moment. Certainly, working with Catherine Fitzmaurice enabled a big shift for me in understanding breath, particularly the relationship between breath and felt perception, breath and intuition, and breath and imagination. The ability to listen deeply with your entire being is crucial to enabling responsiveness in the moment; it facilitates the process of tapping into intuition. And awareness of breath is key to this.

What would your words of advice be to your younger self?

Remain curious. I come back to the importance of having your own practice and expanding on that practice. I've learned to explore with my own body first and make discoveries before going into the classroom. This is important. It's important to feel what it feels like for *you* in your body and in your spirit, really feel, before you venture out to experiment with *other* bodies. Trust in your intuition, go slowly, and let go of the need to "get it right." You don't have to achieve everything all in one go, all in one year, even in three or four years of training. It's within you; it's *in* you. Trust this.

What interests you now?

I'm really interested in exploring the integration of breathwork as it is taught in mindfulness practice and voice. I am currently studying to be a breathwork practitioner. I'm interested in working with women, outside of the context of performance, to understand what it means to find voice, philosophically and pragmatically. I don't believe there is anyone who is voiceless. We all have a voice. All that is needed is for us to access tools that will assist us in finding our voices. I think that breathwork practices provide a solid foundation for this. I am interested in working with women in leadership positions and women in communities. Currently, I'm working with a group of sex workers as part of a research project, and I've been doing voice work with them as a way into performance-making. The experience has been incredible. We've engaged in tremor work, free-writing, and poetry creation to explore the idea of voice as a generative tool. It's been fantastic working with people outside of the context of formal actor training or performance. This is certainly something I would like to explore more.

SCOTT MILLER

You don't have to know how that's going to happen; you don't have to know when that's going to happen. Just know that it's going to happen and be open for it and to it.

You've coached actors and professional voice users and trained teachers. You've done all of it. So, how do you identify yourself in the field?

What we teach is communication, right? So, I don't ever call myself a "vocal coach" because the title becomes very limiting. And, I have no way of getting inside their history to understand what that means to them at all. So, if they see me as a specific thing that's a title, suddenly there will be incredible biases associated with the interaction. And there's incredible biases associated regardless, just by them looking at me, by them hearing my voice. I'm dealing with years and years of history for both of us in this interaction. It's an interesting question when I'm dealing with non-actors or professional voice users, which is fundamentally almost everybody, frankly. (laughs)

Even in a silent meditation, you're still using your voice.

Exactly. So, for non-actors, what I'm most interested in doing is affecting, impacting leaders of the world, people who are making systemic decisions that affect large masses. I'm trying to get the work that I do to them, with the hope that when they're in the work they will be exposed to information that will influence their decision-making.

It sounds to me like it's important that the voice has an element of listening to it.

Absolutely. Voice is the vehicle by which I can get into the room, but ultimately, it's breath. Breath is inhaling and exhaling, or holding: doing neither. And neurologically we find there are specific things that happen when you're inhaling, when you're exhaling, and when you're doing neither. We find that that's deeply connected to decision-making, interpretation, bias, anxiety, and sensorial information: the way we literally take in information through our skin, which is the biggest information taker.

So, if I can get in these rooms and work with these people, I'm not trying to sell them anything. I don't have a stake in the game. As a scientist, it's not my job to sell dogma or policy. My job is to share information. And I believe, once that information is shared, different outcomes will occur.

What qualities are important for a voice coach to cultivate?

I think, fundamentally, it's not so much for coaching or teaching. It's about being human, which is… I mean, how deep do we want to go here?

Why not, right? (laughs)

I believe we all have a wound growing up, because we're in the powerless position of being a child for a long time, eighteen years or so. And we develop an adaptation from the wounds. Depending on what that adaptation is, that adaptation becomes your superhero skill because you're redundantly using it. You've become a master of it. Most of the time, it's in the survival direction because you're trying to gain power where you can. So, a lot of times that superhero power, that adaptation as you grow up and go out into the world, gets used in a kind of negative or survivalist way. If you're fortunate enough to understand what your superpower is, you can actually use it in the other way, which is more upbuilding, generative, growing. It's really important for whomever the individual is that wants to go into teaching to know what their superpower is. You can start to find it by what you're curious about and about what people keep saying, "Wow, you're really good at this."

Don't be distracted by the circumstantial title of the job, because that has nothing to do with it. It's not the "vocal coach" part. What within vocal coaching are you obsessed about? Are you like, "Don't people see this? Why isn't anybody talking about it?" Or "I am so interested in this for some reason." And that will become your "way in." That will be *your* contribution to the world because you will become an expert. Because that's your point of view, that's how you see everything. Instead of getting too lost on, "Okay, what job title am I good for?" Because that's how people are talking to you generally: "Oh, you're going to be a lawyer, you're going to be a doctor." But what *kind* of lawyer are you going to be? What *kind* of doctor? What *kind* of teacher?

Know that you're always going to have one main bias that you really love. And usually, those people who have your learning style will be your favorite students. They'll be those students that are like, "They're so smart! They seem to get it!" And other students will be the resistance students: "Oh, my God, how clear do I have to be? What's their problem?" Know that that's just you, it's all coming from you. It has nothing to do with them.

So, you see teaching as a collaborative experience?

Oh, yeah. There's nothing else going on. This is what I would say to people: if you understand what I'm saying to you, then you already knew it. If you didn't know it, how can you understand what I'm saying to you? It doesn't make any sense, logically. So, if that's true, if you already know what I'm "teaching" you, then what am I actually doing here? I may be reminding you; I may be repositioning information in a way that different synapse connections happen in your brain. But that's fundamentally all I'm doing and I'm hoping you're doing the same to me.

So, when you challenge me on something or when you ask me to explain in a different way because you don't quite understand, that's giving me the opportunity to reorganize *my* brain in a different way, in a different perspective. That's the kind of, like, quid pro quo. You give me 100% of your attention, you do your homework, you come curious, I'll do the same thing and this explosion will happen, and then we'll go home. And that's it. And if we can keep doing that day after day, we will build a knowledge base of the way we approach the world, of ourselves, of others.

I'm thinking about your teaching of breath. Maybe it's your therapeutic background meeting your intellectual curiosity meeting whatever's in the room in front of you.

Yeah, absolutely. And that's why we do this thing [in the Miller Voice Method] called "the act of breath" because what we find is, when we're in our cardiovascular experience, flow is happening, right? It's a life and death experience. You're not holding your breath when you're running. There's a primal, fundamental understanding of the brain: "Don't stop the flow or else we're going to die." Fundamentally, in the way the world deals with itself organically, that's the basic structure: stop moving and you die. When flow stops in anything, death is pretty close and disease starts.

So, we start from that place of getting the breath continuously moving. Neurologically what we found over time is that, when the breath is continuously moving, we tend to be more in the right side of our brain: the somatic, present, creative part of the brain taking in present information. When we're holding our breath or interrupting the flow, it gives us greater ability to go into the left part of our brain, which is the more analytical, the language center, the past, the future.

For acting and maybe even for life, that's not super helpful because we're not going to take present information in. And, most importantly for acting, we're going to start to regurgitate, in a way, our rehearsal and present what we did in the past. I have this image of the cat that brings in the bird it just killed and drops it on the floor. This is what I see actors do all the time: they're bringing in the rehearsal that they've experienced, which is dead now, and they drop it on the stage and say, "Here, audience, look, aren't I great? Isn't this a great idea that I worked on?" And it's not the way we experience life.

We want to see them chase the bird.

Exactly. In acting what I see a lot, or in presentation, is that we're in this old idea of self, thinking that the present idea of self won't be enough. And so, there's a kind of desperation that happens. The listener feels that, unconsciously or consciously. (Pamela laughs)

What brings you joy in your teaching?

I define joy as 100% occupation of my attention. Predominantly in one thing. I don't experience a lot of joy when I'm distracted, when I'm trying to multitask. I express a lot of anxiety in that place. Fundamentally, I'm trying to put my attention 100% on one thing at a time. And that's it. So, teaching becomes, to me—and the art of teaching is—can I bring 100% of my attention to the task at hand so that the only thing that presently exists is the thing in front of me? And when that can happen, there's a real sharing and collaboration of information. It suddenly opens up. When I'm thinking teaching is, "I'm here to give, in obligation, as an authority figure, as a status, in a sense of hierarchy," all these ideas are detachments from collaboration. I'm trying to constantly break those things down as quickly as possible in the room from the people that are projecting that onto me, and most fundamentally, in myself.

If you could speak to your younger self and give him some advice, what would you say to him?

You know, the person before you is the manifestation of a lot of asking those kinds of questions. They're incredibly important questions to ask oneself continuously. The person that you're talking to right now no longer asks that question because I fundamentally understand that I'm perfect, but for everything that has happened in my life in exactly the way it's happened. If someone said, "Okay, this is it. Tomorrow—in the next five minutes—you're gone." I'd feel like, "Well, I've had an amazing life and I'm so ready to go." *And* I'm so ready to stay. I'm so ready for whatever is in front and behind.

So, I would say it's okay. You cannot make a mistake. There are *no* mistakes. You're on a path, it's intentional, it's the only thing that can happen. And when thoughts come in to think otherwise, that's just you refusing to be curious. Sometimes you need to do that to survive and that's okay. It doesn't matter what you think about it. (laughs) You will just keep moving forward and making the choices you need to make with the life that you've been given.

Beautiful. Is there anything else I didn't ask you that you wanted to share?

I love that quote—whether he said it or not—from Einstein supposedly on his deathbed: "If only I had more math!" (Pamela laughs) Which is beautiful to me, because it's a recognition that we're *all* limited by the time and space we're born into. It's not that Meisner, Hagen, all these master teachers from the last century were wrong. It's just that they didn't necessarily have the information that we have. And frankly, considering the lack of this kind of information, it was amazing that they were onto some of the stuff they were onto. I feel the same way on some level. I feel like, "Oh, I just wish I were born a hundred years from now, the memory science and the neuroscience then! Oh, if I only had more of that now!"

So, there is this flow of intense satisfaction, joy, and release into the perfection of who I am in the moment, *and* an incredible sense of *dis*satisfaction and hunger for the experiences that I don't have. They both live together. It's not one or the other. Look, you can be incredibly joyful in your suffering. You can be incredibly joyful in your sadness, meaning you can be 100% occupied. Live in it, feel it, experience it, release it. And you will release it when it's more painful to hold on to it. You don't have to know *how* that's going to happen; you don't have to know *when* that's going to happen. Just know that it's going to happen and be open for it and to it.

STAN BROWN

Love is the breath that I'm taking in to speak the words that I'm speaking to you right now. It's my responsibility to remind myself that every breath I take is loving myself.

How do you identify as a voice coach?

I identify primarily as a coach in the college and university training system, but I do coach in the professional sector. I also teach teachers who have vocal exhaustion, attorneys, the occasional rock singer, someone who wants to give a speech at a wedding, that kind of thing, but primarily in a university.

What was your trajectory as a voice coach?

I grew up in a family of public speakers: teachers and preachers and musicians. My mom said I started singing solos in choir when I was three. Voice lessons came before college, and that kind of thing. And then when you start getting paid for doing it, of course, you start to have a relationship with your voice so that you can continue to get paid for doing it. (laughs) There's an awareness you develop about your voice. Then I went into broadcast journalism in college, and a number of things happened: my dad died unexpectedly, I got pneumonia, and all this stuff happened. So, I sat there and I thought, "Do you really want to be a journalist?"

And so, I went major shopping and theatre was the first place I went because the theatre department was the closest to my dorm. (laughs) I met with someone who ultimately became one of my mentors, and I just never looked back. I remember there was a moment when I realized that I wanted to teach *and* be an actor. I've never been happy *just* teaching or *just* acting. If I can have a little balance, then I'm good. And so, it just seemed logical and more familiar that, if I was going to teach, I should probably do what I've been doing most of my life and that is to focus on voice.

I understand Cicely Berry was one of your mentors.

Yes. I usually tell this story to my senior theatre majors: I was taking a trip home to the US [from London] for a gig. I was already out of the door of my flat, I was on my way, and I turned around and went back and got two books.

Which two books?

One of them was a dusty green speech pathology book, I can't remember the title of it. The other was *The Actor and His Text*—it was still called "*his* text" and [Cicely's] daughter made her change that later. But those are the two that I grabbed. I went to Coventry and caught the train, walked through several cars, and found the empty seat that was right across from her, not knowing it was her. I was reading the book in front of her and she saw me read the book. That started the whole thing where she invited me to a workshop, and then another, and then another, and then she invited me to be an assistant at an international voice conference. I was there for everything, until she said, "Darling, you really don't have to keep coming to these things." I think she was somewhat embarrassed that I was seeing the same thing over and over again sometimes. And I'm like, "I don't care."

It's never the same, though, is it?

No. She not only gave me a language and a way of being able to navigate what it means to support somebody as a voice person. She was my champion; she was there whenever I was going up for jobs and that type of thing.

Share with me, if you will, what love means to you in your practice as a voice coach.

Well, first of all, thank you for asking me that. That mentor that I went to when I was getting over pneumonia and becoming a theatre major—she's a very Southern lady from an old rich Southern family. She's still a dear friend. She said this at one time, and I practice it in my own teaching as well: "If I teach you, I have to love you." If I'm in the room with you, I have to love you. It's really just about how information flows when you are in that place versus how it flows when you're not. Loving is multifaceted. I'm not talking about the same thing you feel for a partner or child, but it's something similar. It's definitely about giving people do-overs, forgiveness, maintaining a flow and making space for a person and seeing their potential. And knowing that, regardless of what's going on in this moment, that life is going to teach them what it is that they might or might not be getting right now.

It sounds very healthy: "I love me and I'm here, and I love you and we're here."

I mean, love is the breath that I'm taking in to speak the words that I'm speaking to you right now. It's my responsibility to remind myself that every breath I take is loving myself. If I could do that—not even for an entire day—if I could do that for five minutes, that would help my mental health. Because I wouldn't be living at a deficit and wondering, "Where is love? Where is comfort? Where is encouragement?" I realize, "Oh, it's always there." If it wasn't there, I wouldn't be there. But we do live in a world where... we've been distracted from that "truth" into an external, physical reality where identity is "out *there*." And so, it sometimes takes tragedy for us to turn in and realize, "Oh, there's another whole wing of this house that we live in that we've been neglecting."

One of the things I preach to my students is, "If you can think of inner and outer reality as your home" —and I say that's 100%— "If you can have at least 51% turned inward and 49% turned outward, then you're doing okay." We do need the exterior. But we're never going to get our identity from "out *there*." Who I am and what I do are just two different things. My job is never going to feed my spirit in the way that cultivating an alignment with who I am can feed my spirit. I can enjoy my job, I can have lots of fun, it can enrich my life and all of that. But I am not my job. I am not going to be wishing that I worked longer hours on my deathbed. That's just not going to happen, you know?

What gives you the most joy in coaching?

It's that reoccurring moment when what I'm offering facilitates an inner connection for the student or client, and they realize that they can do something, or they know something that they didn't know, prior to the connection. That never gets old; that is always gratifying. One of the things that I say over and over again, and it gave me a great amount of peace early on, is that my goal as an educator is to become obsolete in the lives of my students.

How do you identify in this world of Equity, Diversity, Inclusion, and Accessibility? How do you help make yourself obsolete to your students in terms of them understanding who they are and how to be in the world more ethically and with more awareness?

I believe that I am not the path on which my students are walking. At best, I'm a pebble on that path. (Pamela laughs) I don't think it's my responsibility to teach somebody how to give and receive love. I can put you on the playground where you can discover that for yourself. I keep coming back to the fact that, whether or not one believes it, comprehends it, or accepts it, the universe is expanding. Full stop. We are always, always encountering that which we have not encountered before. There's always going to be new stuff coming at us. Is your belief aligned with that one truth that the universe is expanding? Are you consciously participating in your own evolution or are you being dragged along, kicking and screaming, and desperately clinging on to what used to be and what *should* be—what Stevie Wonder calls the "pastime paradise"? If one can just align with that, [that the universe is always expanding,] then they're doing their best with regard to diversity, equity, and inclusion.

It's not about perfection. It's not about being totally competent in every culture out there. It's understanding—what's that Stephen Sondheim lyric—"there's more to learn of what you know." Are you a student? Is learning still a part of who you are? Or is it about knowing? That's a big one. There are people who are so busy knowing [that] they don't have time to learn. It might give confidence, but for me it's the confidence of a stopped clock: It's going to be right twice in twenty-four hours, but it's still a stopped clock. It makes some people [feel] secure because they tell themselves, "I've got these answers." But it really is about one's ability to learn, not just one's ability to always know and have answers ready.

If you could look back and be the person on that train who put a hand on the shoulder of a young boy, what advice would you give your younger self?

I would've just listened to my heart more. We want the people we love to love us. So very often we will separate ourselves from what our hearts are telling us to do and we will do what other people want us to do. By doing that, we betray and become less acquainted with our intuition and with what ultimately guides us. Our inner GPS. If you really listen to your heart, your heart is not always going to tell you what you want to hear but it is never going to lie to you. If you can just get on board with that, that is the best possible place from which to drive the car. Anything that one would fear from following one's heart is miniscule compared to what one would [and should] fear if one betrays their heart's desire and chooses to do what someone else wants them to do.

That's a wonderful piece of advice. What would you say to an aspiring voice coach who's getting ready to start out?

In the field of bioethics, there is an oath that people take. I've often wished that teachers could take it as well. It begins with, "Do no harm." By harm, I think one has to define what that is. The focus of the work is comparable to the back of your head: you have a more intimate relationship with the back of your head than anybody else, but you see it less than other people see it. I, in my detached position, can tell you about the back of your head, can give you information about it, so that you can adjust it. But there are some people out there who [for the sake of manipulation and control] will make things up about what they see when they look at the back of your head. Perhaps, "Oh, you have a snake on the back of your head." That, for me, is harm. And so, if you know you have that perspective, then be incredibly responsible to it. When one gets that piece of paper—that degree, that certification—I believe that a good thing to buy into is, "Now the learning begins." If one truly is an expert, then I think one needs to be expert in learning.

WALTON WILSON

If you want to possess a voice that truly reaches an audience and, as they say, "disturbs the air," then you have to find your own voice and not an imitation of someone else's.

What brought you to teaching voice?

My first experience of doing voice work was at a workshop at Shakespeare and Company in 1981. Kristin Linklater was teaching there and I was early on in my professional life as an actor. That month with her not only opened me up, but opened up a world that I was unfamiliar with. A decade later into my career I had an opportunity to return to work with Kristin again at Shakespeare and Company. It was at that particular workshop that it struck me that this may be something I wanted to pursue.

So basically, I upended my life, sold everything I had, and moved back to New York and apprenticed with Kristin and one of her senior teachers, Andrea Haring, for several years. I was designated and started teaching soon after that. Some years later, I met Catherine Fitzmaurice and studied privately with her for about a year, and then was a member of her first certification class. I've worked a lot with other voice teachers, like Patsy Rodenburg and Richard Armstrong, and so I've always connected voice work to acting and I've always seen it as not "separate from" but just another "way in" to acting.

You came to voice coaching in an old school way of mentor-student. Right?

It was very much an apprentice-master teacher relationship that I had, certainly with Kristin and to some degree with Catherine. I felt a bit like that with Richard Armstrong, as well. It was always connected to my work as an actor. I mean, I don't have an MFA and I barely have a BFA. (they laugh) My real training as an actor was back in the day when regional theatres still had resident acting companies. It was, again, the kind of apprentice-journeyman model. If I was early on in my career today, I don't know that I would be able to teach in many institutions because I lack an advanced degree.

So, you felt a connection to individuals and wanted to learn how they do what they do?

Look, even though I'm a designated Linklater voice teacher, I am teaching *my* version of it. We all model ourselves after our teachers in the beginning, but if I don't continue to grow and develop, I'm going to be so bored and I'm not really doing the work because the whole purpose of the work is to go deeper and expand my capacity as a human being. If I'm just teaching a rote version of what it is that I've learned, I'm not really teaching. In the end, I've discovered—and this is not original by any means—that you teach who you are more than what you know. Yes, you share your experience, or your wisdom, or things that you have learned. But as a voice teacher, you're trying to reach something that is essential to that person in front of you. You're trying to teach something to their *person* more than to their brain. You're trying to teach to the individual rather than, "Here's a set of skills."

You can't ever let yourself get bored or stale because then you're not modeling that growth.

I'm constantly trying to renew myself. And particularly, if you do a lot of teaching, the tank runs dry a lot. You're learning a lot from your students, but you also need to be a student.

And you need time for synthesis, right?

Exactly. Time to walk away from it.

Sometimes walking away means walking *into*, you know?

Yes, exactly.

You said voice very much relates to acting for you.

Richard Armstrong talks about the voice as "the muscle of the soul": an audible manifestation of the state of being. It's a bridge between the inner world of the psyche and the outer world. It communicates the inner life of the individual to the outer world of the listener, both in life and on stage. This word has a lot of different connotations, but if the voice is *free*, (laughs) then it can reflect the inner world with great accuracy, revealing each actor's unique response to text, character, given circumstances. If you want to possess a voice that truly reaches an audience and, as they say, "disturbs the air," then you have to find your *own* voice and not an imitation of someone else's. The voice is unique, like a snowflake or a fingerprint.

I sense from you a quest to keep uncovering your own voice in service of your teaching and coaching.

Right. There's no one right way to do anything. Part of my job as a person who teaches actors is that I want to give the actor as many doors into the room, metaphorically speaking, as possible. If I say, "This is the *one* door you can go through," some people are not going to be able to access or even see the door. There are many extraordinary teachers who teach a single methodology, but my particular interest is broader than that. The divisions between these various vocal techniques are much more porous than what some people understand them to be. And that's become part of my practice as an actor, a person, and a teacher.

You are creating different lenses through which to teach and perceive.

Yes, and part of the way I do that is to see how their bodies—because the voice comes out of the body—to see how their psychophysical selves respond to different images, different stimuli, different directions. Some actors are going to gravitate toward one way or the other, and I have to then follow where the student is going and help guide them in that direction. Because that's what their instinct or their body is telling them: "Oh, this is helpful to me." But if I say, "No, you can't" and I have to, like, yank them back and push them through *this* door, that's not actually serving them in the way that I want to serve them. So, whatever technique I'm teaching has to be flexible enough to accommodate the individual standing in front of me. In the end, you can't teach everything you know.

In this particular cycle of my life as a teaching artist, I have been reducing things to, "What are the essential principles? What are the essential experiences that I want to give students?" Because when you're grounded in the fundamental principles and experiences, then you can do *anything*. So, that's been interesting to me in terms of identifying what is at the center of what we call "voice work" or "voice training" or "voice coaching" for the actor.

How much do you focus on anatomy with the people you teach?

I'm teaching actors; I'm not training them to be voice teachers. It's easy to overwhelm students with too much information. All the physiological structures that we're talking about are responding to thought, feeling, impulse. So, can I just get out of my own way so the body can figure out how to work on its own. If I say to someone, "This particular element in your anatomy isn't functioning as it needs to be," what the hell are they going to do with that?

I want to give actors enough basic information about how the voice works and why it works, and why it *doesn't* work sometimes. But my teaching has always been much more focused on imagery: using imagery to evoke a certain kind of physiological response, rather than saying, "This is exactly how this works in your body," which is prescriptive and can sometimes be overwhelming. This is my bias, right? If someone's interest is in teaching accents and dialects, I suspect an anatomical knowledge of that kind might be more useful to the student. But as someone whose basic focus is on voice production and text work, I'm not as concerned that they don't have that detail of information.

It seems like using images is really important in helping students connect to freeing their voices.

Well, the approach to voice training that I teach requires dealing with cause rather than effect. So, the exercises, the games, or the tools that I use are concerned more with rethinking usage than remaking sounds. Kristin would say, "You have to sacrifice your desire for results to the experience of causes." So, what I think of as "successful" voice work relies as much on mental attention and focus as it does on physical effort. If you try to achieve anything through physical effort alone, you're going to end up using more muscle than you need and there's a very good chance that you won't necessarily use the best muscles for the job.

Would you say "it's more mind than muscle"?

Yes! Because I played sports, it's a bit like if you're playing tennis you try to visualize the entire stroke of the racket. And then the brain turns that image into some physical action. The brain is given the pattern and left to work out the best way to achieve that activity, which usually means it engages the best muscles for the job. Right? When you're playing tennis, you're not thinking, "Oh, reach my right elbow back." You just do it. The great thing about teaching voice is that unless there's been some profound, psychophysical damage, people already know how to speak! They've *been* speaking for most of their lives. I'm not teaching anyone anything they don't already know on some level, but perhaps it's been forgotten or it's been covered up by years of socialization of some kind, or way of rethinking.

So, I think a lot of what I'm trying to do is help people redirect their energy, redirect their thinking in a way that's going to serve them. You're creating new neurological pathways from the brain to the body. Imagery, I think, is a really useful way to do that. And if you can do that without extraneous force or effort, then the results will be more in line with what it is I'm hoping to accomplish, which is a more free, open, connected, personal voice. So, I think imagery is vital. I think physical touch is vital. Imagery and what I think of as a sort of attitude, maybe. I think voice work is best done in a state of almost carelessness. Like, "I can do this" kind of confidence. Like, (snaps fingers) "Oh, yeah, I can do that! This is easy!" That mental attitude provides energy.

It's not pushed.

Yeah. Enabling the muscles to commit with appropriate force rather than holding, rather than withdrawing or pushing. It's a kind of energetic state of mind that comes from commitment and interest.

You talk about ease, an energetic state of mind, being able to have a wealth of metaphors, poetic language, inspiration, and a sense of physicality. These all sound to me like qualities that would be important for someone who's aspiring to coach to embody, connect to, and understand.

Yes, yes, yes. I'm trying to model this embodiment that I'm looking for, that I'm asking for. You know, I had a great acting teacher who ended up being a very successful director. He said, "I was a terrible, terrible actor" but he could *teach* acting. I think it's somewhat different as a voice teacher. I think it's true that you want to be able to embody what it is you're talking about, or at least be able to show the way through your own instrument.

NOTE

1   "I do not approve of anything that tampers with natural ignorance. Ignorance is like a delicate exotic fruit; touch it and the bloom is gone" (Oscar Wilde, *The Importance of Being Earnest*).

Appendix

Pamela's Vocal Health Care Tips

The suggestions below are to be used when the voice is strained and modified when the voice feels fine. THIS IS NOT MEANT TO OVERRIDE ANY MEDICAL ADVICE.

   ALWAYS check with your doctor if you have concerns.

1. **Drink 10–12 glasses of WATER DAILY** – this is really important! Room temperature is best.

2. **Avoid ICE or COLD WATER** – negatively impacts vocal fold flexibility.

3. **Avoid ALCOHOL** – dries out the vocal folds.

4. **STEAM inhalations** – take hot showers and inhale through both the mouth and nose to help moisturize the vocal folds.

5. **LOZENGES – No Mint or Menthol** – they can dry out your voice. Instead, use black cherry pastilles, lifesavers, honey flavored, etc. Zinc lozenges if you feel a cold coming on.

6. **Vocal Rest** – that means NO speaking and NO whispering.

7. **No Throat Clearing** – avoid coughing – swallow instead.

8. **Gargle with warm salt water** – not too hot.

9. **NO SMOKING** or vaping.

10. **Use a Neti-Pot or Saline Nasal Wash** to clear the nasal passages in the morning and/or evening. Great for opening up sinus resonators!

    • ALWAYS Use Distilled/Bottled or Boiled water. NEVER use tap water.

    • I like to follow this with "Nasya Oil" drops. Very healthy and keeps your nasal passages moist.

11. If your stomach is acidic, your physician might recommend Maalox or Mylanta. Check with your doctor.

12. If you are producing a lot of phlegm, your physician might recommend Robitussin Guaifenesin Syrup or Mucinex – without any added ingredients! Check with your doctor.

13. Eat dinner at least 3–4 hours before you go to sleep.

14. **Avoid excess CITRUS** products – creates phlegm.

15. **Avoid excess DAIRY** products – creates phlegm.

16. **Avoid excess COFFEE** – it is drying.

17. Slippery Elm tea is soothing for the throat ("Throat Coat").

18. Boil water with chunks of fresh peeled ginger. 10 min or so … then simmer it … add favorite citrus as well … Strain ginger and drink the warm liquid. Or just grate it fresh and then eat it. It is an elixir and very healing! Soothing for the throat. This has actually helped me get my voice back when it's totally gone.

19. Tinctures that I use when I feel illness coming on: Echinacea & Goldenseal (combined) and Ginger. Drop these into warm water with a little cranberry juice or lemon and honey and drink.

20. **Throat Sprays**: Singer's Saving Grace, Throat Power.

21. **The "Malva Nut" or Pang Da Hai or Sterculia** – A weird looking dried seed that you put in boiling water. It turns into a flowering slimy drink. Use three of the seeds in a large cup—you can add a bit of honey if you like. Drink the liquid—not the nut—very good if you are suffering from vocal exhaustion and/or are losing your voice. May use this for 2–3 days consecutively and see if it helps!

22. **Honeysuckle Tea** – traditionally used for inflammation and upper respiratory tract infections including colds, influenza, and pneumonia, and other viral and bacterial infections. It can be a calming addition to a vocal hygiene plan.

23. **My Vocal Mist: Nebulized Saline** – unique because it delivers cool saline mist to vocal folds. https://myvocalmist.com

This compilation is based on things that have worked for me over the years and is by no means a comprehensive list. Please do your own research and consult with your physician if you have any questions or if for any reason you seem to experience any chronic vocal challenges.

   __Always check with your physician before taking any medication__.

   Last updated December 2022

Interviewee Biographies

The biographies below feature every individual interviewed for this book, including the interviewees' professional websites, where relevant.

Asterisked names indicate those whose Words of Wisdom are included in the printed publication. The complete collection of interviews can be found in this book's online Support Materials.

Abimbola Stephen-Adesina

Abimbola Stephen-Adesina is a lecturer and a speech, accent, and dialogue coach at the Department of Theater Arts, University of Ibadan, Nigeria. She is a Lessac Kinesensics practitioner. Apart from being an advocate for genuine accent realization in performances on stage and in films, she continues to carry out health projects to sensitize the public through Theater for Development. Abimbola desires to build a vibrant voice and speech community in Nigeria and also a community for job creation.

Amy Hume

Amy Hume is Lecturer in Theatre (Voice) at Victorian College of the Arts and voice and dialect coach for theatre, film, and TV. She has taught at the National Institute of Dramatic Art, the Australian Theatre for Young People, and founded Viva Voice. Most recent theatre credits include *Six* and *Billy Elliot the Musical* (LWAA). Television credits include *The Unlisted* (ABC/Netflix) and *The Secrets She Keeps* (Lingo Pictures). www.amyhume.com.au

Amy Stoller*

Amy Stoller is a dialect designer for New York, regional, and touring stage productions, including Broadway's *Beautiful*. She is a long-term resident dialect designer at Off-Broadway's Mint Theater Company and personal dialect coach to Anna Deavere Smith on projects including "Notes from the Field" and "Let Me Down Easy." Other screen credits include *Selma*; *Zola*; *Mozart in the Jungle*;

Nurse Jackie; and *Dora the Explorer*. Amy also coaches performers in private practice. www.stollersystem.com

Andrea Caban

Andrea Caban is the Co-Director and a Master Teacher of Knight-Thompson Speechwork™ and Head of Voice & Speech at Cal State University, Long Beach. She also holds a research appointment at the UCI Department of Neurology. An award-winning academic writer and playwright, Andrea is interested in the intersection of actor-training and arts-based approaches to patient-centered care. She has been an invited master teacher at RCSSD in London, National Institute of Dramatic Art (NIDA) in Sydney, and the University of Cape Town. www.andreacaban.com

Andrea Haring*

Andrea Haring has served as Executive Director of The Linklater Center in NYC, US coordinator for Linklater voice teacher training, and is a Founding Member of Shakespeare and Company. Broadway plays coached include *American Buffalo, Fool for Love,* and *Hello, Dolly!* Andrea is on faculty at Fordham University and The New School and has taught at Yale, Columbia University, and Circle in the Square. She has given workshops in Germany, the UK, Ireland, Spain, Mexico, Italy, and Iceland. www.thelinklatercenter.com/andrea-haring

Andrew Keltz

Andrew Keltz, M.S., CCC-SLP, is a speech-language pathologist (SLP) specializing in voice and upper airway disorders. Before becoming an SLP, Andrew worked as a singer and actor for over a decade, performing in plays, musicals, and concerts in the US and abroad. After finishing his graduate studies at New York Medical College (NYMC), Andrew completed a clinical fellowship in voice, upper airway, and swallowing disorders at the Lakeshore Professional Voice Center in Michigan. Andrew currently serves as an adjunct assistant professor at NYMC, teaching the graduate level voice disorders course.

Ann Skinner*

Ann Skinner is Head of Voice Emerita at the Stratford Shakespeare Festival in Ontario, Canada. She trained with Kristin Linklater, in the Voice Diploma program at the Royal Central School of Speech and Drama, and at the Roy Hart Theatre. She is recognized as one of the founders of Canadian voice training, having been a voice instructor at George Brown College and the National Theatre School of Canada. Ann is a co-creator of BodySoul Rhythms. www.mwfbodysoulrhythms.org

Antonio Ocampo-Guzman*

Antonio Ocampo-Guzman is an actor, director, and theatre teacher from Colombia and Chair of the Department of Theatre at Northeastern University. Antonio trained as an actor with Teatro Libre de Bogotá; earned an MFA in directing from York University in Toronto; furthered his training under David Smukler, receiving a graduate diploma in voice; and completed his training with Kristin Linklater, adapting her practice into Spanish: *La Liberación de la Voz Natural: el Método Linklater*. www.thelinklatercenter. com/antonio-ocampoguzman

Barry Kur*

Barry Kur is Professor Emeritus at Penn State University School of Theatre, and Master Teacher and Past-President of the Lessac Training and Research Institute. He has had teaching residencies in the USA, South Africa, New Zealand, UK, and Croatia. Barry is the author of *Stage Dialect Studies*: *A Continuation of the Lessac Approach to Actor Voice and Speech Training* and is a founding board member and Past President of the Voice and Speech Trainers Association. www.lessacinstitute.org

Ben Furey

Ben Furey is a dialect/accent and voice coach for theatre, TV and films. He has worked on 125 professional theatre productions. Broadway highlights include *Curious Incident …*, *INK*, *Matilda*, *The Last Ship*, *The Encounter*, and *Billy Elliot*. US tours include *Gentleman's Guide …*, *Billy Elliot*, *Mamma Mia*, *Spamalot*, and *Hamilton*. TV/ Film credits include *Elementary*, *Hunters*, *Blindspot*, *Vine Talk*, and *Lost City of Z*. Ben has taught at UNCSA, Juilliard, SMU, and Gaiety School of Acting (Dublin). www.benfurey.com

Beth McGuire*

Beth McGuire has worked as a vocal and accent/dialect coach for over thirty years. She has served on faculty at Yale School of Drama and the Juilliard School. Her book, *African Accents: A Workbook for Actors*, is the first practical comprehensive analysis of the genre. Projects include *He Brought Her Heart Back in a Box* at Theatre for a New Audience in NYC, *Twelfth Night* at Yale Rep, *US* directed by Jordan Peele, and Marvel's *Black Panther*.

Betty Moulton

Betty Moulton (VASTA President 2016–2018) has been an actor, voice teacher, and coach for over forty years. Her teaching credits include SMU, University of Washington, University of Victoria, and the University of Alberta, where she devised and ran the Theatre Voice Pedagogy MFA program. Professional credits include, *Nevermore*, Catalyst Theatre; *Pride and Prejudice, As You Like It, The Three Musketeers,* and *Little Women* at the Citadel Theatre/Banff professional training program, and ten seasons for the Colorado Shakespeare Festival.

Bonnie Raphael*

Bonnie Raphael has taught and coached professional voice users for over thirty years, including at the University of North Carolina, the American Repertory Theatre (ART) and its Institute for Advanced Theatre Training at Harvard, the National Theatre Conservatory, Northwestern University, and the University of Virginia. Bonnie has coached hundreds of productions, at PlayMakers Repertory Company, ART, Missouri Repertory Theatre, Dallas Theater Center, Denver Center Theatre, Repertory Theatre of St. Louis, Colorado Shakespeare Festival, and elsewhere.

Christina Shewell*

Christina Shewell, MA, FRCSLT ADVS, is a spoken voice teacher and speech/language therapist for clients in both voice therapy and development, with expertise in performers and professional voice users. She was a senior lecturer in voice and counseling skills at University College London for eleven years and has spoken at conferences internationally. Christina's book, *Voice Work: Art and Science in Changing Voices*, is a core text for a wide range of voice practitioners. www.shewellvoice.com

Cynthia Santos-DeCure*

Cynthia DeCure is on faculty at Yale School of Drama. She is a certified associate teacher of Fitzmaurice Voicework® and certified in Knight-Thompson speechwork. She has taught at Cal Arts, UC Santa Barbara, University of Southern California, NY Film Academy, and CSULA. Some dialect coach credits: South Coast Repertory's bilingual play *The Long Road Today/Diálogos,* Chance Theater's *In the Heights,* UCSB: *In the Red and Brown Water, Untitled by Ruth Markovsky,* USC: *Broken Eggs, Anna in the Tropics.* www.cynthiadecure.com

Daron Oram*

Daron Oram served as a principal lecturer in voice for the BA Acting Collaborative and Devised Theatre Course and the MA/MFA Voice Studies course at the Royal Central School of Speech and Drama. Daron's research focuses on the development of anti-oppressive approaches to actor training. Daron was awarded a National Teaching Fellowship in 2019 and is a Senior Fellow of the Higher Education Academy and a Designated Linklater teacher. www.thelinklatercenter.com/daron-oram

David Carey*

For forty years, David Carey has worked in higher education and professional theatre, including four years assisting Cicely Berry at the Royal Shakespeare Company during the 1980s. He became Course Leader of the Voice Studies program at RCSSD in 1986, and in seventeen years trained over 200 voice teachers. David and his wife, Rebecca, have published *Vocal Arts Workbook and Video*, *The Shakespeare Workbook and Video*, and *The Dramatic Text Workbook and Video*. www.vocalandverbalarts.com

David Smukler*

David Smukler is the Director of the Canadian National Voice Intensive and founding director and Professor Emeritus of York University's MFA in Theatre, where he established and led the Voice Teacher Diploma course from 1992 to 2016. David was in the first group that Kristin Linklater trained and spent his first four years as a teacher working alongside Kristin at NYU. His teaching experience includes stints at Carnegie-Mellon University, LAMDA, the Toneelschool (Amsterdam), and The University of Calgary. www.thelinklater-center.com/david-smukler

Douglas N. Honorof

Douglas Honorof works full-time as a dialect coach in film and television, remaining active as an actor and writer between shows. Doug trained, most formatively, at the Yale School of Drama, The Actors Center, and The Barrow Group, and holds five degrees in linguistics with a focus on phonetics, including an undergraduate degree from the University of Chicago (1985) and a Ph.D. from Yale University (1999). He is also a loyal member of SAG-AFTRA. www.dialectdoug.com

Eric Armstrong

Eric Armstrong teaches voice, speech, accents, and text at York University in Toronto; he has taught full-time in universities for twenty-five years in the US and Canada. He has presented frequently at the annual VASTA conference and published articles and reviews in the *Voice and Speech Review*. His research interests lie in the pedagogy of accent training for diverse populations, and his most recent project focused on accents and language for Indigenous performers. www.voiceguy.ca

Erik Singer*

Erik Singer is a freelance dialect coach for film and television. He is a master teacher of Knight-Thompson Speechwork and regularly teaches voice, speech, accents, phonetics, and text. His videos for *Wired* discussing accent work in films have been viewed over nine million times and won a Webby award. A former associate editor for the *Voice and Speech Review*, Erik is a graduate of the Webber Douglas Academy of Dramatic Art in London and of Yale University. www.eriksinger.com

Fran Bennett*

Fran Bennett was trained by Kristin Linklater in her first teaching training program, was a teacher with Shakespeare and Company, and was an associate of Company of Women. She was a voice coach and actress for the Guthrie from 1966 to 1978 and has led workshops at the universities of Minnesota, Wisconsin, Mississippi, Iowa State, Fisk, Carnegie-Mellon, and LAMDA. She taught voice at CalArts from 1978 to 2014, was Head of Acting/Director of Performance from 1996 to 2003, and was made Faculty Emeritus in 2016.

Hilary Blair

Hilary Blair, co-founder of ARTiculate: Real&Clear, incorporates her professional voice over and stage training techniques into her re-framing of executive presence and leadership communication. She sees beyond habits and learned behaviors to what is unique and authentic in groups and individuals. She's certified in Conversational Intelligence (CIQ) and CultureTalk. She holds an MFA in acting from the National Theatre Conservatory and a BA from Yale University. www.articulaterc.com

Jan Gist

Jan Gist has coached hundreds of equity productions in professional theatres around the US, as well as Graduate Theatre productions as Head at Voice at Alabama Shakespeare Festival in the 1990s and for twenty years at The Old Globe/University of San Diego. Gist has taught special workshops on Shakespeare, Shaw, and expressive vocal variety for many American theatres and training programs, RCSSD, and an International Voice Teachers Exchange at the Moscow Art Theatre.

Jane Boston

Jane Boston has worked for over thirty years as a voice practitioner, acting coach, director, poet, performer, and researcher in theatre, the acting conservatoires, and higher education. After a decade as Senior Voice Tutor at RADA, she is now Principal Lecturer at the Royal Central School of Speech and Drama, leading the MA/MFA in voice studies and the International Network in Voice. Her book, *Voice: Readings in Theatre Practice*, was published in July 2018.

Jenny Kent

Jenny Kent is renowned as one of Australia's leading voice and dialect coaches. She trained initially as a speech pathologist and actor, then in voice studies at

NIDA and went to London to pursue further training in dialects. Since then, she has taught at various drama schools and now primarily works as a freelance coach in television, film, and theatre. Film credits include *Aquaman* and *Hotel Mumbai*; television credits include *Wentworth* and *Barracuda*; theatre credits include *War Horse* and *Mary Poppins*. www.jennykent.com.au

Joanna Cazden

Joanna Cazden, MFA, MS-CCC, is a licensed speech-language pathologist at Cedars-Sinai Medical Center in Los Angeles, a holistic voice coach in private practice, and the author of *Everyday Voice Care: The Lifestyle Guide for Singers and Talkers* (Hal Leonard Books, 2012). Her certifications include Fitzmaurice Voicework and Performing Arts Medicine Association (Healthcare). She lectures in the USA and internationally and is an advocate for artists' wellness and respectful communication among voice professionals. www.joannacazden.com

João Henriques

João Henriques is a Portuguese voice director, teacher, and opera director, with collaborations in more than fifty new theatre/opera productions, namely at Sao Joao National Theatre, Porto, where he worked for sixteen years. He teaches voice at Lisbon Theatre & Film School, and holds graduate and undergraduate degrees in subjects ranging from voice performance to political science. Directing credits include Bartok's *Bluebeard's Castle*—Barbican Hall, Barbican Centre with the BBC Symphony Orchestra, London (2015).

Katerina Moraitis

Katerina Moraitis is Head of Voice at NIDA, has been the Course Leader for the MA Voice Studies program at RCSSD, and was Head of the International Centre for Voice. Her article "Unlocking the Voice inside Rochester Young Offenders: The Impact of Lessac Voice Training within a Socially Excluded Community" expounds the implications of voice training on the behavior of young offenders in a socially excluded environment.

Kristin Linklater*

Kristin Linklater was Artistic Director of the Linklater Voice Centre in Orkney, Scotland, inaugurated in 2014. She trained at LAMDA in the 1950s and was Professor of Theater Arts at Columbia University from 1997 to 2013. Kristin has taught at NYU, Emerson, the Stratford Festival, the Guthrie, the Negro Ensemble Company, and from 1978 to 1990 for Shakespeare and Company. In the 1990s she was Artistic Director of Company of Women. Her book, *Freeing the Natural Voice*, has sold over 150,000 copies.

Leith McPherson

A graduate of RCSSD, Leith has worked as a voice, dialect, and acting teacher and coach in theatre, films, and television for twenty-five years. Her film work includes four years as dialect coach on *The Hobbit* trilogy directed by Sir Peter Jackson. Leith has worked on shows for the National Theatre (London), Royal Shakespeare Company, Opera Australia, Melbourne Theatre Company, and for Harry Potter and the Cursed Child (Australia). Leith is also a director and an award-wining voiceover artist. www.leithmcpherson.com

Louis Colaianni*

Louis Colaianni coaches for films, television, and stage, is on the faculty of Yale School of Drama, and has taught at drama schools from coast to coast. He has written several books and articles on voice, speech, accents, phonetics, and Shakespeare. He has coached productions on Broadway, off-Broadway, and in theatres throughout the US and has taught in the UK, US, Germany, Finland, and Australia. Colaianni lives in Manhattan, where he maintains a private studio. www.joyofphonetics.com

Mary MacDonald

Mary MacDonald is a director, voice over actor, and dialect coach for films, TV, and theatre. She is an AFTRA and SAG member and represents Portland, Oregon, as SAG's national board member and AFTRA's president. Her theatrical dialect coaching work includes Oregon Shakespeare Festival, Portland Center Stage, and Reprise Theatre Company in Los Angeles, with individual clients all over the United States. Her on-camera dialect coaching work includes Maverick Films' *Twilight* and TNT's *Leverage*. www.marymac.com

Micha Espinosa*

Micha Espinosa is a professor, a coach, an award-winning editor, and an internationally recognized teaching artist and performer. She works with leading actors and directors, coaching voice and text with a focus on identity-conscious character design. She works with private clients to empower them to find their authenticity and communicate effectively. Whether working with attorneys on litigation techniques or executives' onscreen presence, Micha offers her clients liberation practices that lead to life-long skills of confidence and presence. She is currently Lead Trainer and Artistic Director for the Fitzmaurice Institute: www.michaespinosa.com

Michael Lerner

Dr. Michael Lerner is a laryngologist at Yale School of Medicine and Director of the Voice Center at Greenwich Hospital. His practice focuses on the diagnosis and management of vocal fold disease related to professional and performing voice use, as well as neurologic voice disorders. Dr. Lerner is passionate about achieving the best possible results for his patients, utilizing a multidisciplinary approach together with highly trained speech-language pathologists, employing the latest minimally invasive surgical techniques.

Michael Morgan*

Michael Morgan teaches voice, speech, text, and applied theatre at UC Santa Barbara. His other teaching credentials include Yale School of Drama, Temple University, Theatre Conservatorium in Brussels, Royal Conservatoire in Liege, Shakespeare and Company, Shanghai Theatre Academy, and Theatre of Changes in Athens. Morgan spearheaded *The Odyssey Project*, https://odyssey. projects.theaterdance.ucsb.edu, an initiative centering on incarcerated teens finding their voices through theatre. He is the author of *Constructing the Holistic Actor: Fitzmaurice Voicework*. www.michaelmorgan.online

Nancy Houfek

Nationally recognized theatre educator Nancy Houfek presents workshops throughout the US, Canada, and Europe. She was Head of Voice & Speech at Harvard's ART from 1997 to 2014. She has held positions at the University of Washington, the Drama Studio of London, SMU, and the University of Minnesota. Publications include articles in *Voice & Speech Training in the New Millennium: Conversations with Master Teachers*, *The New England Theater Journal*, *The Voice & Speech Review*, and *The Complete Voice and Speech Workout*. www.nancyhoufek.com

Oscar Quiroz

Oscar Quiroz is an actor and theatre trainer from Tegucigalpa, Honduras. He graduated from the National School of Dramatic Art in 2012 and earned his bachelor's degree in theatre at the University of Guadalajara. He studied voice at CEUVOZ in 2017 and has performed in several productions with Teatro Memorias and Proyecto Escénico Kemé. Oscar, a proud member of VASTA, teaches acting, voice and speech, and Spanish classical theatre at the National School of Dramatic Art.

Patsy Rodenburg*

Over the past forty-five years, Professor Patsy Rodenburg OBE has become a world expert on teaching voice, speech, and presentation skills across corporate and creative industries. She has held senior positions at the Royal Court Theatre, the Royal Shakespeare Company, the National Theatre, and Guildhall School of Music and Drama. Through her work with Shakespeare, she developed her leadership techniques and the concept of the Three Circles of Energy© to focus on personal power and impact. www.patsyrodenburg.co.uk

Patty Raun

Patricia Raun is Director of the Center for Communicating Science at Virginia Tech and Professor of Theatre in the School of Performing Arts. During her years as a professional actor, Raun was inspired to develop skills for connection and communication in scientists, engineers, and health professionals. She promotes positive transformation by developing healthy and varied voices. Credentials include ART at Harvard University, the Royal Shakespeare Company, and the Alda Center for Communicating Science at Stony Brook University.

Paul Meier*

Paul Meier is a leading dialect coach, with his books and coaching services for the arts and business available through Paul Meier Dialect Services: www.paulmeier.com. He has taught at RADA, LAMDA, and UNCSA. He has dialect-coached numerous feature films, and over 200 plays and musicals in more than a dozen countries. His audiobooks include *Of Mice and Men* for the BBC. He is the founder and director of the International Dialects of English Archive (IDEA).

Rachel Coleman

Rachel Coleman is a licensed speech-language pathologist (SLP) specializing in the treatment of voice disorders. She provides therapy and coaching through her private practice, RC Speech and Voice. Rachel is also a senior SLP at the Sean Parker Institute for the Voice at Weill Cornell Medicine. With a bachelor's degree in linguistics, a master's degree in speech pathology, and years of classical theatre training, Rachel's work combines the art of performance with evidence-based clinical expertise. www.rcspeechandvoice.com

Rena Cook

Rena Cook is a Professor Emerita, TEDx speaker, and founder of Vocal Authority, a consultancy helping corporate clients use their voice in more authentic ways. She is the author of *Empower Your Voice; Voice and the Young Actor*; and *Her Voice in Law*. She has an MA in voice studies from RCSSD, an MFA in directing from the University of Oklahoma, and an MA in guidance and counseling from the University of Tulsa. www.myvocalauthority.com

Ros Steen*

Emeritus Professor Ros Steen, FRCS, MA, DSD, established Nadine George Voice Work as the core of training at the Centre for Voice in Performance at the

Royal Conservatoire of Scotland. As Voice Specialist/Director for Theatre, Film, and TV for over thirty years, her credits include National Theatre of Scotland and BBC. Productions include Alan Cumming's *Macbeth* and *Black Watch* (NTS). Actors trained include David Tennant and James McAvoy. www.voicestudiointernational.com/portfolio-items/ros-steen/

Sara Matchett*

Sara Matchett is Director of the Centre for Theatre, Dance & Performance Studies at the University of Cape Town, Co-Director of The Mothertongue Project women's Arts Collective, an Associate Teacher of Fitzmaurice Voicework®, and the African Regional Co-ordinator of the Fitzmaurice Institute. Her teaching includes voice, acting, performance-making, applied theatre, and performance analysis. Her interests are in embodied practices that focus on presencing, co-sensing, co-llaborating, and co-generating as a way of transforming "egosystems to ecosystems."

Scott Miller*

With four decades of experience as a coach and teacher, Scott Miller developed the Miller Voice Method®, a transformational way to embody presence and empathy for peak performances that sustain both the audience's and speaker's attention. In addition to teaching at NYU Tisch's Graduate Acting for almost two decades, Scott has coached communication skills at corporations, law firms, film sets, political headquarters, recording studios, and theatres around the world. www.MillerCommunicationConsulting.com

Shane-Ann Younts

Shane-Ann Younts is Associate Arts Professor in the Graduate Acting Program at NYU Tisch where she teaches Techniques of Voice and Text. In her private practice, she teaches applying voice, speech, and text work to Shakespeare. Professionally she has coached Broadway tours of *Newsies, Mary Poppins,* and *Mamma Mia!* She is the co-author of *All the Words on Stage: A Complete Pronunciation Dictionary for the Plays of William Shakespeare*. www.shaneannyounts. com

Stan Brown*

Stan Brown is the director of graduate studies for the MFA Acting program at Northwestern University's School of Communication. He received his MFA from the University of South Carolina and was named a graduate acting fellow at the Shakespeare Theatre in Washington, D.C. Previously, Stan taught acting at the University of Warwick in Coventry, England, and worked with the voice department of the Royal Shakespeare Company. He has been a professional actor for over thirty years in American and British theatre, film, television, and radio.

Tom Burke

Tom Burke, MS CCC-SLP, is a speech pathologist and singer, specializing in the performer's voice and consulting with children. He also works with TedX speakers and business executives for Google. He was a coach for a Bravo TV social experiment, produced by Viola Davis, helping four women explore the world of gender bias by going undercover as men. He is co-owner of Burkestone Estate in Hudson, NY and runs Six Figure Voice Studio. www.tomburkevoice.com

Walton Wilson*

Walton Wilson is a Designated Linklater Voice Teacher and Associate Teacher of Fitzmaurice Voicework ©. He currently serves as Chair of Acting and Head of Voice and Speech at the Yale School of Drama, where he has been teaching since 1999. Walton has served as a voice, text, and dialect coach for numerous productions on and off-Broadway, and in regional theatre. He has also taught overseas in Bali, Bulgaria, Norway, Portugal, and Singapore. www.thelinklater-center.com/walton-wilson

Bibliography

INTERVIEWEE SELECTED PUBLICATIONS

Abimbola Stephen-Adesina

Stephen-Adesina, Abimbola A. 2019. "Answer the Question: Voice Trainings Transplanted, Recycled, and Repurposed in the Nigerian Context." *Theatre, Dance and Performance Training* 10(3): 305–306. doi:10.1080/19443927. 2019.1667180

Stephen-Adesina, Abimbola A. 2022. "On the Effect of Honey, Bitter Kola, Ginger, and Alligator Pepper for Voice Care: A Case Study on the Perception of Undergraduate Actors." *Voice and Speech Review* 16(1): 22–32. doi:10.108 0/23268263.2021.1959012

Amy Hume

Hume, Amy. 2021. "The Australian Accent and Actor Training: The Current State of Play." *Voice and Speech Review* 12(3): 396–404. doi:10.1080/19443927.2021. 1957565

Hume, Amy and Jennifer Innes. 2020. "Dreaming the Future: Evolving Traditions, Sydney, Australia." *Voice and Speech Review* 15(1): 99–103. doi:1 0.1080/23268263.2021.1854477

Amy Stoller

Ryker, Karen. 2005. "Internet Resources for Voice and Speech Professionals Edited by Amy Stoller." *Voice and Speech Review* 4(1): 381–381. doi:10.1080 /23268263.2005.10739497

Stoller, Amy. 2003. "Marni Nixon: More Than You Know." *Voice and Speech Review* 3(1): 143–152. doi:10.1080/23268263.2003.10739394

Stoller, Amy. 2022. "Links." Accessed March 14. https://www.stollersystem. com/links

Stoller, Amy and Paula Hoza. 2009. "Essay Teaching Consonants through a Straw: A Learning Object for Introducing Three Manners of Articulation to Beginners." *Voice and Speech Review* 6(1): 425–428. doi:10.1080 /23268263.2009.10767603

Stoller, Amy, Eric Armstrong, Kim James Bey, Doug Honorof and Adrianne Moore. 2014. "Speech Stereotypes: Good vs. Evil." *Voice and Speech Review* 8(1): 78–92. doi:10.1080/23268263.2013.826077

Andrea Caban

Caban, Andrea. 2018. "Accent Modification, Voicework, and ALS: A Case Study in Prolonging the Ability to Speak." *Voice and Speech Review* 12(2): 175–192. doi:10.1080/23268263.2018.1480171

Thompson, Philip, Andrea Caban and Erik Singer. 2017. "Vocal Traditions: Knight-Thompson Speechwork." *Voice and Speech Review* 11(3): 329–338. doi:10.1080/23268263.2017.1402560

Antonio Ocampo-Guzman

Dietrich, Simone and Antonio Ocampo-Guzman. 2005. "Teaching Shakespeare Bilingually: An Exchange of Ideas, Experiences and Discoveries." *Voice and Speech Review* 4(1): 27–32. doi:10.1080/23268263.2005.10739443

Ocampo-Guzman, Antonio. 2007. "Essay the Journey of a Bilingual Voice Teacher: Linklater Voice Training in Spanish." *Voice and Speech Review* 5(1): 305–308. doi:10.1080/23268263.2007.10769776

Ocampo-Guzman, Antonio. 2009. "Essay Adventures in Bilingual Shakespeare." *Voice and Speech Review* 6(1): 346–351. doi:10.1080/23268263.2007.10769776

Ocampo-Guzmán, Antonio. 2018. *La Liberación De La Voz Natural: El Método Linklater*. 3rd ed. Mexico: Universidad Nacional Autónoma De Mexico.

Barry Kur

Munro, Marth, Deborah Kinghorn, Barry Kur, Robin Aronson, Nancy Krebs and Sean Turner. 2017. "Vocal Traditions: Lessac Kinesensics." *Voice and Speech Review* 11(1): 93–105. doi:10.1080/23268263.2017.1370834

Kur, Barry. 2005. *Stage Dialect Studies: A Continuation of the Lessac Approach to Actor Voice and Speech Training*. Barry Kur.

Beth McGuire

McGuire, Beth. 2016. *African Accents: A Workbook for Actors*. New York: Routledge.

Betty Moulton

Knight, Steve, John Staniunas, Carol Pendergrast, Betty Moulton, Anne C. Schilling and Janet Rodgers. 2005. "Glimpses Around the Globe." *Voice and Speech Review* 4(1): 96–99. doi:10.1080/23268263.2005.10739452

Moulton, Betty. 2007. "Peer Reviewed Article International Performers and Voice Teachers Speak: Diverse Methods for Integrating the Disciplines of the Spoken and Singing Voice." *Voice and Speech Review* 5(1): 367–380. doi: 10.1080/23268263.2007.10769789

Moulton, Betty and Jane MacFarlane. 2019. "Betty Moulton: My Journey to Now." *Voice and Speech Review* 14(3): 348–359. doi:10.1080 /23268263.2020.1698839

Bonnie Raphael

Freed, Sharon, Bonnie Raphael and Robert T. Sataloff. 2005. "The Role of the Acting-Voice Trainer in the Medical Careof Professional Voice Users" in *Treatment of Voice Disorders*. Robert T. Sataloff, ed. 105–114. San Diego: Plural Publishing Group.

Raphael, Bonnie N. 1984. "Preparing a Cast for a Dialect Show." *Communication Education* 33(1): 43–51. doi:10.1080/03634528409384716

Raphael, Bonnie N. 1986. "Improving the Singer's Speaking Voice." *Journal of the National Association of Teachers of Singing* 43: 9–13.

Raphael, Bonnie. 1989. "The Sounds of Violence–Part I: The Real Thing." *Fight Master* 12(1): 12–15.

Raphael, Bonnie. 1989. "The Sounds of Violence–Part II: Vocal Safety and Technique." *Fight Master* 12(2): 8–13.

Raphael, Bonnie. 1989. "The Sounds of Violence–Part III: Topping the Competition." *Fight Master* 12(3): 8–10.

Raphael, Bonnie N. 1995. "Screaming without Suffering." *Voice Talk* 1(3): 9.

Raphael, Bonnie N. 1997. "A Consumer's Guide to Voice and Speech Training" in *Vocal Visions*. Marian Hampton and Barbara Acker, eds. 203–213. New York: Applause Books.

Raphael, Bonnie N. 2000. "Case Study: Hyperfunctional Voice in an Actor" in *Voice Therapy: Clinical Studies* 2nd ed. Joseph C. Stemple, Ph.D., ed. 409–421. San Diego: Singular Publishing Group.

Raphael, Bonnie N. 2000. "Peer Reviewed Article Dancing on Shifting Ground." *Voice and Speech Review* 1(1): 165–170. doi:10.1080/23268263.2000.10761401

Raphael, Bonnie N. 2001. "Staged Violence: Greater Than the Sum of Its Parts." *Voice and Speech Review* 2(1): 22–29.

Raphael, Bonnie. 2005. "A Voice for Owen Meany." *Voice and Speech Review* 4(1): 167–169. doi:10.1080/23268263.2005.10739463

Raphael, Bonnie N. 2006. "Special Considerations Relating to Members of the Acting Profession" in *Professional Voice: The Science and Art of Clinical Care* 3rd ed. Robert T. Sataloff, ed. 387–390. San Diego: Singular Publishing Group.

Raphael, Bonnie N. 2007. "Theatre Voice Coaching" in *Western Drama through the Ages*. J. Kimball King, ed. Vol 2. 558–561. Westport, CT: Greenwood Press.

Raphael, Bonnie N. 2010. "Hyperfunctional Voice in an Actor" in *Voice Therapy: Clinical Studies* 3rd ed. Joseph C. Stemple, Ph.D. and Lisa Thomas Fry, eds. 377–382. San Diego: Plural Publishing Inc.

Raphael, Bonnie N. and Robert T. Sataloff. 1991. "Increasing Vocal Effectiveness" in *Professional Voice: The Science and Art of Clinical Care*, Robert T. Sataloff, ed. 359–374. New York: Raven Press.

Raphael, Bonnie N. and Robert T. Sataloff. 2005. "Increasing Vocal Effectiveness" in *Treatment of Voice Disorders*. Robert T. Sataloff, ed. 46–57. San Diego: Plural Publishing Group.

Raphael, Bonnie N. and Ronald C. Scherer. 1987. "Voice Modifications of Stage Actors: Acoustic Analyses." *Journal of Voice* 1(1): 83–87.

Rubin, Lucille S., Ruth Epstein, Catherine Fitzmaurice, Bonnie Raphael and Pamela Lynn Harvey. 1991. "Common Speaking Voice Problems: Case Studies with Optional Solutions." *Journal of Voice* 4(4): 321–327.

Scherer, Ronald C. and Bonnie N. Raphael. 1986. "Voice Projection: An Electroglottographic Study of Theatre 'Call' Technique." *ASHA* 28(10): 70.

Christina Shewell

Carding, Paul, Eva Carlson, Ruth Epstein, Lesley Mathieson and Christina Shewell. 2000. "Formal Perceptual Evaluation of Voice Quality in the United Kingdom." *Logopedics Phoniatrics Vocology* 25(3): 133–138. doi:10.1080/14015430050175860

Shewell, Christina. 1998. "The Effect of Perceptual Training on Ability to Use the Vocal Profile Analysis Scheme." *International Journal of Language & Communication Disorders* 33(1): 322–326. doi:10.3109/13682829809179444

Shewell, Christina. 2009. "Peer Reviewed Article the Voice Skills Perceptual Profile: A Practical Tool for Voice Teachers." *Voice and Speech Review* 6(1): 171–184. doi:10.1080/23268263.2009.10761519

Shewell, Christina. 2009. *Voice Work: Art and Science in Changing Voices.* Chichester: Wiley-Blackwell.

Shewell, Christina. 2020. "Poetry, Voice, Brain, and Body." *Voice and Speech Review* 14(2): 143–166. doi:10.1080/23268263.2020.1743502

Cynthia Santos-DeCure

DeCure, Cynthia. 2015. "Monologues for Latino/a Actors." *Voice and Speech Review* 9(1): 102–104. doi:10.1080/23268263.2015.1016721

Espinosa, Micah and Cynthia Decure. 2019. *Scenes for Latinx Actors: Voices of the New American Theatre.* Hanover, NH: Smith & Kraus.

Daron Oram

Oram, Daron. 2018. "Losing Sight of Land: Tales of Dyslexia and Dyspraxia in Psychophysical Actor Training." *Theatre, Dance and Performance Training* 9(1): 53–67. doi:10.1080/19443927.2017.1415955

Oram, Daron. 2020. "The Heuristic Pedagogue: Navigating Myths and Truths in Pursuit of an Equitable Approach to Voice Training." *Theatre, Dance and Performance Training* 11(3): 300–309. doi:10.1080/19443927.2020.1788272

Oram, Daron. 2015. "Research and Practice in Voice Studies: Searching for a Methodology." *Voice and Speech Review* 9(1): 15–27. doi:10.1080/23268263.2015.1059674

Oram, Daron. 2018. "Finding a Way: More Tales of Dyslexia and Dyspraxia in Psychophysical Actor Training." *Voice and Speech Review* 12(3): 276–294. doi:10.1080/23268263.2018.1518375

Oram, Daron. 2019. "De-Colonizing Listening: Toward an Equitable Approach to Speech Training for the Actor." *Voice and Speech Review* 13(3): 279–297. doi:10.1080/23268263.2019.1627745

Oram, Daron. 2019. "Identity and Dialect Performance: A Study of Communities and Dialects." *Voice and Speech Review* 13(2): 251–253. doi:10.1080/23268263.2018.1537220

Oram Daron. 2020. "The Expressive Voice in Performance: Chekhov's Techniques for Voice and Singing." Chap 3 in *Michael Chekhov Technique in the Twenty-First Century: New Pathways* 93–106. Cass Fleming and Tom Cornford, eds. London: Methuen Drama.

Oram, Daron. 2021. "Decentering Listening: Toward an Anti-Discriminatory Approach to Accent and Dialect Training for the Actor." *Voice and Speech Review* 15(1): 6–26. doi:10.1080/23268263.2020.1842455

David Carey

Carey, David and Rebecca Clark Carey. 2009. *Vocal Arts Workbook and Video: A Practical Course for Vocal Clarity and Expression*. London: Methuen Drama.

Carey, David and Rebecca Clark Carey. 2015. *The Shakespeare Workbook and Video: A Practical Course for Actors*. London: Methuen Drama.

Carey, David and Rebecca Clack Carey. 2019. *The Dramatic Text Workbook and Video: Practical Tools for Actors and Directors*. London: Methuen Drama.

Carey, David. 2000. "Essay towards a Career in Voice Teaching the Work of the Central School of Speech and Drama." *Voice and Speech Review* 1(1): 189–190. doi:10.1080/23268263.2000.10761403

Carey, David. 2003. "Dialect Coaching for Film and Television: An Interview with Penny Dyer." *Voice and Speech Review* 3(1): 99–105. doi:10.1080/23268263.2003.10739386

Carey, David. 2003. "Interviews with Patsy Rodenburg and Cicely Berry." *Voice and Speech Review* 3(1): 227–235. doi:10.1080/23268263.2003.10739407

Carey, David. 2011. "Scanning Shakespeare: The Epic Caesura." *Voice and Speech Review* 7(1): 52–54. doi:10.1080/23268263.2011.10739519

Carey, David. 2013. "In Search of Shakespeare's Use of the Period-Stopped Line: A Folio Punctuation Investigation." *Voice and Speech Review* 8(1): 93–99. doi:10.1080/23268263.2013.829708

Carey, David. 2019. "Vocal Traditions: Cicely Berry and the Central School Tradition." *Voice and Speech Review* 14(1): 86–95. doi:10.1080/23268263.2019.1673995

David Smukler

Smukler, David. 2003. "Dialogue Coaching for Film: One Part of My Work." *Voice and Speech Review* 3(1): 44–49. doi:10.1080/23268263.2003.10739376

Smukler, David. 2019. "David Smukler: My Journey to Now." *Voice and Speech Review* 13(3): 360–369. doi:10.1080/23268263.2019.1573005

Doug Honorof

Honorof, Douglas N. 2003. "Reference Vowels and Lexical Sets in Accent Acquisition." *Voice and Speech Review* 3(1): 106–122. doi:10.1080/23268263.2003.10739387

McCullough, Jill, Barbara Somerville, ed. Douglas Honorof. "Comma Gets a Cure." Copyright 2000 Douglas N. Honorof, Jill McCullough and Barbara Somerville. https://research.ncl.ac.uk/necte2/documents/comma.pdf

Stoller, Amy, Eric Armstrong, Kim James Bey, Douglas Honorof and Adrianne Moore. 2014. "Speech Stereotypes: Good vs. Evil." *Voice and Speech Review* 8(1): 78–92. doi:10.1080/23268263.2013.826077

Eric Armstrong

Armstrong, Eric. 2001. "Interview Earning the Role: The Company Voice Coach." *Voice and Speech Review* 2(1): 148–154. doi:10.1080/23268263.2001.10761462

Armstrong, Eric. 2003. "This Is *Normal?*: A Theatre Coach Works in Film." *Voice and Speech Review* 3(1): 33–43. doi:10.1080/23268263.2003.10739375

Armstrong, Eric. 2005. "Hybrid Dialects." *Voice and Speech Review* 4(1): 251–260. doi:10.1080/23268263.2005.10739477

Armstrong, Eric. 2009. "Peer Reviewed Article Embodying Meter." *Voice and Speech Review* 6(1): 243–253. doi:10.1080/23268263.2009.10767575

Armstrong, Eric. 2015. "IPA Keyboards for iOS." *Voice and Speech Review* 9(1): 96–102. doi:10.1080/23268263.2015.1062598

Armstrong, Eric. 2015. "The Accent Kit." *Voice and Speech Review* 9(1): 94–96. doi:10.1080/13669877.2015.1014190

Armstrong, Eric. 2016. "Efficacy in Phonetics Training for the Actor." *Voice and Speech Review* 10(1): 36–52. doi:10.1080/23268263.2017.1282676

Armstrong, Eric and Paul Meier. 2005. "R and Its Articulation." *Voice and Speech Review* 4(1): 237–250. doi:10.1080/23268263.2005.10739476

Armstrong, Eric, Shannon Vickers, Katie German and Elan Marchinko. 2020. "Accent and Language Training for the Indigenous Performer: Results of Four Focus Groups." *Voice and Speech Review* 14(3): 1–21. doi:10.1080/23268263.2020.1727640

Stoller, Amy, Eric Armstrong, Kim James Bey, Doug Honorof and Adrianne Moore. 2014. "Speech Stereotypes: Good vs. Evil." *Voice and Speech Review* 8(1): 78–92. doi:10.1080/23268263.2013.826077

Erik Singer

Thompson, Philip, Andrea Caban and Erik Singer. 2017. "Vocal Traditions: Knight-Thompson Speechwork." *Voice and Speech Review* 11(3): 329–338. doi:10.1080/23268263.2017.1402560

Hilary Blair

Blair, Hilary. 2011. "Business Culture – Code Switching." *Voice and Speech Review* 7(1): 250–253. doi:10.1080/23268263.2011.10739547

Blair, Hilary and Robin A. Miller. 2021. *Articulate at Work: How Performance Techniques Bring Business Communication to Life*. Denver, CO: ArticulateRC Press.

Jan Gist

Gist, Jan. 2000. "Poetry." *Voice and Speech Review* 1(1): 148–316. doi:10.1080 /23268263.2000.10761393

Gist, Jan. 2001. "Poetry Six Poems on the Theme of Domestic Violence." *Voice and Speech Review* 2(1): 39–49. doi:10.1080/23268263.2001.10761445

Gist, Jan. 2021. "Voicing Poems." *Voice and Speech Review* 15(2): 235–238. doi: 10.1080/23268263.2020.1784547

Jane Boston

Boston, Jane. 1997. "Voice: The Practitioners, Their Practices, and Their Critics." *New Theatre Quarterly* xiii: 248–254.

Boston, Jane. 2014. "Poetic Text in Contemporary Voice Training: A Repositioning." *Voice and Speech Review* 8(2): 131–148. doi:10.1080/23268263.2014.906957

Boston, Jane. 2018. *Voice: Readings in Theatre Practice*. London: Macmillan Publishers, Ltd.

Boston, Jane. 2019. "Pitch and Gender in Voice Training: New Methodological Directions." *Theatre, Dance and Performance Training* 10(3): 332–336. doi:1 0.1080/19443927.2019.1660523

Boston, Jane and Rena Cook, eds. 2009. *Breath in Action: The Art of Breath in Vocal and Holistic Practice*. London: Jessica Kingsley Publishers.

Turner, J. Clifford. 2007. *Voice and Speech in the Theatre*. 6th ed. Jane Boston, ed. London: Methuen Drama.

Joanna Cazden, S.L.P.

Cazden, Joanna. 2003. "Dionysus, Demi Moore, and the Cult of the Distressed Voice." *Voice and Speech Review* 3(1): 243–246. doi:10.1080 /23268263.2003.10739409

Cazden, Joanna. 2007. "Essay When Bodies Bring Forth More Than Speech: Voice Teachers and Pregnancy." *Voice and Speech Review* 5(1): 300–304. doi :10.1080/23268263.2007.10769775

Cazden, Joanna. 2012. *Everyday Voice Care: The Lifestyle Guide for Singers and Talkers*. Wisconsin: Hal Leonard.

Cazden, Joanna. 2017. "Stalking the Calm Buzz: How the Polyvagal Theory Links Stage Presence, Mammal Evolution, and the Root of the Vocal Nerve." *Voice and Speech Review* 11(2): 132–153. doi:10.1080/23268263.2017.1390036

Cazden, Joanna. 2019. "Complete Vocal Fitness: A Singer's Guide to Physical Training, Anatomy, and Biomechanics." *Voice and Speech Review* 13(3): 373–375. doi:10.1080/23268263.2019.1588505

Cazden, Joanna. 2020. "Joanna Cazden: My Journey to Now." *Voice and Speech Review* 15(1): 104–113. doi:10.1080/23268263.2020.1776473

Kristin Linklater

Linklater, Kristin. 1972. "The Body Training of Moshe Feldenkrais." *The Drama Review* 16(1). Available at: https://www.linklatervoice.com/resources/-articles-essays/35-the-body-training-of-moshe-feldenkrais

Linklater, Kristin. 1990. "The Incredible Shrinking Shakespearean." *American Theatre Magazine*. October. https://www.linklatervoice.com/resources/-articles-essays/36-the-incredible-shrinking-shakespearean

Linklater, Kristin. 1992. *Freeing Shakespeare's Voice: The Actor's Guide to Talking the Text*. New York: Theatre Communications Group.

Linklater, Kristin. 1997. "Thoughts on Theatre, Therapy and the Art of Voice" in *The Vocal Vision: Views on Voice by 24 Leading Teachers, Coaches, and Directors*. Marion Hampton and Barbara Acker, eds. 3–12. London: Applause Books.

Linklater, Kristin. 2000. "Essay Word Music: The Soul of the Theatre." *Voice and Speech Review* 1(1): 193–194. doi:10.1080/23268263.2000.10761405

Linklater, Kristin. 2003. "Vox Eroticus." *American Theatre Magazine*, April. https://www.linklatervoice.com/resources/articles-essays/38-vox-eroticus

Linklater, Kristin. 2007. *Freeing the Natural Voice: Imagery and Art in the Practice of Voice and Language*. London: Nick Hern Books.

Linklater, Kristin. 2009. "The Alchemy of Breathing" in *Breath in Action*. Jane Boston and Rena Cook, eds. 101–112. London: Jessica Kingsley Publishers.

Linklater, Kristin. 2010. "The Importance of Daydreaming." *American Theatre Magazine*. https://www.americantheatre.org/2010/01/01/the-importance-of-daydreaming/

Linklater, Kristin. 2018. "Our Vocal Heritage." November. https://www.linklatervoice.com/resources/articles-essays/147-inheritance-of-acting-techniques-and-their-innovative-developments

Linklater, Kristin. 2018. "Vocal Traditions: Linklater Voice Method." *Voice and Speech Review* 12(2): 211–220. doi:10.1080/23268263.2018.1444558

Linklater, Kristin. 2019. "The Embodied Voice." August 28. https://www.linklatervoice.com/resources/articles-essays/161-the-embodied-voice-pevoc-019

Linklater, Kristin. "Moments of Nothing." https://www.linklatervoice.com/resources/articles-essays/160-moments-of-nothing

Linklater, Kristin. "The Art and Craft of Voice (and Speech) Training." https://www.linklatervoice.com/resources/articles-essays/42-the-art-and-craft-of-voice-and-speech-training

Louis Colaianni

Anderson, Claudia and Louis Colaianni. 2002. *Bringing Speech to Life: A Companion Workbook to Louis Colaianni's The Joy of Phonetics and Accents.* New York: Joy Press.

Colaianni, Louis. 1999. *Shakespeare's Names: A New Pronouncing Dictionary.* New York: Drama Publishers.

Colaianni, Louis. 2000. "Editorial Column Pronunciation, Phonetics, Linguistics, Dialect/Accent Studies." *Voice and Speech Review* 1(1): 19–20. doi:10.1080/23268263.2000.10761382

Colaianni, Louis. 2000. "Interview with Rosina Lippy-Green." *Voice and Speech Review* 1(1): 21–22. doi:10.1080/23268263.2000.10761383

Colaianni, Louis. 2000. *The Joy of Phonetics and Accents.* New York: Joy Press.

Colaianni, Louis. 2001. "Bearing the Standard: Issues of Speech in Education." *Voice and Speech Review* 7(1): 199–208. doi:10.1080/23268263.2011.10739541

Colaianni, Louis and Cal Printer. 2004. *How to Speak Shakespeare.* Solana Beach, CA: Santa Monica Press.

Micha Espinosa

Espinosa, Micah. 2005a. "Inner Voices and Tsunamis." *The Journal of Intergroup Relations* 32(1): 85–87.

Espinosa, Micah. 2005b. "Insight into the Challenges Latino Students Face while Training in Theatre." *Voice and Speech Review* 4(1): 129–143. doi:10.1080/23268263.2005.10739458

Espinosa, Micah. 2011. "A Call to Action: Embracing the Cultural Voice or Taming the Wild Tongue." *Voice and Speech Review* 7(1): 75–86. doi:10.1080/23268263.2011.10739524

Espinosa, Micah. 2014. "Teaching in Cuba: A Voice Teacher's Awakening to the Effects of Commodification on the Learning Process." *Voice and Speech Review* 8(2): 157–168. doi:10.1080/23268263.2014.905098

Espinosa, Micah, ed. 2014. *Monologues for Latino/a Actors: A Resource Guide to the Contemporary Latino/a Playwrights for Students and Teachers.* New Hampshire: Smith & Krause.

Espinosa, Micah. 2016. "The Expressive Actor, Integrated Voice, Movement, and Actor Training." *Voice and Speech Review* 10(1): 83–85. doi:10.1080/23268263.2016.1228795

Espinosa, Micah and Cynthia Decure. 2019. *Scenes for Latinx Actors: Voices of the New American Theatre.* Hanover, NH: Smith & Kraus.

Espinosa, Micah and Antonio Ocampo-Guzman. 2010. "Identity Politics and the Training of Latino Actors" in *The Politics of American Actor Training.* Ellen Margolis and Lissa Tyler Renaud, eds. 150–161. New York: Routledge.

Meier, Paul. 2020. "Episode 26 (Spanishes): A Conversation with Micha Espinosa." *In a Manner of Speaking* from Paul Meier Dialect Services, March. https://www.paulmeier.com/2020/03/01/episode-26-spanishes/

Michael Morgan

Morgan, Michael. 2005. "Vocal Health with Chinese Medicine." *Voice and Speech Review* 4(1): 362–374. doi:10.1080/23268263.2005.10739494

Morgan, Michael. 2009. "Qi Gong Breathing" in *Breath in Action*. Jane Boston and Rena Cook, eds. 147–160. London: Jessica Kingsley Publishers.

Morgan, Michael. 2012. *Constructing the Holistic Actor: Fitzmaurice Voicework*. Scotts Valley, CA: CreateSpace Publishing.

Nancy Houfek Brown

Houfek, Nancy. 2001. "Illustrated Guide to the Exercises." *The Act of Teaching: Parts I & II*. Cambridge, MA: Derek Bok Center for Teaching and Learning at Harvard University. http://bokcenter.harvard.edu/fs/docs/icb.topic650252.files/actguide.pdf

Houfek, Nancy. 2001. "Strategies to Avoid 'Burnout'." *The VASTA Voice* 15(2): 9–10.

Houfek, Nancy. 2002. "The Advanced Triangle Pose." In *The Complete Voice & Speech Workout*. Janet Rodgers, ed. 19–20. New York: Applause Books.

Houfek, Nancy. 2005. "Oedipus' Aiee's: Using Ancient Greek on the American Stage." *Voice and Speech Review* 4(1): 173–180. doi:10.1080/23268263.2005.10739465

Houfek, Nancy. 2010. "Life in the Voice Lane." *New England Theatre Journal* 21(21): 135–157.

Houfek, Nancy. 2014. "You Can Go Home Again." *Voice and Speech Review* 8(1): 57–77. doi:10.1080/23268263.2013.829355

Houfek, Nancy. 2022. "Nancy Houfek: My Journey to Now." *Voice and Speech Review*. doi:10.1080/23268263.2021.2008628

Saklad, Nancy. 2011. "An Interview with Nancy Houfek" in *Voice and Speech Training in the New Millennium: Conversations with Master Teachers*, 125–134. Wisconsin: Hal Leonard.

Patsy Rodenburg

Carey, David. 2003. "Interviews with Patsy Rodenburg and Cicely Berry." *Voice and Speech Review* 3(1): 227–235. doi:10.1080/23268263.2003.10739407

Rodenburg, Patsy. 2005. *Speaking Shakespeare*. London: Methuen Drama.

Rodenburg, Patsy. 2009. *Power Presentation: Formal Speech in an Informal World*. London: Penguin.

Rodenburg, Patsy. 2009. *Presence: How to Use Positive Energy for Success*. London: Penguin.

Rodenburg, Patsy. 2015. *The Right to Speak: Working with the Voice*. 2nd ed. London: Methuen Drama.

Rodenburg, Patsy. 2018. *The Need for Words: Voice and the Text*. 2nd ed. London: Methuen Drama.

Rodenburg, Patsy. 2019. *The Actor Speaks: Voice and the Performer*. 2nd ed. London: Methuen Drama.

Rodenburg, Patsy. 2022. *The Woman's Voice*. London: Bloomsbury Press.

Patty Raun

Raun, Patricia. 2009. "Essay Transformational Identification: Empathy through Poetry and Text." *Voice and Speech Review* 6(1): 320–323. doi:10.1080/23268263.2009.10767584

Raun, Patricia. 2019. "Let Your Life Speak: The Art of Connecting across Difference." *Voice and Speech Review* 14(1): 49–55. doi:10.1080/23268263.2020.1668713

Paul Meier

Armstrong, Eric and Paul Meier. 2005. "R and Its Articulation." *Voice and Speech Review* 4(1): 237–250. doi:10.1080/23268263.2005.10739476

Bennett, Leslie and Paul Meier. 2009. "Essay the Actor's Ecology: Integrating Movement and Voice." *Voice and Speech Review* 6(1): 38–43. doi:10.1080/23268263.2009.10761503

Foy, Kate and Paul Meier. 2001. "Peer-reviewed Article Vocal Clarity in the Outdoor Theatre." *Voice and Speech Review* 2(1): 210–222. doi:10.1080/23268263.2001.10761469

Meier, Paul. 2000. "Peer-Reviewed Article Structure and Substance in Shakespeare's Verse." *Voice and Speech Review* 1(1): 209–218. doi:10.1080/23268263.2000.10761410

Meier, Paul. 2003. "Interviews with Three Film and Television Coaches: Carla Meyer, Gillian Lane-Plescia, and David Alan Stern." *Voice and Speech Review* 3(1): 57–71. doi:10.1080/23268263.2003.10739379

Meier, Paul. 2007. "Essay Training the Trainers." *Voice and Speech Review* 5(1): 53–67. doi:10.1080/23268263.2007.10769741

Meier, Paul. 2011. "A Midsummer Night's Dream: An Original Pronunciation Production." *Voice and Speech Review* 7(1): 209–223. doi:10.1080/23268263.2011.10739542

Meier, Paul. 2012. *Accents and Dialects for Stage and Screen*. Adelaide: Paul Meier Dialect Services.

Meier, Paul. 2017. "Paul Meier: My Journey to Now." *Voice and Speech Review* 12(1): 105–115. doi:10.1080/23268263.2018.1409944

Meier, Paul. 2020. *The Charts of the International Phonetic Alphabet: An Interactive Animation*. CD-ROM. Paul Meier Dialect Services.

Meier, Paul. 2020. *Voicing Shakespeare*. Ebook. Paul Meier Dialect Services.

Zazzali, Peter and Paul Meier. 2014. "Trust and Communication in the Director/Voice Coach Collaboration: A Case Study of *Much Ado About Nothing* at the University of Kansas." *Voice and Speech Review* 8(3): 250–260. doi:10.1080/23268263.2014.968342

Rena Cook

Boston, Jane and Rena Cook, eds. 2009. *Breath in Action: The Art of Breath in Vocal and Holistic Practice*. London: Jessica Kingsley Publishers.

Cook, Rena. 2001. "Peer-reviewed Article You've Got to Be a Chameleon: Interviews with Leading Vocal Coaches." *Voice and Speech Review* 2(1): 155–168. doi:10.1080/23268263.2001.10761463

Cook, Rena. 2005. "A Week with Andrew Wade." *Voice and Speech Review* 4(1): 88–95. doi:10.1080/23268263.2005.10739451

Cook, Rena. 2018. *Empower Your Voice: For Women in Business, Politics and Life*. Oklahoma: Total Publishing and Media.

Cook, Rena. 2018. *Voice and the Young Actor*. London: Methuen Drama.

Cook, Rena. 2021. "Rena Cook: My Journey to Now." *Voice and Speech Review*. doi:10.1080/23268263.2021.1989876

Cook, Rena and Laurie Koller. 2020. *Her Voice in Law: Vocal Power and Situational Command for the Female Attorney*. Chicago, IL: American Bar Association.

Ellis, Matthew E. and Rena Cook. 2007. "Essay Voice Coach & Fight Coach: A Collaboration in Physical Effort, Free Breath and the Open Voice." *Voice and Speech Review* 5(1): 187–191. doi:10.1080/23268263.2007.10769758

Kayes, Gillyanne and Rena Cook. 2009. "Essay Breath and the Vocal Folds—a Musical Theatre Perspective." *Voice and Speech Review* 6(1): 443–444. doi:10.1080/23268263.2009.10767607

Ros Steen

Meier, Paul. 2020. "Episode 25: Tongues of Scotland, with Ros Steen." Podcast *In a Manner of Speaking*. Paul Meier Dialect Services.

Steen, Ros and Joyce Deans. 2009. "Essay What We May Be: The Integration of Lecoq Movement and George Voice Work at the RSAMD." *Voice and Speech Review* 6(1): 286–302. doi:10.1080/23268263.2009.10767579

Steen, Ros. 2005. "Helena, Hitler and the Heartland." *Voice and Speech Review* 4(1): 43–58. doi:10.1080/23268263.2005.10739445

Steen, Ros. 2005. Speech "Voices of Scotland." VASTA Conference *Breaking Boundaries: Crossing the Cultural Divide*. Glasgow, Scotland.

Steen, Ros. 2007. "Essay Seein Oursels as Ithers See Us." *Voice and Speech Review* 5(1): 281–290. doi:10.1080/23268263.2007.10769772

Steen, Ros. 2012. "Earthing the Electric: Voice Directing the Directors." *Theatre, Dance and Performance Training* 3(3): 375–388. 10.1080/19443927.2012.719831

Sara Matchett

Cloete, Nicola, Nandita Dinesh, Rand T. Hazou and Sara Matchett. 2015. "E(Lab)orating Performance: Transnationalism and Blended Learning in the Theatre Classroom." *Research in Drama Education: The Journal of Applied Theatre and Performance* 20(4): 470–482. doi:10.1080/13569783.2015.1065723

Halligey, Alex and Sara Matchett. 2021. *Collaborative Conversations: Celebrating Twenty-One Years of the Mothertongue Project*. Cape Town: Modaji Books.

Hassim, Shireen, Shereen Essof, Aili Mari Tripp, Elaine Salo, Jennifer Radloff, Sara Matchett and L. Muthoni Wanyeki. 2005. *Feminist Africa 4: Women Mobilised*. Issue 4. January 1. University of Capetown: African Gender Institute.

Matchett, Sara. 2009. *Breathing Space: Cross-Community Professional Theatre as a Means of Dissolving Fixed Geographical Landscapes*. Republic of Moldova: Lambert Academic Publishing.

Matchett, Sara. 2012. "Breath as Impulse, Breath as Thread: Breath as Catalyst for Making an Autobiographical Performance in Response to 'Corrective Rape' and Hate Crimes Against Lesbians." *South African Theatre Journal* 26(3): 280–291. doi:10.1080/10137548.2013.803670

Matchett, Sara. 2018. "Mapping a Classic: Body Mapping and Koodiyattam Rasa Breath Patterns as a Way of Embodying Character and Analysing Text in a Production of *The Trojan Women* with Second Year Acting Students from the University of Cape Town's Drama Department." *South African Theatre Journal* 31(1): 86–97. doi:10.1080/10137548.2017.1417742

Matchett, Sara. 2019. "Breath-Body-Self: Reflections on Performance-Based Approaches to Breath through a Women's Theatre Project in South Africa." *Voice and Speech Review* 13(3): 265–278. doi:10.1080/23268263.2019.1591097

Matchett, Sara and Phoebe Kisubi Mbasalaki. 2020. "Butoh Gives Back the Feeling to the People." *Agenda* 34(3): 74–86. doi:10.1080/10130950.2020.1775102

Matchett, Sara and Rehane Abrahams. 2020. "The Application of a Translational Performance Method Using Archival Material, Personal Narrative, Mythology and Somatic Practices: The Making of *Womb of Fire*." *South African Theatre Journal* 33(1): 34–51. doi:10.1080/10137548.2020.1742780

Scott Miller

Miller, Scott, John Patrick, Liam Joynt and Kristi Dana. 2018. "Vocal Traditions: Miller Voice Method" *Voice and Speech Review* 12(1): 86–95. doi:10.1080/23268263.2018.1435610

Shane-Ann Younts

Cash, Cassidy. 2019. "Episode 82: Shane Ann Younts on Iambic Pentameter." Podcast *That Shakespeare Life*.

Scheeder, Louis and Shane Ann Younts. 2003. *All the Words on Stage: A Complete Pronunciation Dictionary for the Plays of William Shakespeare*. New Hampshire: Smith and Kraus.

Scheeder, Louis and Shane Ann Younts. *Audio Shakespeare Pronunciation App*. https://www.audioshakespearepronunciationapp.com

SignatureTheatreNY. 2019. "How to Sound Like You're in a Horton Foote Play with Dialect Coach Shane Ann Younts." *YouTube*. https://www.youtube.com/watch?v=phuBeevSWyM&feature=youtu.be

Stan Brown

Brown, Stan. 2000. "Column the Cultural Voice." *Voice and Speech Review* 1(1): 17–18. doi:10.1080/23268263.2000.10761381

Brown, Stan. 2001. "Column the Cultural Voice: An Interview with Danny Hoch." *Voice and Speech Review* 2(1): 124–128. doi:10.1080 /23268263.2001.10761456

Tom Burke, S.L.P.

Burke, Tom. 2014. "Holistic Vocology: A Four-Part Framework for Voice Training and Rehabilitation." *Voice and Speech Review* 8(2): 217–219. doi:10 .1080/23268263.2014.887250

OTHER RECOMMENDED PUBLICATIONS

Brown, Brené. 2021. *Atlas of the Heart: Mapping Meaningful Connection and the Language of Human Experience*. New York: Random House.

Brown, Brené. 2018. *Dare to Lead*. New York: Random House.

Burnes, Bernard. 2009. *Managing Change*. 5th ed. Harlow: FT Prentice Hall.

Campbell, Joseph. 2008. *The Hero with a Thousand Faces*. Novato, CA: New World Library.

Chödrön, Pema. 2002. *The Places That Scare You: A Guide to Fearlessness in Difficult Times*. Boston: Shambhala.

Clear, James. 2018. *Atomic Habits: An Easy & Proven Way to Build Good Habits & Break Bad Ones; Tiny Changes, Remarkable Results*. New York: Avery.

Cuddy, Amy. 2015. *Presence: Bringing Your Boldest Self to Your Biggest Challenges*. New York: Little, Brown Spark.

Fairbanks, Grant. 1960. *Voice and Articulation Drillbook*. New York: Harper & Row.

Ferriss, Timothy. 2017. *Tribe of Mentors: Short Life Advice from the Best in the World*. New York: Houghton Mifflin Harcourt.

Gould, Stephen Jay. 2007. *Punctuated Equilibrium*. Cambridge, MA: Belknap Press.

Hendricks, Gay. 2021. *The Genius Zone: The Breakthrough Process to End Negative Thinking and Live in True Creativity*. New York: St. Martin's Publishing Group.

Hixon, Thomas J. 1987. *Respiratory Function in Speech and Song*. London: College Hill Press.

Hixon, Thomas J. 2006. *Respiratory Function in Singing: A Primer for Singers and Singing Teachers*. San Diego, CA: Plural Publishing.

Hof, Wim. 2020. *The Wim Hof Method: Activate Your Full Human Potential*. Louisville, CO: Sounds True.

Knight, Dudley. 2000. "Standard Speech: The Ongoing Debate." *Voice and Speech Review* 1(1): 31–54. doi:10.1080/23268263.2000.10761385

Knight, Dudley. 2012. *Speaking with Skill: An Introduction to Knight-Thompson Speechwork*. London: Methuen Drama.

Myers, Thomas W. 2021. *Anatomy Trains: Myofascial Meridians for Manual Therapists and Movement Professionals*. 4th ed. Amsterdam: Elsevier.

Nestor, James. 2020. *Breath: The New Science of a Lost Art*. New York: Riverhead Books.

O'Connor, Joseph Desmond 1980. *Better English Pronunciation*. 2nd ed. Cambridge: Cambridge University Press.

Saklad, Nancy. 2011. *Voice and Speech Training in the New Millennium: Conversations with Master Teachers*. New York: Applause Books.

Singer, Michael A. 2007. *The Untethered Soul: The Journey Beyond Yourself*. Oakland, CA: New Harbinger.

Skinner, Edith. 1990. *Speak with Distinction: The Classic Skinner Method to Speech on the Stage*. Lilene Mansell, ed. New York: Applause Theatre Book Publishers.

Taylor, Trey. 2013. "The Rise and Fall of Katharine Hepburn's Fake Accent." *The Atlantic*, August 8. https://www.theatlantic.com/entertainment/archive/2013/08/the-rise-and-fall-of-katharine-hepburns-fake-accent/278505/

Wells, John Christopher 1982. *Accents of English 1: An Introduction*. Cambridge: Cambridge University Press.

Wells, J. C. 1982. *Accents of English 2: The British Isles*. Cambridge: Cambridge University Press.

Wells, J. C. 1928. *Accents of English 3: Beyond the British Isles*. Cambridge: Cambridge University Press.

Whyte, David. 2014. *Consolations: The Solace, Nourishment and Underlying Meaning of Everyday Words*. Washington, DC: Many Rivers Press.

ADDITIONAL RESOURCES AND TRAINING METHODOLOGIES

Alexander Technique: www.alexandertechnique.com

Feldenkrais Method: www.feldenkrais.com

Fitzmaurice Voicework: www.fitzmauriceinstitute.org

Knight-Thompson Speechwork: www.ktspeechwork.org

Linklater Voice: www.linklatervoice.com

Miller Voice Method (mVm): www.millervoicemethod.com

Nadine George Voice Work: www.voicestudiointernational.com

Research in Drama Education: The Journal of Applied Theatre and Performance: www.tandfonline.com/journals/crde20

Roy Hart Theatre: www.roy-hart-theatre.com

Six Figure Voice Studio: www.expressyourgenius.com/sixfigurevoicestudio

The American Laryngological Association (ALA): www.alahns.org

The Association for Theatre in Higher Education (ATHE): www.athe.org

Theatre, Dance and Performance Training: www.tandfonline.com/journals/rtdp20

The Australian Voice Association (AVA): www.australianvoiceassociation.com.au

The British Voice Association (BVA): www.britishvoiceassociation.org.uk

The International Dialects of English Archive (IDEA): www.dialectsarchive.com

The International Phonetic Association (IPA): www.internationalphonetic association.org

The Lessac Training and Research Institute: www.lessacinstitute.org

The National Center for Voice and Speech (NCVS): www.ncvs.org

The Pan American Vocology Association (PAVA): www.pavavocology.org

The Performing Arts Medicine Association (PAMA): www.artsmed.org/ membership

The Speech Accent Archive: https://accent.gmu.edu

The Summer Vocology Institute: www.vocology.utah.edu/svi/index.php

The Visual Accent and Dialect Archive (VADA): www.visualaccentdialectarchive.com

The *Voice and Speech Review*: www.tandfonline.com/journals/rvsr20

The Voice and Speech Trainers Association (VASTA): www.vasta.org

The Voice Foundation: www.voicefoundation.org

Vibrant Voice Technique: www.vibrantvoicetechnique.com

Voice and Speech Resources Facebook Group: www.facebook.com/groups/ voicespeechresources

Index